Communicating for Survival

Communicating for Survival

Coping With Diminishing Human Resources

E.W. BRODY

PRAEGER

New York
Westport, Connecticut
London

Library of Congress Cataloging-in-Publication Data

Brody, E. W.
    Communicating for survival.

    Bibliography: p.
    Includes index.
    1. Communication in personnel management.
2. Communication in organizations.   I. Title.
HF5549.5.C6B69 1987   658.3'00141   87-11774
ISBN 0-275-92652-4 (alk. paper)
ISBN 0-275-92808-X (pbk. : alk. paper)

Library of Congress Catalog Card Number: 87-11774

ISBN: 0-275-92652-4
      0-275-92808-X (pbk)

First published in 1987

Praeger Publishers, One Madison Avenue, New York, NY 10010
A division of Greenwood Press, Inc.

Printed in the United States of America

The paper used in this book complies with the
Permanent Paper Standard issued by the National
Information Standards Organization (Z39.48-1984).

10 9 8 7 6 5 4 3 2 1

For Kris, Susan, Glenn,
Lisa and Peggy

CONTENTS

PREFACE

The economic future of the United States in the mid-1980s was less than certain. The nation was caught up in a period of rapid systemic change. Manufacturing industry was in decline. Service businesses were growing. The circumstances suggested that the nation was in transition from the industrial to the postindustrial periods. The economy was in transition in another way, from national to global.

A legion of problems attended the two transitions. Among them, international trade disparities and deficit spending were proving to be most intransigent. These difficulties were compounded by a sort of national political gridlock. The nation's elected officeholders appeared unable to achieve a consensus on ways and means to successfully attack any of the primary problems of the day.

In the absence of national policy and national priorities, commerce, industry, and institutions were caught up in struggles for individual survival. Manufacturers exported jobs and demanded protectionist legislation. Overproductive farmers called for new governmental solutions to their economic problems. The several components of the health care industry battled among themselves for consumer dollars and with governmental agencies over cost containment. The underlying issues—whether health care should be a right or a privilege, and who should pay—were largely ignored.

The same sorts of conflicts were endemic across the nation, and workers found themselves paying a disproportionate part of the price of change. Plant closings, layoffs, wage and benefit give-backs, and a host of other measures adopted by businesses struggling for survival were producing economic pain for a declining middle class.

They were also being blamed for the nation's competitive woes. U.S. products had indisputably been losing their positions of market dominance. In consumer electronics, in the automotive industry, in office automation, and elsewhere the problem was the same. The Japanese, the Germans, the Koreans, the Swedes, the Italians, and many others were carving out growing portions of domestic markets. They were doing so with products that Americans found superior in quality and competitive in price.

These conditions had generated no little contention over the blame. Business blamed workers. Workers blamed business. There was no shortage of blame, but little willingness to attack underlying issues. National productivity had been declining in quantitative and qualitative terms, due to a historically adversarial relationship between organizations and their employees. Each had sought to enhance economic return at the expense of the other and to gain further advantages by enlisting the power of government in its behalf.

While this pattern persisted in the United States for most of the century, a far different approach was developing around the globe. In the nations listed above and in most others a new philosophy had developed. Government, management, and labor had joined hands to advance their mutual interests and the United States was suffering as a result.

Reversal of these trends, which many deem essential to the nation's economic welfare, will require far different organizational philosophies than those that prevail today—philosophies that will become increasingly attractive in the next decade as basic demographic change engulfs the economy. For the first time since World War II, a seller's market in labor will develop in the United States. Employers in the next few years will be competing for a declining number of entry-level workers. To attract and retain these workers they will be forced to radically modify traditional approaches to human resources management.

Fair, equitable treatment of employees will be a prerequisite to success. To assure such treatment, most organizations will be forced to design and develop compensation, performance-appraisal, and disciplinary systems atypical of those that predominate today. More important, they will have to successfully communicate the existence and efficacy of these systems to employees and prospective employees who have learned to view organizations and their managements as "the enemy."

This book was written in an effort to provide guidance for those farsighted enough to see the problems on the contemporary horizon and prepare for a new era in labor relations and organizational communication. It is a product of several decades of consulting to organizations of all kinds; of exposure to success and failure predestined by the relative willingness of senior managers to accept and respond to social change.

The title was chosen out of conviction that human resources management will be the key to organizational success or failure for the remainder of the century and beyond. The content evolved out of an equally strong conviction that organizational survival will depend on senior managers' ability to accept and treat their workers as a primary stakeholder group—granting them equal status with customers, shareholders, and others. Only in this manner can today's largely adversarial relationships be supplanted by mutual effort toward enhanced productivity for mutual benefit.

The latter task will not be easily accomplished. Few organizations today are credible in the eyes of their workers. Most are deservedly considered exploitative, unfeeling, and uncaring. These conditions can be reversed only through managerial commitment and appropriate action.

Equitable compensation, performance appraisal, and disciplinary policies fairly applied will be prerequisite to success. Only when these are in place and organizations have demonstrated their commitment to fairness and equity will workers respond. Only then will they abandon their "us against them" attitudes and accept membership in the organizations of which they are a part. As the barriers are removed, communication can begin, and the damage of several decades can be repaired.

Thus, the chapters that follow deal in sequence with the nature of the problem, removal of the barriers, and only finally with the process and techniques of communication. Their content is designed to provide insight into the breadth and depth of the problem at hand and into the several steps that must be taken in its solution. It is a distillation of information and experience gained over several decades, intended to help organizations build a better tomorrow for themselves and their workers.

The book would not have been written without encouragement and support from many sources. Members of the College of Communication and Fine Arts and the Department of Journalism at Memphis State University have been especially helpful. I am particularly indebted to Dean Richard R. Ranta and Dr. John DeMott for their encouragement and the freedom to pursue the project.

My colleagues in organizational communication and public relations have also been generous in their assistance. Corporate Communications Manager Richard K. Long of Dow Chemical and Thomas R. Martin, Federal Express Corporation's managing director for employee communication, were especially helpful.

I am indebted to Professor Michael B. Hesse of the University of Alabama and to William J. Corbett, vice-president for communication at the American Institute of Certified Public Accountants, for their comments and suggestions in reviewing the manuscript.

Their guidance as well as that of Alison Bricken and her colleagues at Praeger Publishers were vital in bringing the project to completion.

E. W. BRODY
Memphis, Tennessee

Communicating for Survival

1
THE CHALLENGE OF A NEW CENTURY

Communication is one of the most complex processes in which humans engage. It assumes myriad forms beyond verbal and visual transmission of messages. Humans communicate as much through tonal inflection, facial expression, and manual gesture as through words. These accompanying signals often alter basic meanings. Seemingly straightforward statements can be radically modified with the wink of an eye or the shrug of a shoulder.

The process is even more complex where organizations are involved. Meanings of messages transmitted to customers, shareholders, employees, and others are modified by many intervening variables. Most important among them are conflict and credibility.

Conflict refers to levels of consistency within and across sets of messages. It arises in immediate and historic terms. Response to management's call for fiscal austerity, for example, is influenced by immediately associated actions. The acquisition of a new corporate jet aircraft is apt to discourage compliance with the austerity message. Canceling a shareholder cocktail party, on the other hand, would underscore the austerity message and tend to induce the desired response. The organization's historic handling of similar pronouncements also intervenes. A history of vacillation or frequent policy changes encourages procrastination. Credibility plays a similar role. Where management is known for consistent policy enforcement, compliance is usually forthcoming; where a history of inconsistency exists, wait-and-see attitudes are more probable.

Management credibility and consistency are universally accepted as desirable organizational attributes. They vary in degree among organizations. Resulting problems have been of only moderate magnitude, however, for the past several decades. Managers' primary concerns have been capital and land, which have been scarcer and more costly than the human component of production for more than 30 years. Labor has been relatively plentiful. Personnel have been viewed as a consumable resource, to be used and replaced as necessary.

The ensuing decades will see a reversal of these conditions. Labor will become the scarcest and most expensive component of production. Human resources problems will come to overshadow those on which managers historically have focused their attention.

A NEW CHALLENGE

The United States for almost a decade has been attempting to cope with multiple intractable problems. Budget deficits and foreign-trade imbalances have created difficulties in the domestic economy. So have environmental problems, drug trafficking, inner-city decay, and deterioration of the nation's infrastructure—roads and bridges, sewage and water facilities, and the like.

The list could go on at considerable length. Birth control, health care, organ transplants, comparable worth, the space shuttle, Nicaragua, Iran, and a host of other issues have intermittently preoccupied the nation. Human rights, women's rights, employee rights, and gay rights have been debated at length. So have immigration, food additives, and nuclear power.

These problems share a common attribute: Given adequate time and resources, each can be more or less resolved. Other difficulties are less amenable to human solution, however, and one of the most pervasive and intractable among them will soon be upon us: the most severe labor shortage the nation has experienced since World War II.

ORIGINS

The first tangible signs of the problem appeared in the mid-1980s. During the summer of 1986, minimum-wage jobs in New York and New England went unfilled because employers were unwilling to pay $6 to $7 an hour or to import labor. One of the nation's leading fast-food chains found it necessary to transport employees from New York City to Connecticut to staff turnpike restaurants. Another made a similar effort in Massachusetts, busing workers from a depressed area to a more affluent community some 90 minutes away.

These companies were seeing the first signs in the labor market of what has become known as the "baby bust." Between 1965 and 1979, after some of the most fertile years in the nation's history, the domestic birth rate plummeted. Now, more than 20 years later, the leading edge of the baby-bust generation is coming into the labor force.

The First Wave

Today's developing labor shortage was inevitable and predictable. Elementary and secondary schools have been coping with the baby bust for years. The numbers of children between the ages of 6 and 18 declined by 14 percent between 1975 and 1985. Schools closed and teachers were laid off.

By the mid-1980s the leading edge of the bust had arrived at the doors of the nation's colleges and universities and at the threshold of the labor force. The number of 16– to 19–year-old workers declined by 20 percent between 1978 and 1985 and the 20– to 24–year-old group was beginning to shrink as well. Data from the Bureau of Labor Statistics indicated that the supply of teenage workers would continue to drop at an average rate of 1 percent annually through 1995.

The problem may subside quantitatively thereafter, but qualitative difficulties will apparently perpetuate employers' problems. Some easing in the supply of entry-level workers may occur by the late 1990s. The baby bust ended in 1970, and a boomlet, sometimes called the "baby-boom echo," then developed. The echo generation promises to be better educated than its predecessors and will probably be more prone to avoid uninteresting or unchallenging work.

The latter circumstances are implied in the relative success enjoyed by the higher education community in meeting the challenge of the baby bust. Educators met the vanguard of anticipated declines in student enrollment without great difficulty. While numbers of high school graduates declined 12 percent between 1984 and 1985, college and university enrollment dropped only 2 percent. More aggressive recruiting of adults and of high-school students apparently was responsible. The net result, however, may compound employers' difficulties.

The New Worker

Tomorrow's workers will be better educated and fewer in number. More and more will be products of an educational system that honors inquiry, challenge, and change, rather than passive acceptance of subordinate roles. This mental set will have been superimposed over already changed values and life-styles. Quality of life is fast becoming the primary concern of the U.S. worker. Material rewards are no longer sufficient. Workers seek a sense of accomplishment as well as compensation. Proprietorship—psychic if not economic—is becoming essential to motivation. Employers will thus have to cope with a more demanding (and smaller) labor pool.

Their success or failure will be primary determinants of organizational futures. Human resources will be the scarcest component of production. Economic rewards will be insufficient to attract and retain qualified personnel. In a seller's labor market, there will always be a competitor ready and willing to pay a higher salary. Where employers fail to provide the sort of nurturing environment new workers demand, enterprises will inevitably fall short of meeting their potential. At worst they may collapse, as workers "vote with their feet" for more attractive situations.

Insightful managers have long accepted a tenet that rejects the status quo as indicative of success. Organizations progress or retrogress, they declare.

There is no middle ground. Those that want to continue to succeed have no choice but to adjust to changing circumstances.

Rivers of Change

Contemporary organizations are at the confluence of three rivers of change, says *Industry Week* editor Perry Pascarella. They must cope with a global rather than a national economy, with accelerating technological change and with explosive change in values and life-styles. The latter "have exploded into such diversity that old assumptions about the people who produce and consume have become hopelessly inadequate."

Organizational responses may be no better. Payrolls can be cut, but durable improvement can come only through enhanced productivity on the part of those who remain. New technologies can be created, but their acceptance is a function of human factors—interpersonal skills and individual readiness to accept change. Participative and strategic management systems can be installed, but their success or failure again is a function of human relationships.

Organizational problems. Value and life-style conflicts also arise in organizations, usually in more intractable form. "Often," Pascarella says, "when top management wants change, it loses sight of the fact that it is making incongruous demands on *organizations designed to reinforce long-established ways of doing things* [emphasis added]. It wants people to do new things while their experience, training and compensation programs support the old thing."

This conflict between new management demands and old organizational systems is more complex than it appears. While organizations have been struggling to deal with economic and technological change, workers also have been changing. They no longer are motivated to work as efficiently or effectively as they have in the past. They find work less satisfying and management promises less convincing.

Deteriorating attitudes. Sixty percent of workers in the late 1960s looked on their work as a source of personal satisfaction, according to researcher Daniel Yankelovich. By the early 1980s, only 43 percent believed that "hard work always pays off." Only 13 percent found their work meaningful and more important than leisure pursuits.

Thus, worker commitment is deteriorating, as organizations awaken to the breadth and depth of their quality and productivity problems. Employers face a monumental task in inducing workers to recommit themselves to the organizations by which they are employed.

The task will be rendered doubly difficult by lack of commitment among many managers. They tend to subscribe to conventional wisdom, which holds capital investment, technology, and management systems more important than individuals and their motivations.

LITIGATION AND CREDIBILITY

Evidence of worker perceptions of employers and employer motivations abounds in the legal arena. The volume of litigation filed by workers against employers has grown with each passing year. The number of National Labor Relations Board cases and arbitration proceedings has increased apace.

While superficially inconsequential in an overly litigious society, the data underscore the suspicion, distrust, and contentiousness that pervade the workplace. These will be major obstacles to management efforts to bridge a credibility gap of immense magnitude.

Simply put, credibility is the individual condition that produces believability or trustworthiness. Individuals whose behaviors induce credibility have the confidence, faith, and trust of colleagues and subordinates. Where words induce doubt, behavior produces suspicion, and motives generate skepticism: credibility is rapidly eroded. Charles D. Flory and R. Alec McKenzie describe the results:

The credible manager not only believes; he is believable. He not only has confidence; he is worthy of confidence. When credibility gaps then distrust, doubt, disbelief and misgivings have found their way into the lines of communication and most likely of all onto the grapevine. When managerial action is unbelievable there is a full sweep of no confidence in the organization.

This concept applies to organizations as well as managers. Individual behaviors are critical, but the ubiquitous "they" quickly attaches to any organization that harbors even a few whose actions belie their words.

Worker Predispositions

The few "bad apples" rot the barrel by providing tangible evidence in support of vocal workers whose experiences make them suspicious of all employers. They consider themselves the victims of a host of unfulfilled promises. The promises usually are of diverse origin and were made over a period of years, but they nevertheless destroy morale and productivity.

Broken promises for many U.S. workers extend back to childhood tales in which good inevitably triumphed over evil and "they all lived happily ever after." Similar words too often came readily to the lips of parents anxious to instill the work ethic in children: "Hard work produces success."

More promises. Armed with such glowing prospects, individuals enter a work environment peculiarly designed to compound a potential for difficulty. Human resources departments under pressure to fill vacant positions often oversell their organizations: "This is a great place to work. The people are wonderful. The raises and promotions come often to those willing to work." First-line managers or supervisors, concerned with short-term productivity improvements, follow suit: "We reward productivity around here. Work hard and you'll go a long way with this organization."

Disillusionment. The promises are casually given and quickly forgotten by all but the workers involved. Broken promises for them are the ultimate evidence that managers and management are not to be trusted. It matters not that those who made the promises exceeded their authority, that they lacked the power to make good their words. Workers view them as authorized representatives of an uncaring authority.

The result is a level of distrust that can only have been compounded in recent years. Consider, for example, the perspective of employees who supported wage/benefit give-backs to preserve jobs, only to have their companies collapse, nevertheless. Consider also headline-making cases of employees terminated just short of retirement, of canceled pensioners' health-care benefits, of jobs lost through mergers or acquisitions.

These factors are complicated by two others. One is the complexity of the contemporary organization, which creates barriers for those seeking to attach meaning to their occupational roles. The other consists of "need to know" internal information systems. Information is provided only to those who require it to discharge their duties. The potential for commercial or industrial espionage is reduced in the process, but so is the potential for workers to identify their jobs with a worthwhile enterprise.

The Ultimate Trap

Workers' distrust and inability to identify with their organizations is further reinforced by what might best be termed "organizational doublespeak." It exists in most organizations and destroys any potential for substantive improvement. Philosophically, it involves paying lip service to one concept but honoring another. In organizations it involves rewarding counterproductive behaviors.

Short term versus long term. Senior managers, for example, are entrusted with long-range decision making, but usually are compensated for short-term results. Their bonuses are based on annual performance. They therefore tend to sacrifice investment in personnel and equipment to produce short-term profit. Their organizations stagnate as a result.

Middle managers presumably should be rewarded for economy and efficiency. Those who create inefficiency are granted larger budgets, however, while colleagues who reduce expenditures find budgets cut for ensuing years. The system penalizes the productive and rewards the counterproductive, all the while calling for increased productivity.

More conflict. Conflicts are similarly resolved in offices and plants. Clerical job security is a function of paper work. Production worker compensation is generated by hours worked; predictable result—more of both. Clerks generate more paper and production workers do just enough to avoid being fired.

Organizations are awash in such contradictions. They demand long-term solutions, but reward quick fixes. They seek quality, but reward quantity. They call for teamwork, but reward one player at the expense of another. They ask for loyalty, but best compensate the most recently hired or those who threaten to leave.

TOWARD A SOLUTION

As human resources diminish through the mid 1990s, organizations more and more will find themselves involved in highly competitive manpower situations. A seller's market in labor is rapidly developing in the United States. There soon will exist more jobs in many categories than there are employees to fill them. Employers who adjust to these new realities will succeed; others will fail. The difference between success and failure may mean life or death to the enterprises involved.

How can organizations best respond? Their responses must be simultaneously simple and complex. Simplistically, to paraphrase a dated but meritorious definition of public relations, they must "do a good job and get credit for it."

The problem is complex because a good job requires more than executive decisions followed by traditional subordinate response. Contemporary management systems discourage change, however, by creating no linkage between performance and rewards. Workers withhold their best efforts in these circumstances, and 75 percent of the U.S. labor force, by some estimates, consists of withholders.

Management's first challenge, then, is systemic change. Tradition dies hard, especially in organizations. Change requires altering organizational values, mores, and folkways. The process can require years unless reward mechanisms are changed to support behavioral standards. From the moment of decision, however, communication becomes the organization's primary need.

Communication is vital in developing the new culture, in conveying underlying concepts, and in delivering "due notice" of essential behavioral changes to all involved. The latter step is especially difficult in traditional organizations. They are too often well known among their employees for tolerating significant differences between policy and performance or for too frequent policy changes. These behaviors compound both organizational inertia and communication problems.

THE ROLE OF COMMUNICATION

Communication is a complex process. More often than not, as organizations repeatedly demonstrate, it is inadequately understood. Several functional factors are important to those who would communicate successfully. Most significant among them:

1. The communication process is controlled by the receiver. When messages are not received, understood, believed, or acted upon, communication fails.
2. Inconsistency destroys credibility. Where organizations transmit one message to one constituency and a conflicting message to another, neither is apt to be believed.
3. Source, message, and channel all contribute to the credibility—or incredibility—of communication.

Credibility

Of the three concepts, the latter is the most important. Employees tend to be skeptical, especially where they earlier have been—or believe they have been—misled. One or the other occurs too often in most organizations. Where this has been the case, managers must be prepared for a time-consuming and often painful process. Credibility can be restored only by demonstration. "Where personnel have learned to discount management pronouncements," says one consultant, "it's sometimes necessary to leave a little blood on the floor."

This should not suggest that organizational change must be punitive. As much can be accomplished with rewards as with penalties. "It's necessary always to remember," the consultant adds, "that the purpose of organizational policy is compliance rather than punishment. Compliance is best achieved, however, where reward and/or penalty are perceived as inevitable." This is the case only where management perseveres.

Consistency

Consistency can be as much a problem in communication as in handling rewards and penalties. Credibility is at stake in both areas. Communication problems are more difficult to control, however, due to prevalent methodologies.

Communicators view organizations as sets of stakeholder groups. Employees, shareholders, customers, and suppliers are included, together with members of the media and financial communities. Groups are viewed in terms of informational needs and motivations. Their diversity in these areas can result in each being examined without regard for others. This, in turn, can lead to conflict among messages fashioned for disparate groups, with potentially destructive results.

Conflicts develop because group memberships overlap. Employees are often consumers of the organization's products or services. Some may be shareholders as well. Thus, exaggerated advertising claims aimed at consumers may produce negative reactions among employees. Where high product quality is claimed in the face of poor manufacturing processes, employee credibility suffers. The same might be true where profit declines are attributed in an annual report to competitive factors, while employees are aware of considerable internal waste.

Control

Managerial consistency and credibility precondition employees to control communication in a highly predictable manner. Where managers are credible and consistent, messages tend to be accepted and acted upon. Where credibility and consistency levels are lower, message acceptance and action levels deteriorate accordingly.

Credibility and consistency suffer most where organizational value and control systems are in conflict. Value systems may be formal or informal. They are sometimes reduced to writing, as in mission statements. More often, they are implied in aggregate organizational performance—negative or positive.

Conflicts. Conflict can arise in either case. Senior management tolerance of waste belies any written commitment to efficiency and productivity. Demonstrated willingness to see superior employees depart, rather than adequately compensate them, destroys the credibility of contrary statements, written or verbal. Employees faced with such conflicts respond to experience rather than policy. Tolerance of waste produces more waste. Employees rewarded only with promises follow their predecessors to greener pastures.

Behavior communication. A simple truth is critical: Behavior communicates. Where behavior contradicts pronouncements, credibility attaches to behavioral messages. Painstakingly constructed statements of organizational philosophy and mission at best will be ignored. At worst, they will be considered evidence of organizational duplicity.

Managements committed to organizational survival in what will become the nation's worst labor shortage since World War II ultimately will be forced to a painful choice. Counterproductive human resources management policies must be reversed or acknowledged. The first option almost inevitably will be traumatic and may not succeed. In recent years many chief executives have resigned in frustration over their inability to modify organizational values. The second option will be equally painful and inevitably fatal.

The Solution

The path to organizational success in an era of diminishing human resources will not be an easy one. Performance must precede communication. The good job must be done before personnel will grant credit. Consistency is prerequisite to credibility. Policy and procedure must be brought into conformity with stated organizational values.

Employees and middle managers will experience varying degrees of difficulty in adapting to change, and a degree of management tolerance is essential during the transition. All involved will need time to learn that new policies and procedures will be enforced—fairly and equitably, but without exception.

As consistency restores credibility, compliance supplants resistance to logical and rational policy and procedure. Logic and reason are vital—and atypical—commodities in many organizations. Control systems have traditionally been oriented toward punishing nonperformance rather than rewarding performance. Reversing this practice almost invariably is the first step toward successful human-resources management.

REWARD AND PUNISHMENT

The axiom that "you get what you pay for" is as applicable in organizations as in commerce. Where management strategies fail, the cause is almost invariably ignorance or neglect of this concept. The relative efficiency of Japanese manufacturers, for example, has been studied ad nauseam in recent years, profiting only the authors. The superior results of the Japanese can safely be attributed to basic systemic differences. Their workers are employed for life. As much as 40 percent of their compensation is based on organizational productivity. U.S. workers have no job security and most are paid by the hour rather than on the basis of production, sales, or profits.

Similar and identical problems pervade most organizations in the United States. Workers are rewarded for hours on the job instead of productivity; middle managers for empire building rather than efficiency; senior managers for short-term profits rather than long-term growth. Other than in sales, few organizations use incentive systems. Virtually none have installed integrated reward mechanisms that base every member's compensation on individual and group productivity.

Integrated Systems

Integrated compensation systems incorporate accountability at every organizational level. Individuals are compensated on the basis of productivity, preferably with bonuses rather than wage increments. Supervisory compensation is similarly structured and is based on the sum of subordinate productivity. Middle managers, in turn, are compensated for the performance of organizational components directed by their supervisors. At each level superiors control subordinates' compensation.

The underlying concept is simplicity itself. Where contribution to organizational success governs rewards, performance follows. Put another way,
if you're going to get what you pay for, you should pay for what you want.

Potential Problems

Performance-based compensation systems are not without potential problems. Fortunately, however, problem potential is readily minimized if not
eliminated. Given an integrated system, the greatest potential for difficulty
arises out of performance measurement.

Quality versus quantity. Quantitative and qualitative standards are necessary if systems are to create optimal results. Quality of work is apt to
suffer where quantitative standards are used exclusively, and the reverse is
equally true. Supervisors and managers must define "minimum acceptable
performance" in both contexts, a task that is not inherently difficult. It is a
major challenge to the uninitiated, however, which can be met only by
retraining those involved.

Individual versus group. Problems may also arise where individual enterprise is permitted to govern unchecked. Interpersonal friction appears
when salesmen compete for prospects or assembly-line personnel speed
their operations to the detriment of other individuals or the tasks to which
they are assigned.

The Japanese approach, involving only group rewards, would eliminate
such difficulties, but not without its price. Two factors are involved. The
U.S. focus on individualism rather than team play suggests a need for individual incentives. More important, the Japanese approach requires greater
credibility levels than exist in many if not most U.S. enterprises.

Group reward advantages. Finally, group incentives introduce another
valuable element indigenous to Japanese systems but lacking in the United
States: The systems become self-policing. Peer pressure engenders productivity levels no other reward or disciplinary system will produce. It also
helps compensate for managers' erroneous perceptions of workers.

Most humans are prone to judge others by themselves—to assume that
"what motivates me will motivate them." Such assumptions are ill advised.
Traditional incentives still work for about 56 percent of the worker population, Yankelovich estimates, but fail for the remaining 44 percent. His
first group consists of "go getters" (15 percent), those who put work before
pleasure (19 percent), and habitual workers (22 percent). The second
includes "turned off" workers (27 percent) and middle managers (17 percent).

The latter group may be ill placed by Yankelovich in terms of the performance-based compensation system proposed here. It consists of "young,
highly educated, managers and professionals, hungry for responsibility and
challenge, seeking interesting and vital work." Responsibility and challenge

invariably attach to performance-based compensation systems. They attract interest in concept and implementation as well as rewards.

VARIABLE BENEFITS

Variability is as much an asset in employee benefit programs as compensation systems. It serves employers and employees by insuring that wage and benefit expenditures generate optimally attractive packages for all personnel. The concept is best exemplified by the so-called cafeteria plan, which permits individuals to select the benefits that most appeal to them.

Cafeteria Programs

The cafeteria concept came into vogue as more and more women entered the work force in the early to mid-1980s. Increasing numbers of two-wage-earner households produced duplicative sets of benefits, which tended to reduce their value. Cafeteria and similar programs can be expected to grow in popularity through the end of the century. With the number of younger workers declining, retirees have started taking their places in part-time jobs. They prefer compensation in the form of benefits, rather than wages. Many need not be counted as taxable income, which would reduce retirement and Social Security benefits.

Benefits as Incentives

Another nontraditional program makes benefits a variable in the compensation mix. Under this system workers earn benefits at predetermined rates based on the number of hours worked in each compensation period.

The system was conceived to meet two objectives. First, absenteeism and tardiness are discouraged where benefits are based on hours worked rather than hours paid. Second, the plans often permit cash payments in lieu of benefits, excepting only those mandated by state or federal governments. The latter feature creates an advantage for employers in competitive labor markets without increasing their costs. Further innovations can be expected as demographic patterns change and the marketplace becomes more competitive.

Changing Demographics

Graphic representations of the U.S. population have traditionally been more or less pyramidal in form. Large numbers of young people are at the base of the pyramid, while small numbers of the elderly form the apex. Contemporary trends indicate that future representations will be more akin to rectangles, with more nearly equal numbers of individuals in each age group.

The need for more flexible benefit programming will be compounded with more seniors and fewer 18– to 24–year-olds in the work force. Benefits as well as compensation ultimately may be linked to productivity. Some systems already permit exchanging compensation for additional benefits, which works to the advantage of senior workers. Such programs, of course, will require more precise performance measurement.

MEASUREMENT SYSTEMS

Design and installation of performance-based compensation systems is readily accomplished. Existing productivity levels are usually acceptable to all involved as "minimum acceptable performance." They also are generally acceptable to senior managers in that costs increase only with productivity and, presumably, profit levels. Equally important, the system affords organizations an opportunity to "rehumanize" jobs.

Men and Machines

Organizations in the United States have historically applied identical management techniques to human beings and heavy machinery. Simplification and repetition engendered optimum productivity, but at staggering cost in human pride, dignity, and gratification. An oft-told tale is illustrative.

The superintendent of a construction project sought to determine why three equally qualified masons were producing work of varying quality. One was performing below acceptable standards. The second barely met job requirements. The work of the third was exceptional. He decided to ask each, in, order, to tell him what they were doing. "Laying bricks," answered the first mason. "Building a wall," said the second. "Creating a temple," responded the third.

Workers' perceptions of the roles they play in organizations influences the quality of their work. Job redesign in the United States has enhanced productivity in quantitative terms. Qualitative results were another matter, however, and the impact of associated change on workers was negative in the extreme.

Reengaging the Worker

To achieve optimum productivity, managers must reengage the interest and pride of employees. Compensation systems must deal in intrinsic as well as extrinsic rewards. Simply stated, but difficult to achieve? Perhaps, but nevertheless achievable, as demonstrated by IBM. The computer giant has been, without question, the most profitable organization in the industry. It has also pioneered in such diverse areas as robotics and human-resources management.

Total responsibility. When IBM installed state-of-the-art robots in a Kentucky plant in the mid-1980s, management made and fulfilled a commitment to retrain and retain every displaced worker. This was but another logical step, in the IBM Office Products Division, to earn and maintain the support of personnel. The company early led in what IBM alumnus Clair F. Vough described as a "total responsibility" or "vertical management" approach to job design and development. He used a janitor to illustrate.

The end product of his work is a clean plant. His complaint was that he performed a single *function* toward that end and that he had no control over the other functions. As a sweeper for the entire plant, his job was designed horizontally. What he wanted was *vertical responsibility*—control of all the cleaning functions in one part of the plant. Logically, he would then report to a manager in charge of the entire plant's cleanliness, who in turn might report to the plant's maintenance chief. If, on a given morning, most of the plant was clean but a small part of it was not clean, the cleaning manager would know exactly where the failure was, exactly the person whose work had to be improved.

Multiple benefits. The vertical responsibility concept also rehumanized the sweeper's job. The quality of his work was more evident to all. He could take greater pride in it, and it was more readily measured and rewarded. The same principle, applied throughout the IBM division, was equally productive from a management perspective. Individual and organizational performance improved, and work was accomplished with fewer echelons of supervision or management.

Others are seeking the same results, stripping away entire management echelons in the interests of productivity and profitability. Whether they accomplish these objectives without encountering unforeseen human resources problems only time will tell. Communication will be a critical factor in any event.

COMMUNICATION SYSTEMS

Communication systems contribute to organizational success or failure. They amplify the good and underscore the evil. Perhaps evil is too strong a word—perhaps not. Communication systems are neutral. They have no philosophy. They create no messages. At best—and at worst—they reflect their organizations.

Best and Worst

The best occurs where leaderships are enlightened, credible, and committed to growth and development with—rather than through—employees. Communication systems in such organizations accelerate information distribution. Any and all information—good or bad—that impacts the organization and its members is fully and rapidly disclosed. In these circumstances, messages are received, understood, and acted upon by members who have confidence in credible leaderships.

Worst results occur where manipulative leaderships use communication systems to influence employee behavior for organizational benefit rather than mutual gain. Bad news in such systems is anathema. Organizations and managements are portrayed as perfect or better. Reading such an organization's employee publication has been aptly compared to going down for the third time in a sea of maple syrup.

Alternative Reactions

Communication systems of this sort produce one of two reactions among message recipients, each contributing to organizational failure. Intended recipients most often simply "tune out" the messages. They discard newsletters unread, ignore bulletin board memos, and sleep through employee meetings. In the alternative, messages may become a source of organization-wide speculation as to hidden meanings or concealed motives, as to "what they're trying to do to us now." They are not only disbelieved but become a source of rumor and speculation, which at best is counterproductive.

THE ROAD TO RECOVERY

Restoring credibility and employee confidence in these circumstances must become the organization's first priority. Change is time consuming and to some extent painful. No one enjoys admitting error. The process nevertheless is essential to assure survival into the new century.

It consists of a series of simple steps. The first is a clear mandate from senior management to middle managers and supervisors: Dealings with all employees shall be based on the truth, the whole truth, and nothing but the truth. Where management is suspect, change of the magnitude necessary to restore credibility and confidence first produces suspicion and disbelief. Old practices must demonstrably have been abandoned before credibility returns and confidence is restored.

Defining the Problem

The second step requires defining the problem management is seeking to remedy. The depth, breadth, and severity of the situation must be established through valid research. Where levels of suspicion are high or where internal resources are lacking, external counsel should be called upon to administer an instrument such as Gerald Goldhaber's ICA Communication Audit. Results provide basic information to senior management, identify unusual problem areas, and generate baseline data through which programmatic effectiveness can be assessed.

Third, every member of senior management must become directly involved in the turnaround effort. The process involved has been called "management by walking around." It requires that senior managers *regularly* get out of their inner sanctums and into the organization's plants and offices. It is primarily a *listening* process through which senior managers become privy to the thoughts and concerns of others in the organization.

Inevitably, "management by walking around" leads to the fourth step in the rebuilding process: action responsive to the needs and concerns of organizational personnel; interest in and commitment to improvement, expressed through tangible response.

System Redevelopment

Where this process is accompanied by parallel redesign and redevelopment of the employee communication system, management credibility and employee confidence can be restored over time. System components—newsletters, bulletin boards, luncheon meetings, and so on—are of little consequence as long as the messages they contain reach intended recipients.

The messages, however, are critical. Truth, candor, and consistency are of paramount importance; adequate feedback mechanisms are also vital. Senior managers' walking-around procedures should continue. They can be accompanied by periodic executive luncheons with representative employee groups, a functional suggestion system, and other devices through which successful managers monitor their organizations.

SUMMARY

Communication is a complex process, especially in organizations. It takes many forms and is highly dependent on managerial credibility and employee confidence in the organization and its leadership. Associated problems will be compounded as the baby bust of the 1960s produces a radical decline in the entry-level work force of 1990–2000.

Potential management problems are compounded by change in workers. Most will be better educated and more prone to challenge conventional employee–employer relationships. They will arrive at employers' doors already challenged by a global economy, accelerating technological developments, and explosive change in human values and life-styles.

They will come to their first jobs skeptical of management promises and more prone to litigation than their predecessors. Continued organizational doublespeak, through which counterproductive behaviors are rewarded, can only compound their potential as problem generators.

Enlighted managements will respond with new reward and communication systems designed to reestablish credibility and employee confidence. Performance-based compensation mechanisms and variable compensation systems almost certainly will be among them.

ADDITIONAL READING

Flory, Charles D., and R. Alec McKenzie. *The Credibility Gap in Management.* New York: Van Nostrand Reinhold, 1971.

LeBoeuf, Michael. *The Greatest Management Principle in the World.* New York: Putnam, 1985.

Pascarella, Perry. "Making Change a Way of Life," *Industry Week,* April 14, 1986, pp. 59–66.

Supple, Terry Stevenson. "The Coming Labor Shortage," *American Demographics,* September 1986, pp. 32–35.

Vough, Clair F., with Bernard Asbell. *Tapping the Human Resource: A Strategy for Productivity.* New York: AMACOM, 1975.

Yankelovich, Daniel. "Yankelovich on Today's Workers: We Need New Motivational Tools," in *How to Be a Better Leader.* New York: Penton, 1983, pp. 79–84.

2
PATTERNS OF CHANGE

Impending problems in the workplace grow out of four conflicting trends. Two involve change in national demographic patterns. Substantially fewer workers will be coming into the labor force through the early years of the next century, the first tangible signs of which appeared in 1986. The composition of the work force will be changed as well. It will be more heavily female and more of these females will be interrupting their careers for childbearing.

Changing values, expectations, and aspirations among workers constitute the third significant trend. Workers are becoming increasingly frustrated, alienated, and counterproductive. Their needs and interests conflict with the fourth trend, an ongoing restructuring of organizations fighting for survival in increasingly competitive circumstances. The long-term welfare of workers, organizations, and the national economy may hinge on the collective ability of those involved to adjust to new circumstances.

DEMOGRAPHIC TRENDS

The magnitude of the approaching human resource shortage is readily established through Census Bureau data dealing with population projections and educational attainment. Educational statistics, arguably, may be imprecise. Enrollment in postsecondary institutions has historically varied with factors other than age and may do so again. Population projections are beyond argument. The number of 18– to 24–year-olds—the group from which entry-level employees are largely drawn—has been fixed for the next 18 to 24 years. All of them have already been born; their number will not increase, nor will it decline, short of war or natural disaster.

Educational Data

The number of high school graduates enrolling in U.S. colleges and universities has increased steadily since 1967. Percentages of high school graduates in college, however, have fluctuated in a narrow range. Some 7.6

million or 33.2 percent were enrolled in 1984 compared to 5.1 million or
33.7 percent in 1967. The number increased steadily in intervening years,
but percentages remained between 35.0 percent in 1969 and 29.7 percent
in 1973.

Total college enrollment increased from 9.1 million in 1972 to 12.3
million in 1982, but then stabilized through 1984. The number of younger
students started to decline after 1983, while enrollments in older age groups
increased. The latter trend softened the impact of the baby bust on colleges
and universities. It will have no bearing, however, on the number of 18–
to 24–year-old job seekers who will be graduating in the next 18 or more
years.

Increases in the number of older students occurred in two areas. Two-
year colleges, which are more likely to serve older and part-time students,
accounted for 30 percent of the total undergraduate enrollments in 1984.
Graduate school enrollment continued to rise and encompassed 21 percent
of the student population. Educational data are thus only superficially encouraging from the standpoint of employers. Significant increases in the 18–
to 24–year-old cohort cannot be expected before the turn of the century.

While birth rates turned upward in 1976, elementary school enrollment
continued to decline through 1984. Total enrollment at that point was 7.1
million or 21 percent below the 1970 peak. Those born in 1976 will not
reach high school age until 1991. Few will complete their college educations
before 2000.

Population Data

By the turn of the century, members of the post–World War II baby-boom
generation will be in their mid-life years. Members of the baby bust group
that followed will be in their twenties. The aging of the nation's population
will be accelerating. Raw numbers of 18– to 24–year-olds will start to
increase, but they will remain a smaller percentage of the total population
than in earlier years (see Figures 2.1 and 2.2).

Census Bureau population projections involve several variables. The data
are based on estimates and were projected forward using the cohort–component method with alternative assumptions for fertility, mortality, and net
immigration levels.

Ultimate lifetime births per woman were estimated at 1.6 to 2.3, the
middle assumption being 1.9. Life expectancy at birth was estimated from
77.4 to 85.9 years, with the middle assumption at 81.0 years. Yearly immigration estimates ranged from 250,000 to 750,000 with a middle assumption of 450,000. The assumptions are shown graphically in Figure 2.3.
The potential variation is not significant for employers, however, in that
population distribution over age ranges shown in Figure 2.2 would not vary
significantly.

Figure 2.1. Percent Distribution of U.S. Population by Age and Sex, 1982–2080.

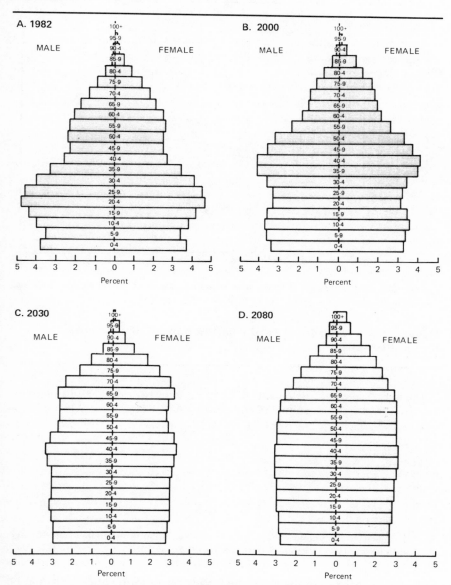

Source: Bureau of the Census, "Projections of the Population of the United States by Age, Sex and Race, 1983 to 2080," Series P-25, No. 952, May 1984.

Figure 2.2.   Estimates and Projections of Total Population; 1950–2080

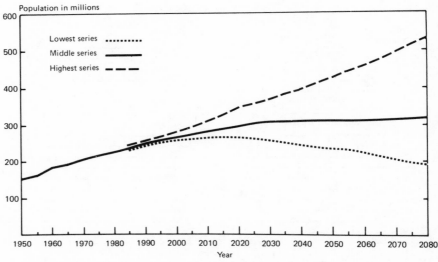

Source: Bureau of the Census, "Projections of the Population of the United States by Age, Sex and Race, 1983 to 2080," Series P-25, No. 952, May 1984.

Figure 2.3.   Percentages of Total Population in 18- to 24-year Age Group, 1985–2080.

Year	Lowest Series	Middle Series	Highest Series
1985	12.0	12.0	12.0
1990	10.4	10.3	10.3
1995	9.3	9.1	9.0
2000	9.4	9.2	9.0
2010	9.4	9.8	9.9
2030	7.9	8.6	9.2
2050	7.5	8.3	9.1
2080	7.4	8.1	9.0

Source: Bureau of the Census, "Projections of the Population of the United States by Age, Sex and Race, 1983 to 2080," Series P-25, No. 952, May 1984.

Variation at the extreme, from the lowest series to the highest, would be only 1.6 percent. The result, as illustrated in Figure 2.4, will be steady decline in the 18– to 24–year-old component of the population through most of the twenty-first century. A seller's market in entry-level labor thus becomes inevitable.

Figure 2.4.   U.S. Population by Age: 1980, 1990, and 2000.

(in thousands, based on Census Bureau estimates)

Age	1980	1990	2000	Percentage Change 1980–1990	Percentage Change 1990–2000
Under 5	16,448	19,200	17,624	16.7	-8.2
5 - 9	16,595	18,599	18,758	12.1	0.9
10-14	18,277	18,599	18,758	-8.0	16.4
15-19	21,123	16,957	18,950	-19.7	11.8
20-24	21,605	18,567	17,126	-14.1	-7.8
25-29	19,763	21,503	17,380	8.8	-19.2
30-34	17,824	22,003	19,007	23.4	-13.6
35-39	14,126	20,004	21,736	41.6	8.7
40-44	11,752	17,841	21,982	51.8	23.2
45-49	11,047	13,973	19,753	26.5	41.1
50-54	11,687	11,418	17,341	-2.3	51.9
55-59	11,619	10,451	13,285	-10.1	27.1
60-64	10,134	10,639	10,494	5.0	-1.4
65-69	8,805	10,006	9,110	13.6	-9.0
70-74	6,843	8,048	8,583	17.6	6.6
75-79	4,815	6,224	7,242	29.3	16.4
80-84	2,972	4,060	4,965	36.6	22.3
85 +	2,274	3,461	5,136	52.2	48.4
Total	227,658	249,731	267,990	9.7	7.3

Source: From Current Population Estimates, Bureau of the Census, based on 1980 Census.

Stakeholder Issues and Strategies' editor Terry Stevenson Supple summarized the impact of these trends on the national labor force.

By 1995, the supply of teenaged workers will be 20 percent below what it was in 1975. Already, the Bureau of Labor Statistics reports that the number of workers aged 16 to 19 is down 20 percent since 1978, and the number of 20– to 24–year-old workers is beginning to drop. These young people are well educated, and they have high expectations for finding good jobs. Employers will have to compete for their services.

Statisticians' Assumptions

While census data are clearly drawn, they are based on assumptions that require employer attention. These include steady economic growth at rates of 2.5 to 3.2 percent; growth rates of about 3.1 percent for other nations; a resurgence in U.S. manufacturing productivity; and a slowing growth rate in the service sector.

The latter premises are especially questionable. Few economists, futurists, or strategic planners would be inclined to accept them at face value. They neglect, for example, radical change in employment that might arise from a significant economic downturn. Substantive variation from other Census Bureau assumptions presumably would result in consequent change in forecast outcomes as well. Only time will validate or invalidate the projections. In the interim, employers must deal with contemporary realities.

EARLY PROBLEMS

While the baby-bust generation is in its teens, the primary impact will be on fast-food and other industries that rely on younger, low-wage workers. They first experienced shortages during the summer of 1986.

The isolated problems of that year attracted increasing attention over a period of months. The problem moved from newspapers' inside pages to page 1 of the September 2, 1986 issue of the *Wall Street Journal*. "Help Wanted: A Shortage of Youths Brings Wide Changes to the Labor Market," said the newspaper's headline. "Opportunities for Poor, Elderly and Handicapped; Pressure for Immigration? Minimum Wage Grows Rarer."

Jobs Go Begging

This article followed others describing problems in New England's resort areas, where "minimum wage" jobs were going begging at $6 and $7 an hour. Other reports recounted difficulties experienced by the fast-food industry in staffing Connecticut expressway restaurants. Solution to the problem: busing workers from New York City. *Newsweek*, on June 16, 1986 (p. 53), described the impact of demographic trends on the nation's hamburger chains: "The industry is slowly learning that no amount of advertising will solve its most pressing problem: labor. In the fast-food business, demography is destiny. And these days demography is dealing hamburger chains a cruel blow. . . . And the problem can only worsen."

A Pattern Taking Shape

The problem was not confined to New England. Atlanta motel operators found the $3.35 minimum wage, in the *Wall Street Journal*'s words, "becoming irrelevant." Other straws in the wind: more pressure for increased automation; more job opportunities for the disadvantaged; aggressive recruitment of older workers.

Teenage unemployment patterns taking shape in scattered areas in 1986 underscored the trend. Overall, the rate was 17.5 percent in mid-summer. In New Jersey, however, it was 5.5 percent. Maryland, Virginia, and Georgia, as well as New England, were experiencing similar shortages.

Bureau of Labor Statistics (BLS) data, like those of the Bureau of the Census, indicate that the trend will continue. For 1990, BLS forecasts 21.3 million workers between the ages of 16 and 24. The total in 1984 was 24 million or 11 percent more.

CHANGING FAMILY STRUCTURES

While basic demographic trends are most significant for employers, several other variables will also influence the composition and predispositions of the national work force. They include family structure, mortality and morbidity patterns, and immigration patterns.

The "changing American family," as it has been called, is rapidly becoming extinct in the old meaning of the term. Marriage rates continue to decline. Planned pregnancies among unmarried women are increasing. Couples are marrying later and divorcing earlier. More children are spending more years in fatherless families. More than half of mothers with preschool children are working.

Origins of change. The changes started in the 1960s, accelerated in the 1970s, and continued through the mid-1980s. Changing U.S. families conformed less and less to traditional stereotypes. They became progressively more diverse and less stable. Apparent departures from social norms involve 75 percent of the population. Experts no longer debate the existence of these structural changes. They argue instead over whether the economic, social, and cultural upheavals involved are continuing or subsiding. Most believe change in marriage and the family is abating. Declining birth rates and increasing divorce rates appear to be moderating. The influx of women into the labor force ultimately must slow as well.

Family structure. While relating in part to changing life-styles, family structure plays a significant demographic role. Contemporary trends continue to be away from the nuclear family. Marriage rates are declining. Birth rates among those who marry continue to decline as well.

The tendency to delay marriage may increase the number of lifelong singles to record levels. Never-marrieds in their twenties and thirties more than doubled between 1970 and 1985 and numbered more than 10 million by 1986.

The trend is rendered doubly complex by an increasing number of married couples electing to remain childless. Childless couples in the 25–29 age group increased from 13 percent in the 1960s to 29 percent in the mid-1980s. One in four never-married women between 25 and 34 was childless in 1986, compared to one in ten in 1960.

Childbearing Patterns

Advances in medicine have extended women's childbearing years into their late thirties or early forties. First pregnancies among women over 35 have been increasing. Other medical advances have reduced the number of women unable to have children, yet birth rates remain relatively low. Childlessness rates in 1986 were at their highest point since the depression.

In a 1984 Family Service of America study, Morton Darrow pointed out that fewer than 10 percent of the nation's households consist of the "typical" family of husband/wage earner, wife, and two or more children. He added:

Though over 90 percent of Americans presently marry, by 2000 this may drop to 85 percent as many of the recent changes take hold. Stemming from the weakening of religious, social and legal taboos, greater sexual freedom will promote continued growth of cohabitation, single-person households, unwed single-parent families and homosexual couples. Over the next few years, despite the moral objections (of those with traditional values), there will be widespread recognition of a family as consisting of two or more people joined together by bonds of sharing and intimacy.

Morbidity and mortality. While the family is changing, life spans are lengthening. The average life-span conceivably could be extended beyond 100 years in the foreseeable future.

Morbidity, or the onset of disabling disease, is another matter. It has proven relatively resistant to advances in medical science. Clement Bezold and his colleagues at the Institute for Alternative Futures argue, however, that older individuals can lead healthier lives to a point much closer to their deaths. This would induce an increase in the number of older individuals and render them healthier and more capable of work.

Immigration. Changes in the nation's immigration laws in 1986 may compound the anticipated worker shortage. Contemporary Bureau of the Census projections were based on assumptions that predated congressional action to limit illegal immigration from Latin America.

The bureau assumed annual immigration rates between 450,000 and 750,000 annually. Some considered them illogical, arguing that the influx would be between 1 and 1.5 million a year. The latter figures appeared at least equally logical until the Congress acted. They now appear more susceptible to challenge, provided the business community is assumed willing to tolerate an ongoing labor shortage. Pressure on legislators to increase immigrant flows can be expected in the face of a declining labor supply and increasing contentiousness among workers.

THE NEW WORKER

Changing organizations almost inevitably will come into conflict with workers aspiring to life-styles congruent with their aspirations in the postindustrial age. They seek in practical terms to extend a pattern of change that has persisted in U.S. society since the founding of the nation.

Early settlers came to North America for a life-style characterized by freedom of choice. They achieved this objective, but paid a price in social, religious, and economic terms. Work from dawn to dusk was essential to survival. Deviation from social norms could produce physical and social ostracism in an era in which expulsion from a community was life threatening.

As the years passed, social rather than physical constraints became dominant. The Protestant Ethic controlled through the early years of the industrial era, when wrenching change first occurred in a young nation. Workers lost the power of choice in the industrial revolution. Their lives were molded to fit the industrial age. From the factory floor to white-collar and professional ranks, workers were increasingly enslaved by the machines that raised their level of existence.

The Postindustrial Era

These conditions prevailed, in the face of increasing worker resistance through organized labor, throughout the industrial period. The era of industry in the United States reached its zenith in the years subsequent to World War II. Pent-up demand fueled a boom in production and productivity. The cold war, the Korean war, and the space race added impetus to economic expansion. Increasing productivity permitted greater rewards for all involved. If ever there were "good old days" in the United States, they were these.

Then came a series of political, governmental, and economic shocks. The assassination of the Kennedys and Martin Luther King were quickly followed by the Watergate scandal and oil boycotts. Productivity waned. So did the nation's sense of well-being. The automotive and steel industries declined. Others followed. The leading edge of the postindustrial age—the age of information—had arrived. With it, however, had come a deepening antagonism toward business. "In the Age of Uncertainty," John Kenneth Galbraith wrote in a book of that name, "the corporation is a major source of uncertainty. It leaves men wondering how and by whom and to what end they are ruled."

Their wonder is expressed in their attitudes toward their employers and their jobs. Conditions during the first half of the decade doubtless accelerated the progressive disillusionment documented in 1979 by the Opinion Research Corporation. The trends were most strongly seen among hourly workers. Lower levels of deterioration in job-related attitudes were recorded among clerical and managerial workers between 1950 and 1977.

Declining Satisfaction

Downward trend lines were found in multiple categories. Included were perceptions of the company as a place to work, as a provider of job security, and as doing something about employee problems. Employers' ratings in regard to their willingness to listen to problems also deteriorated. The most striking decline, however, involved perceptions of employer fairness (see Figure 2.5).

Several factors in Figure 2.5 are noteworthy. Deterioration occurred in

Figure 2.5.   Rating of Company on Fairness in Dealing with Employees.

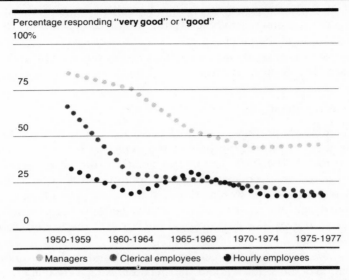

Percentage responding "**very good**" or "**good**"

100%

75				
50				
25				
0				

1950-1959   1960-1964   1965-1969   1970-1974   1975-1977

○ Managers   ● Clerical employees   ● Hourly employees

Source: Reprinted by permission of the *Harvard Business Review*. An exhibit from "Changing Employee Values: Deepening Discontent?" by M. R. Cooper et al. (January/February 1979). Copyright © by the President and Fellows of Harvard College; all rights reserved.

the perceptions of all groups. Clerical workers' attitudes, once significantly different from those of hourly employees, became virtually identical over the period involved. Attitudes of clerical workers and managers declined considerably more than did those of hourly employees. The data suggest disillusionment among those once favorably disposed toward organizational perspectives. "The changes reported here," the authors concluded, "are ubiquitous, pervasive, and nontransient; any reversal is unlikely in the foreseeable future. The goal for management is to be aware of and prepared for new and surfacing employee needs, before it is forced to take reactive, ignorant and resistive posture."

Economic Polarization

A growing national economic polarization will tend to add to worker discontent. The middle class, while in no danger of extinction, is losing ground. Rich and poor in 1986 were growing in numbers in sharp contrast to the 25 years after World War II. The rich grew richer during the latter period, but the middle class also got richer, and grew in numbers as well. The ranks of the poverty-ridden dwindled as well. These trends changed between the late 1960s and the mid 1970s. The economy continued to grow, but gains were inequitably divided.

Growing economic disparity was compounded in the early and mid-1960s by massive layoffs among middle managers and rank-and-file workers alike. While quantitative data are lacking, the number of individuals and organizations involved suggests that significant deterioration in worker morale and loyalty was almost inevitable.

Socioeconomic pressures exacted a high price, in fact, even among those who managed to remain "on the fast track." Wall Street's insider trading scandals and increasing cocaine usage in the business community were exacting a heavy toll. Psychotherapists found many executives losing all sense of balance between work and other aspects of their lives.

Growth of Dissatisfaction

Conditions away from the fast track were no more encouraging. Research suggests that few people find work challenging, exciting, or fulfilling. Those who do are most often in the professions or relatively high in organizational hierarchies. They get involved in their work, derive a great deal of satisfaction from it, and make policy for others on the assumption that they gain similar intrinsic rewards. Among most workers satisfaction is neither expected nor received. Their perspective might best be described as resigned acceptance of the status quo, hardly a prescription for productivity.

The *World of Work Report* (Vol. 6, p. 10) in 1981 reported that long-prevalent dissatisfaction among rank-and-file personnel was spreading to managers as well. "On virtually all counts," the report said, "managers are more dissatisfied with their jobs, their companies, and their opportunities than ever before." A report in the same issue of the publication concerning an early retirement plan installed by Peugeot, the French automaker, supported that contention: "An incredible 79 percent of all engineers and senior management wanted to leave, as did 86 percent of technicians and 91 percent of shopfloor workers."

Changing Workers

Acceptance of new workers' predispositions toward work and the workplace will be critical to future managers' success. The aspirations and expectations of today's workers differ significantly from those of the past. They are more educated, better informed, and more affluent than their predecessors. Their outlooks are broader, their ambitions are higher, and their expectations of employers are greater than in earlier generations. They seek more responsibility and greater opportunity for advancement. The younger among them, especially, view their jobs differently than did earlier generations. They want to be heard and heeded. They are motivated by participation and fulfillment, rather than by fear and compulsion.

Employees' perceptions of work and reward differ fundamentally from those of earlier generations. Once a moral imperative and essential to survival, work now is often viewed as intrusive upon an otherwise idyllic existence. Resentment toward the need to work is compounded by enhanced educational levels. "More abundant education," Judson Gooding pointed out, "makes men aware of abstractions such as freedom and autonomy, and they increasingly demand control over their destinies."

Personal values are changing. Workers' primary interest in survival may remain, but it is survival of a new sort. Rather than economic, as in the early days of the United States, it is psychological, spiritual, and emotional. Impoverishment can occur in any area, and workers are fighting for a new type of survival.

The senior managers of the 1990s will be the last group whose lives were significantly influenced by the economic depression of the 1930s. Middle managers and supervisors will stand between them and a new generation of still better trained and educated workers. The new generation will demand greater responsibility, more challenging work, and more rapid advancement. They will expect participative rather than authoritarian leadership.

They will be aware of the alternatives and opportunities available to them, concerned over personal and professional growth, open to job changes, and less constrained by concepts of company loyalty. Their as yet unknown value systems inevitably will differ from those of their predecessors and can only compound supervisory and managerial problems.

Their deteriorating perceptions of employer organizations received little attention during the early 1980's. Organizations were not oblivious to potential problems. They were preoccupied, however, with economic conditions that threatened the survival of many and produced the collapse of others.

ORGANIZATIONS AND EMPLOYEES

Organizations' efforts to cope with economic problems in the 1980s did nothing to reduce workers' disillusionment. Jobs were exported to countries where wages were lower. Joint ventures were undertaken with European and Asian organizations. Internal belt tightening became the order of the day.

The latter concept produced trends that exacerbated employees' perceptions of the organizations for which they worked. Plants closed, jobs were lost, and unions were weakened. Labor negotiations led to union givebacks. More part-time workers were hired. Employee benefits were curtailed and limited. Dual wage and benefit systems compounded worker resentment.

Organized Labor

By mid-decade, plant closings of the early 1980s created deteriorating conditions for organized labor. Membership declined rapidly. Strikes dwindled in number, and unions won few of them. Hard-won work rules were bargained away. Unions, which had been a protective shield for almost a quarter of the national work force were soon accomplishing relatively little for a total membership half that size.

Government, however, to some extent was assuming a more protectionist role. By mid-decade, right-to-know laws, requiring companies to divulge information on hazardous substances in the workplace, had been enacted in some two dozen states. Many also created statutory protection for corporate and government whistleblowers.

Court decisions steadily eroded the employment-at-will doctrine. First the states and then the Congress outlawed mandatory retirement ages.

Individual privacy rights were strengthened by laws limiting governmental disclosure of data on individuals. Use of the polygraph was curtailed as well. Employees increasingly were given access to their personnel files, and a number of states blocked use of arrest records in the hiring process.

National and state occupational safety laws were strengthened. Discrimination on almost any basis and under any circumstances was barred. Employee rights in pension funds were strengthened, and new increases in the minimum wage were being discussed.

NEW ORGANIZATIONS

Legislative action may provide some protection for workers until declines in their numbers induce greater organizational liberality. In the interim, however, they are apt to become further alienated as organizations continue restructuring to meet the demands of the information age.

These changes extend to basic organizational shapes or profiles, which traditionally were pyramidal in form, with few senior managers, greater numbers of middle managers, and still more rank-and-file workers. Oval patterns appeared early in organizational restructuring processes, as the economy ax fell at lower echelons. As cost cutting extended to middle management, however, organizational profiles more resembled dumbbells. Two factors apparently were responsible. One was economic: Organizations sought to adopt "lean and mean" profiles in the face of economic uncertainty. The other was more systemic but less apparent: Middle management became more and more anachronistic with the advent of the computer. An overabundance of middle managers coupled with a shortage of beginners was emerging as a long-term economic problem.

These circumstances suggest a greater potential for employee violatility than has ever been the case. Dislocations of a magnitude anticipated by economists, congressional planners, and others will inevitably provoke concern, fear, and perhaps even paranoia in much of the nation's labor force. "In such a rapidly changing economy," says Richard Louv, "the need for a sense of belonging and control is intensified—especially in the workplace." Employers, he says, will need to make the workplace a home, and this at a time when work itself is less and less easy to conceptualize.

In the information age, what comes to mind are flickering letters on a video display terminal, or the transient statistics of an investment newsletter—all ephemeral, impermanent. The assembly line stripped manufacturing of much of its satisfaction long ago, but the information age removes even more of the tangible proof of our labor. If what we make does not seem real or solid, or even semi-permanent, then our connections to our work do not seem real or solid. Work is the glue that holds society together; identifiable, role-producing, understandable work....

What this atmosphere of uncertainty suggests is the need for radically different workplaces. One option is to work for yourself, to be an entrepreneur. In an economy that demands flexibility, self-employment can be a way to get a sense of selfhood and potency. While one way of working in America fails, another rises. An America full of self-satisfaction is doing everything it can to create the illusion that work in the future will be full of wonder and security, in places worthy of coming home to. The truth may be different.

The extent to which this pattern will persist is difficult to estimate. Public or private policy shifts in at least five areas could significantly impact the labor market. They include programs to fix or stabilize employment at or near "full employment" levels; worker training or retraining programs; economic revitalization or reindustrialization programs; efforts to redistribute income unlinked to jobs and work; and combinations of two or more of the foregoing.

COMPOUNDING PROBLEMS

The ensuing decade may compound many of the problems described above. The United States will become a "high-risk and high stress society," according to Oxford Analytica, Ltd., a research and consulting firm based at the British university. Results of their research in behalf of several U.S. corporations, published in 1986, suggest that the 1990s will test the confidence of the population.

Less upward mobility, less opportunity, less family stability, and a less effective governmental response to the nation's social needs are in prospect for the nation, the research showed. In the employment area, Oxford Analytica predicted increased competition for relatively fewer senior organizational positions; more early retirement, as frustrated Boomers abandon efforts to reach the top; and younger newcomers receiving fewer pomotions as older, more experienced workers crowd career ladders.

Other problems, such as the growing gap between haves and have nots, were predicted to persist. "American society at all levels...is approaching a period in which the active pursuit of self-interest will be paramount." It will involve a testing of belief in U.S. exceptionalism, competing visions as to the kind of country its citizens want, and a choice of what visions to pursue. These issues inevitably will impact workers and workplaces, compounding what many perceive to be mounting worker dissatisfaction.

The Age of Information

The onset of the age of information thus promises to be a mixed blessing. In practical terms, a way of work life is dying, and new one is coming into being. Steel workers are being supplanted by hamburger servers. The United States appears destined to provide knowledge, information, and services to the world, while less-developed nations assume basic manufacturing functions.

The transition will be painful for organization and worker alike. High technology appears destined to dislocate millions of workers. Estimates range from 15 to 45 million, and the Congressional Budget Office predicts that robots and computers alone will supplant some three million manufacturing workers by 1990.

A NEW APPROACH

What can be done? Leadership and a new management approach are essential, says entrepeneur Ross Perot of Electronic Data Systems Corporation and General Motors. "We must replace bureaucrats with leaders, and we've got to do that quickly," he warns. Because of foreign competition this country is "living on borrowed time." Perot urges reprogramming leaders and managers, eliminating "adversarial relationships" within corporations, where "procedures are more important than results."

The Challenge Defined

Management success in dealing with demographic, technological, and economic factors will vary with the ability to meet human change as well. The challenge was well delineated in Naisbitt and Aburdene's "Ten Considerations in Reinventing the Corporation":

1. The best and brightest people will gravitate toward those corporations that foster personal growth.
2. The manager's new role is that of coach, teacher, and mentor.
3. The best people want ownership—psychic and literal—in a company; the best companies are providing it.

4. Companies will increasingly turn to third-party contractors, shifting from hired labor to contract labor.

5. Authoritarian management is yielding to a networking, people style of management.

6. Entrepreneurship within the corporations—intrapreneurship—is creating new products and new markets and revitalizing companies inside out.

7. Quality will be paramount.

8. Intuition and creativity are challenging the "it's all in the numbers" business-school philosophy.

9. Large corporations are emulating the positive and productive qualities of small business.

10. The dawn of the information economy has fostered a massive shift from infrastructure to quality of life.

Reinventing Work

Organizations' first step in accommodating to these changes, according to Naisbitt and Aburdene, requires "reinventing work." While individual and organizational needs are increasingly compatible in the information society, they point out, the U.S. workplace remains oriented to the industrial society of the 1950s.

The average worker at that point in time was a white male with a wife and children to support. He worked full time in an office or factory and belonged to or would join a union. He was about 40 years old and would retire at 65. He was motivated by job security and steady pay and, whether working in an office or a plant, lived in an industrial society.

Today, the typical worker increasingly is female. She is a 34-year-old baby boomer with two children and a working spouse who plans to work beyond retirement. She neither belongs to a union nor would consider joining one and is willing to accept risk for possible rewards that superior performance would bring. Finally, she is likely to have or prefer some sort of flexible work schedule.

New Age Skills

Theories bearing on organizational efficacy are legion. Some have been subjected to thorough testing. Others are little more than concepts remaining to be explored. None has proven of special merit in resolving contemporary problems or anticipating those of the future. There nevertheless are some obvious steps that will be necessary on the part of virtually every organization. They are outlined concisely by Hickman and Silva, who prescribe six "New Age skills" essential "to achieve excellence in the dynamic future"[1]

Creative Insight: Asking the Right Questions. Insight, which involves adapting a variety of critical perspectives, forces executives to strike at the heart of a problem, not just at its visible symptom. Executives lacking insight see either the forest or the trees, but never both. Without insight, executives waste valuable resources because they don't get at the roots of problems and are therefore unable to design successful solutions. By asking the right questions, you obtain the key to the increased insight that informs superior strategies.

Sensitivity: Doing unto Others. If, in the final analysis, people are an organization's greatest asset, then New Age managers must understand how to bind them together in a culture wherein they feel truly motivated to achieve high goals. Face-to-face communication, ongoing training and development, creative incentive programs, and job security all display the sort of sensitivity that nurtures strong cultures. Every strong culture derives from management's sensitivity. Without it, employees feel unmotivated, underutilized and even exploited. Most executives are sensitive in some ways but not in others.

Vision: Creating the Future. Leaders who develop clear vision can mentally journey from the known to the unknown, creating the future from a montage of facts, figures, hopes, dreams, dangers and opportunities.

Versatility: Anticipating Change. A difficult skill to master, versatility presumes that some goals other than immediately pressing business problems should concern you. Unless you aggressively pursue interests outside your field, you will never be able to comfortably adapt to change.

Focus: Implementing Change. Everything that happens in your organization either contributes to or erodes its efforts to implement change and keep strategy and culture in harmony. Focus enables leaders to invest available resources toward implementing successful and lasting change.

Patience: Living in the Long Term. Executives must rise above the thoughts and actions of others and commit themselves to long-term perspectives of their enterprises. If you believe in your firm's long-term purpose, you must be patient enough to see it through.

The first two of these skills are critical in handling the impending human-resources problem. Insight is essential in defining the scope and impact of prospective difficulties on individual organizations. Their vulnerabilities will be greatest as two basic conflicts develop in the work force. One is intergenerational, pitting the baby boom against the baby bust. The other is structural, producing conflict between management traditionalists and innovators.

[1]From *Creating Excellence* by Craig R. Hickman and Michael A. Silva. Copyright (c) by Craig R. Hickman and Michael A. Silva. Reprinted by arrangement with NAL Penguin, Inc., New York, NY.

SUMMARY

Four conflicting trends are leading to major conflicts in the contemporary work place. First among them is a fast-changing demographic profile in the United States. Numbers of 18– to 24–year-olds are declining, as the baby-bust generation comes into the work place. Concurrently, the number of those in the traditional retirement-age sector is increasing.

The first evidence of resultant human-resources shortages occurred in the mid-1980s, in what traditionally were teenager jobs. Although spotty, these shortages were precursors of worse to come.

The second trend of significance to employers is change in family characteristics and their impact on future workers. As few as 25 percent of households today fit the traditional nuclear family pattern. More and more are childless. Some will remain so, while in others childbearing will come in later years, which also will complicate employers' problems.

These and other elements are contributing to the evolution of a "new worker." This third trend is producing an increasingly dissatisfied, disillusioned, and only marginally productive work force. Worker discontent is compounded by economic change, both organizational and individual.

At the organizational level, disappearing jobs, layoffs, and reduced compensation and benefits are but a few of the causes. Others include multitiered employment systems and economic polarization.

Change in organizations, especially as it has impacted worker security, has in part been offset by protective legislation. Ultimately, however, organizations will be forced by labor shortages and worker discontent to respond internally to compounding levels of dissatisfaction. They will be challenged to create a new organization amidst the turmoil of conflicts pitting baby boomers against baby busters and traditional managers against innovators.

ADDITIONAL READING

Apcar, Leonard M. "Work Rule Programs Spread to Union Plants," *Wall Street Journal,* April 16, 1985.

Bacas, Harry. "Where Are The Teenagers?" *Nation's Business,* August 1986.

Bean, Ed. "Cause of Quality-Control Problems Might Be Managers—Not Workers," Wall Street Journal, August 10, 1985.

Bloom, David E. *How to Respond to the Changing Labor Market.* Ithaca, NY: American Demographics, 1985.

Brannigan, Martha. "Help Wanted: A Shortage of Youths Brings Wide Changes to the Labor Market," *Wall Street Journal,* September 2, 1986.

Bureau of the Census. *Projections of the Population of the United States by Age, Sex and Race: 1983 to 2080.* Washington, DC: U.S. Department of Commerce, 1984.

——— *School Enrollment—Social and Economic Characteristics of Students: October 1984.* Washington, DC: U.S. Department of Commerce, 1985.

Bureau of Labor Statistics. *Occupational Projections and Training Data.* Washington DC: U.S. Department of Labor, 1984.

Carvell, Fred J. *Human Relations in Business.* 3rd. ed. New York: Macmillan, 1980.

Cooper, M. R., et al. "Changing Employee Values: Deepening Discontent?" *Harvard Business Review,* January-February 1979.

Engel, Paul G. "Have You Been 'Sacked' By Your Subordinates?" *Industry Week,* November 24, 1986.

Fishman, Joshua A. "Bilingualism and Separatism," *Annals of the American Academy of Political and Social Science,* September 1986.

Fowler, Elizabeth M. "Low-Level Vs. Middle Salaries," *New York Times,* October 29, 1985.

Goleman, Daniel. "The Strange Agony of Success," *New York Times,* August 24, 1986.

Harwood, Edwin. "American Public Opinion and U.S. Immigration Policy," *Annals of the American Academy of Political and Social Science,* September 1986.

Hickman, Craig R., and Michael A. Silva. *Creating Excellence: Managing Corporate Culture, Strategy and Change in the New Age.* New York: New American Library, 1984.

Hymowitz, Carol, and Thomas F. O'Boyle. "Pittsburgh's Evolution from Steel to Service Sparks a Culture Clash," *Wall Street Journal,* August 21, 1984.

Kantrowitz, Barbara, et al. "Three's a Crowd," *Newsweek,* September 1, 1986.

Kieffer, Jarold. "The Coming Opportunity to Work Until You're 75 . . . ," *Washington Post,* September 9, 1984.

Kiplinger Washington Letter, *The New American Boom.* Washington, DC: The Kiplinger Washington Editors, 1986.

Kotlowitz, Alex. "Labor's Ultimate Weapon, the Strike, Is Mostly Failing," *Wall Street Journal,* October 13, 1986.

Levin, Doron P. "GM Announces Drive to Trim Salaried Staff," *Wall Street Journal,* August 25, 1986.

Louv, Richard. *America II.* Los Angeles: Tarcher, 1983.

Macarov, David. *Worker Productivity: Myths and Reality.* Beverly Hills, CA: Sage, 1982.

Meyers, William. "Child Care Finds a Champion in the Corporation," *New York Times,* August 4, 1985.

Miller, Annetta. "Burgers: The Heat Is On," *Newsweek,* June 16, 1986.

Miller, Michael W. "Computers Keep Eye on Workers and See If They Perform Well," *Wall Street Journal,* June 3, 1985.

Mitchell, Arnold. *The Nine American Life Styles: Who We Are and Where We Are Going.* New York: Macmillan, 1983.

Naisbitt, John. *Megatrends.* New York: Warner Books, 1982.

———, and Patricia Aburdene. *Reinventing the Corporation.* New York: Warner Books, 1985.

Noble, Kenneth B. "Why Walkouts Don't Work as They Used To," *New York Times,* March 24, 1985.

——— "End of Forced Retirement Means a Lot—To a Few," *New York Times,* October 26, 1986.

Oxford Analytica. *America in Perspective*. Boston: Houghton-Mifflin, 1986.

Press, Robert M. "Proposed US law seen as unlikely to stem tide of Mexican illegals," *Christian Science Monitor,* October 17, 1986.

Reich, Charles A. *The Greening of America.* New York: Random House, 1970.

Reinhold, Robert. "Surge in Bogus Papers Predicted in Wake of Change in Alien Law," *New York Times,* October 20, 1986.

Ricklefs, Roger. "Faced With Shortages of Unskilled Labor, Employers Hire More Retarded Workers," *Wall Street Journal,* October 21, 1986.

Russell, Cheryl, and Thomas G. Exter. "America at Mid-Decade," *American Demographics,* January 1986.

Samuels, Phil. "Nine Principles for 'Demotivating' Workers," in Gerald M. Goldhaber, *Organizational Communication,* 4th ed. Dubuque, IA: Brown, 1986.

Serrin, William. "Unionism Struggles through Middle Age," *New York Times,* October 27, 1985.

Solis, Dianna. "Their Ranks Eroded, Unions Try to Recruit Illegal Immigrants," *Wall Street Journal,* October 15, 1986.

Sterngold, James. "On Wall Street, a Greedy New Breed," *New York Times,* July 27, 1986.

Supple, Terry Stevenson. "The Coming Labor Shortage," *American Demographics,* September 1986.

Toffler, Alvin. *The Third Wave.* New York: Morrow, 1980.

Wessel, David. "Growing Gap: U.S. Rich and Poor Increase in Numbers; Middle Loses Ground," *Wall Street Journal,* September 22, 1986.

————. "Promises, Promises: Firms Seek to Cut Insurance for Retirees," *Wall Street Journal,* April 17, 1985.

————. "Do as I Do: More Consultants Quit Profession to Start New Businesses," *Wall Street Journal,* October 15, 1986.

Williams, Winston. "Business Brings Back the Lockout," *New York Times,* October 5, 1986.

3

CONFLICT: GENERATIONAL AND ORGANIZATIONAL

Escalating conflict in the workplace arises primarily out of divergent interests in two areas: generational and organizational. Disparate baby-boom and baby-bust generations find themselves positioned in adversarial occupational roles. The boomers block career ladders that busters seek to climb. Generational values, beliefs, and expectations are thus compounded by economic and hierarchical considerations. Strength of impact and resultant organizational damage can be limited, but only where organizations act to eliminate traditional hierarchical conflicts. In most of them, the conflicts also are a barrier to productivity. Successful intercession in either area will require understanding of the forces involved.

THE BOOMERS

The baby boom was created by a generation reared in the insecurities of the Great Depression and World War II. The preboom generation came to maturity during what may prove to have been the nation's longest and greatest period of economic expansion. Reacting to the optimism of the times, it produced more than 75 million children—the baby boom.

Boomers were reared in a home- and child-centered society. Parents were determined that their children would enjoy "a better life" than their own. Parental sacrifice was the norm. A generation consisting primarily of factory workers and small businessmen sought to launch their children into the professions through higher education.

Economic expansion encouraged parents and children. Parents looked forward to more affluent life-styles for their youngsters. Children took material success for granted and became concerned with and involved in social issues. Their generation became more idealistic, rebellious, and dedicated to personal growth.

A New Challenge

They now are creating a threat to succeeding generations' standards of living. Boomers now in middle age will soon be eligible for old-age benefits the nation may or may not be able to provide.

Congress, in late 1986, was already acting to ameliorate the threat of a "gray-power" revolt. The first step was twofold. Legislation requiring mandatory retirement at predetermined age levels was struck down; and concurrently, employers were required to continue making retirement fund payments for those continuing to work.

Further changes may follow, but conflict is almost inevitable. Boomers will become an unprecedented economic burden for the baby bust generation. Their numbers also will concentrate political power in the elderly.

Fewer workers. The baby-bust generation will be looking for support to a dwindling working population. Concurrently they will be coping with the consequences of an unprecedented federal debt. Declining educational standards and productivity will compound their problem.

An unreserved assumption of future disaster is, nevertheless, not wholly warranted. The national population has been aging for decades as a result of lower fertility rates and increasing longevity. Living standards, however, have continued to improve from generation to generation.

Continuing trend? These conditions developed as a result of ever-improving technological capability. Those who discount prospective problems apparently assume that this trend will continue. The assumption implies that the next generation will be productive beyond belief, or that the nation can continue borrowing from future generations.

Available data suggest otherwise. At present, 3.4 workers support each retiree through Social Security and Medicare. About 30 percent of all federal revenues are expended in this manner. More than half of all 1986 federal spending supported the 11 percent of the population over 65. Yet about a third of them then were living at or near the poverty line.

As boomers reach retirement age and the number of elderly doubles there may be as few as 1.5 workers to support each retiree. Employee and employer payroll taxes supporting Social Security and Medicare are already scheduled to increase to more than 15 percent or a maximum of almost $8,000 per worker by 1990. Further increases appear inevitable, unless workers somehow become more productive than they are today, an occurrence that appears less than likely.

Generational Differences

Contemporary conditions suggest that tomorrow's workers are apt to be less rather than more productive. One of five children in the United States lived in poverty in 1986, an increase of almost 50 percent over the prior 14 years. More than 40 percent of the poor had not reached adulthood, and history indicates that poor children tend to become poor adults.

Educational backgrounds. The younger generation of the 1980s also is likely to be less well educated than those that went before. National expenditures on education in constant dollars declined 30 percent between

1980 and 1985. Perhaps in part as a result, student performance on Scholastic Aptitude Tests (SATs), declined from early baby-boom days through the early 1980s. They improved somewhat—to 1975 levels—by mid-decade, but the improvement appeared more a sign of baby-buster effort to succeed than of taxpayer support.

Changing expenditures. Government expenditures between 1960 and 1984 shifted from the young to the elderly. The spending ratio in dollars reached 10:1 in the latter year, but conditions were more complex than the numbers indicated. Teachers' real incomes declined more than 12 percent during the decade ending in 1983. Their qualifications and performance deteriorated apace. The nation thus will be called upon to shoulder a greater social burden with a less well educated work force, apparently predisposed to poverty.

Discouraging Data

Data generated by the National Taxpayers Union (NTU) and Social Security Administration (SSA) are particularly discouraging. Unfunded liabilities of federal annuity programs, according to NTU data, are approaching $7 trillion. If the national economy follows its pattern of the past 15 years, the SSA estimates, payroll taxes will have to almost triple.

These burdens can be avoided by the next generation in one of only two ways: by cutting future retirement and other benefits for baby boomers or increasing earnings to such an extent that the unprecedented cost will be acceptable to those involved.

Mobility factor. Employers and employees ultimately will have to deal with this problem and with another relating to national demographic characteristics. The second problem: mobility of the baby-boom generation—upward or downward. Analysis of Census Bureau data in 1986 indicates that 72 percent of the boomers were working in jobs paying an average of about $10,000 a year. The young, upwardly mobile professionals or "yuppies" numbered only three million. Boomers for the most part appeared to be a downwardly rather than an upwardly mobile group.

Reduced investment. The root of the problem, says economist Lester Thurow, is relatively simple. National savings and investment rates have not kept pace with the worker population. Increases in the labor supply must be matched by productive investment, or both productivity growth and real wages will decline, he says. Employers may thus be concurrently confronted by new demands from a new generation of workers and a pressing need for greater plant and equipment investment.

THE BUSTERS

The baby-bust generation's early experience differed considerably from that of the boomers. While boomers grew up in increasing prosperity and afflu-

ence, busters were troubled by insecurities and economic dislocations arising out of the Vietnam conflict. Their social fabric was torn repeatedly by
assassination and civil rights strife. Inflation in the late 1960s brought wage
and price controls. An oil crisis, stagflation, yet another oil shortage, and an
extended recession followed.

The bust generation experienced less parental supervision, more divorce,
and attendant problems. Divorce rates increased and almost half the busters
will have spent some time in single-parent households before reaching the
age of 18. More than 35 percent of them were not living with both biological
parents in 1982.

The numbers of children in single-parent households more than doubled
between 1960 and 1982. Concurrently, the number of working mothers
with preschool children almost tripled. Little more than 25 percent were
cared for in their own homes. More than half were cared for at home 20
years earlier.

Change in Perspective

Latent insecurities were to be expected, given the environment in which
the baby-bust generation was reared, but they remained dormant during
the busters' early years. The generation ahead was experiencing prosperity.
The busters anticipated prosperity, more leisure, and a better society, until
the first oil shock. From that point forward, the picture darkened.

Rather than success in the boom generation, the busters saw economic
hardship—overqualified workers struggling in mind-dulling jobs, with housing increasingly beyond their reach. They also were responding to their
environments in ways that suggest problems for prospective employers.

Teenage suicide rates have tripled since 1958, and perhaps a half million
youngsters have attempted suicide but failed. The trend has been attributed
to emotional stress arising out of family break-ups. Members of the baby-
bust generation also appear more prone to other violence, both as victims
and perpetrators. They are involved in more homicides, use more psychiatric and psychological help, and appear more hostile and alienated than
their predecessors. They are more apt to have children out of wedlock and
in most cases elect to rear their offspring.

Greater Diversity

The baby busters also will be a more diverse generation than their predecessors. White-to-nonwhite birth ratios changed from 7 to 1 at the start of
the baby boom to 5 to 1 at the end of the baby bust in 1976. Immigration
of Hispanics from Central and South America and Orientals from Vietnam
and elsewhere enhanced that diversity. Immigration curbs may slow the
process, but the extent of any slowdown remains to be discerned.

Middle-class decline. Decline in the middle class will also contribute to the intergenerational gap. The well educated and well trained have been well compensated, but others have seen incomes deteriorate in relative terms. Decline in manufacturing and increased use of computers and robotics are major causes.

Tax systems, especially at the federal level, served as income redistributors and equalizers. They became less so in the early 1980s and declined further in effectiveness with the tax reform of 1986, adding to income disparity.

Further diversity will arise out of declining social pressures against nontraditional life-styles. Pregnant high school students no longer need leave school. Abortions are performed openly. Gays no longer find it necessary to "closet" themselves, and society may become still more liberal.

Redefining liberalism. Social liberality should not be taken as implying political or economic liberalism. After four presidencies "failed," in their eyes, baby busters became sufficiently impressed by Ronald Reagan to move toward political conservatism. They also appear attracted by Republican economic conservatism and less socially activist government.

Baby busters apparently will be a more ambitious, pragmatic, skeptical, selfish, goal-oriented generation. They seek a society that allows individuals opportunities to do what they want and reap the rewards.

Youngsters of the 1960s sought to overthrow the system through persistent protests. In the 1970s they ignored the system, turning to introspection and inner development. Their objective in the 1980s is to beat the system through individual initiative.

THE DIFFERENCES

Intergenerational change is not new. Seldom has a generation failed to bemoan the behavioral standards and life-styles of its successors. Accelerating social and technological change, however, have broadened intergenerational gaps. Historically they have been bridged through the socialization of younger generations. Hippies, yippies, and yuppies have been successively assimilated into the national social structure without undue dislocation.

Accommodation or Conflict?

Whether this process can create accommodation between the baby-boom and baby-bust generations is open to question. Older generations have traditionally been positioned to control the assimilation process. They have been in controlling occupational positions and until now have been of near equal size. These circumstances enabled them to demand a measure of compliance with social norms; to enforce conformity with "establishment" mores and folkways.

Figure 3.1.   Comparison of Baby-Boom and Baby-Bust Generation Perspectives.

INTERGENERATIONAL DIFFERENCES:
BOOMERS VS. BUSTERS

Characteristic	Boomers	Busters
Economic environment	Expansive and optimistic	Recession and instability
Social context	Civil rights; assassinations; uncertainties	Relatively stable other than in economic areas
Perception of future	Bright	Uncertain to poor
Parental status	Working class	White collar
Parental focus	Home and family	Material success
Parental commitment	To children	To careers
Family stability	Relatively strong	Relatively weak
Education	Relatively good	Relatively poor
Economic success	Sought after and largely achieved	Taken for granted early; now less certain
Social concerns	Secondary to economic	Primary interest early; now less important
Mobility	Generally upward	Stable or downward
Expectations	Often unfulfilled	Being fulfilled

Source: Adapted from Richard Longman, "Richer or Poorer: Will the Baby Boom Live Better than their Parents?" and Mathew Greenwald, "Beyond the Boom: How Will the Baby Bust Be Different?" Speeches to the American Demographic Institute, New York City, June 1986.

Arrival of the baby-bust generation will destroy the numerical balance and place greater power in the hands of the newcomers. With labor a relatively scarce commodity, boomers will be less able to require conformity. They will be forced to accept much of the baby bust generation into the work force on its own terms, despite conflicting backgrounds, values, and life-styles.

Intergenerational differences become apparent in a tabular comparison of the two groups, as shown in Figure 3.1.

The differences suggest multiple problems for organizations and managers. Whether they will materialize is another matter. Demographic projections are only projections. Any number of events can intervene to destroy assumptions that underlie demographic data. Congressional action in late

1986 to bar mandatory retirement and curb illegal immigration, for example, will influence job availability and population growth, unless government intervenes once more.

Behavioral Factors

Behavioral characteristics of individuals are more predictable, especially when the environments in which the individuals grew up are known. This is the case as to both boom and bust generations, permitting logical conjecture as to their predispositions and potential for conflict in the work place. Individual examination of intergenerational differences suggests the following areas of potential friction:

Wages—Baby busters will seek greater economic security to compensate for past insecurities, their perceptions of the future, and added demands that will be made on their generation.

Benefits—Change in family and social structure will lead to demand for more diverse benefit structures.

Working conditions—Equipped with more bargaining power as a result of supply and demand factors, baby busters will press for more salutary occupational environments.

Proprietorship—Psychic or real proprietorship will be among busters' primary requirements. Many will participate in a national entrepreneurial renewal. Employers will find it essential to offer comparable rewards.

Under these conditions, the best and the brightest workers will be attracted to those organizations that foster individual as well as organizational growth. They will be attracted to managers and supervisors who serve as mentors and coaches, rather than overseers.

They will be seeking networking rather than authoritarian management styles and what has been called "intrapreneurship" along the lines pioneered by the 3M Company and others. Such organizations give their personnel latitude to pursue any concept that may prove productive. When they succeed, they are rewarded. Failure, however, is ignored rather than punished. Multiple failures have preceded most of the major scientific and technological discoveries of the century and many of the minor ones as well. The 3M Company's policies, for example, led to the ubiquitous "stick-on" notes that are now used in most offices.

Management of this sort also departs from traditional by-the-numbers approaches and embraces the intuitive and creative. In essence, the productive features that long have launched most major business successes must be reestablished in large organizations. Organizations, as Naisbitt and

Aburdene put it, are becoming "confederations of entrepreneurs" rather than conventional bureaucracies.

What Workers Want

The entrepreneurial small-business boom that has been developing in the United States occurred, workers contend, because "working for most companies is so demeaning to the human spirit that many talented people are forced out the door." The information economy, they declare, is forging a "new work contract," a major revision of the unwritten agreement between worker and employer. It involves a new model of the ideal employee: one who takes responsibility for, initiates, and monitors his or her own work, rather than one who follows instructions well.

What few organizations accept is that the "new workers" are not new. They have been awaiting recognition for some time. Employers have long considered wages and benefits to be primary criteria in employee definition of a "good job." Employees disagree. Surveys taken over the past decade and more have repeatedly demonstrated the fallacy of employer assumptions. Among the more recent of them was a 1983 study undertaken by researcher Daniel Yankelovich for the Public Agenda Foundation. Job security, wages, and benefits were not among the top ten characteristics, listed below, that respondents sought in their jobs.

1. Respect from coworkers
2. Interesting work
3. Recognition for good work
4. Opportunity to develop skills
5. Colleagues willing to listen to ideas for improvement
6. Opportunity for independent thinking
7. Seeing the results of one's work
8. Working for efficient managers
9. Challenging work
10. Being well informed about the organization

Satisfaction of boomer and buster needs will be determined by the extent to which organizations resolve the second major conflict now facing them: traditionalism versus innovation in organizational philosophy and structure.

ORGANIZATIONAL CONFLICT

Conflict in contemporary organizations arises out of several basic issues. Primary among them are control and purpose. Who shall control the organization and what shall be its goals? The issues are complex and inseparable. Traditionalists hold that the purpose of business is business. Contemporary society, on the other hand, demands that business enterprises benefit workers and communities as well as owners and managers.

The issues are complicated by problems described earlier. Workers have changed. So have the nation's demographic and economic structures. The latter factors have created conflict that inevitably impinges on the workplace at all organizational levels.

The Organizational Dilemma

Surviving organizations must create environments in which workers can simultaneously achieve individual and organizational objectives. They are being challenged to accomplish this objective in a society confused by extreme social philosophies. One places the individual above the organization. The other takes a diametrically opposed position.

Traditional organizational bureaucracies estrange workers by excluding them from real involvement. They have no part, for example, in decision-making processes that produce performance standards with which they must comply. Yet managers bemoan their lack of commitment and involvement.

These conditions produce a sort of "us against them" class warfare. Such sense of community as exists occurs in polarized hierarchical groups, detracting from rather than contributing to organizational effectiveness. Non-managers and, indeed, some managers feel no obligation to organizations that fail to promote their involvement and participation.

Managerial Blindness

Senior managers appear blind to the fact that all organizations are essentially political entities in which member involvement is prerequisite to commitment. Worker self-concept suffers where involvement is denied; where workers have no control over jobs and no influence on organizations; where they receive no recognition from management.

Boring and meaningless work with no psychic income destroys motivation. What remains is a level of performance barely adequate to prevent loss of employment. Managers who behave as if worker values, attitudes, and beliefs can be left in the locker room contribute to organizational dysfunction.

Dangerous Assumptions

Worker's problems are created by the most destructive of managerial assumptions: that organizations' problems necessarily are created by worker behavior. Where difficulties arise, workers are assumed to be unable or unwilling to perform as required. Organizations are assumed to be inherently blameless.

Problem-solving efforts that assume organizational omnipotence are unlikely to succeed. At least half of all potential problem sources—and solutions—are ignored. The result often is an effort to conform workers to organizational systems, when the opposite approach would be more appropriate.

Most organizations, according to Lee M. Ozley, fall into one of two categories. The first consists of "working-for" organizations, characterized by

1. Adversarial relationships, carping, bickering and rumor mongering
2. Parochialism and fiefdoms, with each department manager trying to outdo the others
3. Management personnel acting as policemen rather than resources
4. Underuse of internal expertise
5. Bureaucratic mentality in day-to-day operations
6. A don't-give-a-damn attitude about the needs of the organization.

"Working-with" organizations, on the other hand, are oriented toward

1. Tapping total organizational problem-solving potential
2. A win-win climate where everyone gains
3. Joint allegiance to the department, the group, the corporation, and the craft or profession
4. Minimum rigidity, maximum responsiveness
5. A positive, energized work climate
6. High levels of satisfaction among employees and managers alike
7. An attitude of caring about the corporation's success.

MANAGEMENT PERSPECTIVES

Why should organizational orientation be of managerial concern? Because organizational survival is a shared need. Organizations in which workers produce at optimum levels are better equipped to meet competition—foreign and domestic. Organizations prosper when workers are involved in their jobs and in contributing ideas for improvement. They suffer when the reverse is true.

Organizations that recognize employees as stakeholders also tend to experience lower turnover rates and greater employee continuity, fewer labor problems, and greater employee flexibility and cooperation. These are almost inevitable where ethical management practices prevail. Equally welcome is the pleasant, less strained atmosphere that develops in organizations where workers are involved and feel responsible. Absence of tension reduces fatigue and produces better work.

Attempts to maintain traditional management systems in the face of change in the work force inevitably produce adversarial conditions. Cooperative atmospheres, however, are readily created where managers accommodate to change. According to Judson Gooding

The choice comes down to moving with the exigencies of the times—not mollycoddling but accommodating the demands of people for more control over their environments—or existing in a grim atmosphere of discontent or active hatred. Management that fails to involve workers in their jobs also fails to tap production workers' know-how and misses out on the best and richest single source of money and time-saving ideas available.

Origin of Problems

Contemporary human resources problems are often insidious. They develop more out of managerial generation gaps and benign neglect than diabolical design. Managers approach personnel with predetermined concepts of human behavior. When worker behavior fails to conform to stereotypes, managers attempt to change rather than accommodate to them.

New approaches. At least two new approaches to human-resources management have been applied in attempting to enhance worker performance: Participative management techniques have been used during the past decade with varying results; and more recently, executives have sought to modify organizational cultures to create better environments.

Participative management, involving such devices as quality circles, was triggered by efforts to emulate the Japanese. Quality circles, which involve worker group efforts to improve productivity, have produced significant benefits in some organizations but have been short-lived in others. The essential difference between the two groups involved executive commitment. As Perry Pascarella pointed out, "If managers look only to the techniques of participative management, their thinly disguised autocratic styles will only worsen the situation. If they do not buy the underlying philosophy, they will still be trying to adapt people to systems rather than adapting themselves and their systems to the realities of today's people."

Executive support. Quality circles and participative management have succeeded only when applied as long-term techniques with total senior executive support. Otherwise, failure has usually occurred.

Change in organizational culture is more difficult and time consuming to achieve. It is being attempted in many companies, however, with varying degrees of senior executive commitment. Such change is costly. It requires commitment of the sort illustrated by a time-worn description of the ham and egg breakfast: "the chicken was dedicated; the pig was committed."

More than a few chief executive officers have tried and failed to change corporate cultures. Most failures can be attributed to the executives involved. Cultural change requires leadership rather than management. Responsibility can not be delegated and forgotten. Long-term success in most organizations, nevertheless, can best be achieved through such basic change. "Managers will increasingly find," said Pascarella, "that the only way they can be winners is to create winners."

The role of the manager is becoming a transformative one. As a teacher or coach, his or her fulfillment will come increasingly from helping others find fulfillment. Managerial effectiveness, then, depends more upon setting a learning environment than a telling environment. The quality of management is determined by its ability to bring together the best efforts of the entire organization. The most effective managers are not the masters of great systems. In fact, they are somewhat the opposite. In quite unsystematic ways, they stroll through the organization, trolling for information, asking questions, encouraging people to pursue their own ideas, revealing their enthusiasm and commitment to improvement.

Leadership

Leadership rather than management is the one vital ingredient in organizational success. A special type of leadership, in fact, appears to be essential. Successful political leaders were once defined as those sufficiently perceptive to discern the direction in which the public was moving. They then needed only to position themselves in front of the moving throng. Contemporary organizational leadership requires something more, but not necessarily something new. Perhaps the greatest attribute of military leadership, it has been said, is to be found in a single command: "Follow me." The attitude expressed in this command is vital to organizational leaders, for where there is no leader there can be no followers.

"The leader does not create purpose," Pascarella says. "He or she finds common purpose in the organization through deep self-examination and ongoing communication with others to determine what it is they want to achieve. The leader points out the direction in which all can work—toward a purpose that meets both individual and group needs."

Social purpose. What more will be needed to enlist the wholehearted support of personnel in gaining organizational objectives? Social purpose can be an effective motivator, but many corporations would experience difficulty in defining their missions in this context. How then can individuals be motivated? As simple a concept as quality can constitute a worthwhile goal, provided the organization is truly committed to it.

Quality products or services serve worthwhile human ends. They need not be the best of their kind; to proclaim one's product or service the best, when this obviously is not the case, is self-defeating. Employees quickly identify gross exaggeration or deceit. Products or services need only serve well the consumers for whom they are intended—provide good value for value received.

Worker satisfaction and organizational achievement thus become corequisites to organizational productivity. These conditions need not be viewed as a problem. They can instead be taken as an opportunity to gain a competitive edge to the benefit of all involved, while meeting a growing need for individual as well as organizational responsibility.

Tactics. New managerial tactics will be necessary, however, if these objectives are to be achieved. The tactics to be used might best be designed in the light of organizational responses to an important question. Are organizations managing those variables that require management, or are their efforts misdirected? Contemporary conditions suggest the latter. Traditionalist managers appear bent on controlling individual behavior within rigid environmental parameters rather than remolding the environment. This strategy goes contrary to virtually everything man has learned about the universe.

Every lesson of psychology, sociology, anthropology, and biology demonstrates that living organisms adapt to environments to survive. Nowhere in science is there evidence suggesting that such patterns can be modified by command. Lasting behavioral change can be induced only through environmental change, which in organizations can be developed only by applying new management tools or techniques.

Rather than continuing their efforts to manipulate workers, organizations must create environments that induce the evolution of desired behaviors. Managers must be made accountable for outcomes. Uniform ethical standards must be applied across organizations. Clearly defined organizational values must be established, and workers must be given an opportunity to participate in reshaping organizations.

A CENTRAL PROBLEM

Organizations' ability to respond to the new challenges will vary with the abilities of senior executives and their immediate subordinates. Line and middle management have been the most neglected components in contemporary organizational planning. Individuals involved are often products of the so-called Peter Principle, having risen to their levels of inefficiency. Their managerial skills have been acquired by emulating peers or superordinates whose behaviors may not be exemplary of superior management technique. Too often they are products of Frederick Taylor's school of scientific management, a once-honored but contemporaneously inappropriate approach.

Organizations today survive and prosper to the extent that they recognize and respond to management theorist Peter Drucker's admonitions of more than a decade ago: "The major assumptions on which both the theory and the practice of management have been based these past 50 years rapidly are becoming inappropriate." They have been undermined, Drucker said, by five "new realities":

1. All institutions, including business, are accountable for the "quality of life."
2. Entrepreneurial innovation will become the very heart and core of management.
3. It is management's task to make knowledge more productive.
4. Management will have to be considered as both a "science" and a "humanity."
5. Economic and social development are the result of management.

Of Drucker's five new realities, three are especially significant in terms of today's worker and workplace—quality of life, making knowledge more productive, and dealing with management as science and humanity. Quality of life may be most important in that it applies to individuals in all settings.

Quality of life. "Because our society is rapidly becoming a society of organizations," Drucker said, "all institutions will have to make fulfillment of basic social values, beliefs and purposes a major objective of their continuing activities rather than a social responsibility that restrains or lies outside their primary functions." Thus, the values of individuals and the society of which they are a part must become factors in management.

It will increasingly be the job of management to make the individual's values and aspirations redound to organizational energy and performance. It will simply not be good enough to be satisfied—as industrial relations and even human relations traditionally have been—with the absence of discontent ....

We will, within another 10 years, become far less concerned with *management* development (that is, adapting the individual to the demands of the organization), and far more with *organization* development (that is, adapting the company to the needs, aspirations, and potentials of individuals).

Science and humanity. As to management as both science and humanity, Drucker commented,

Management, we now know, has to make productive the values, aspirations and traditions of the individual, the community and the society for a common productive purpose. If management does not succeed in putting to work the specific cultural heritage of a country and of a people, social and economic development can not take place.... As a science and a humanity, management is both a statement of findings that can be objectively tested and validated and a system of belief and experience.

What remains, then, is to put both science and humanity to work to achieve objectives beneficial to organizations, their employees, and the society in which both must continue to function.

SUMMARY

Generational and organizational conflict will arise in the workplace over the next several years. The divergent interests of members of the baby-boom and baby-bust generations and those of traditional and innovative managers inevitably will collide. In large part, the boomers and traditional interests will fall on one side of the battlefield, while busters and innovators will be on the other.

The baby-boom generation will be blocking career ladders that the busters will be seeking to climb. The busters, however, will be few in number and of such value to organizations that their demands may be difficult to resist.

Organizations also will inevitably be involved, directly or indirectly, in the economic burdens that the baby-boom generation will be called on to assume.

Baby busters, as a result and to compensate for past insecurities, will demand greater compensation. Differences in their family circumstances will result in their demanding different benefits, and they can be expected to press for more salutary environments as well.

Perhaps most significant from a management standpoint, they will seek psychic or real proprietorship in their organizations, something few contemporary organizations are prepared to provide.

In reality, these "new" workers are not new. Research over the past decade has demonstrated that security, wages, and benefits are not among their higher priorities. They want respect from coworkers, interesting work, and recognition for their accomplishments.

The essence of organizational conflict involves control and purpose. The issues are complex and intertwined. Organizations today are being called upon to meet social as well as commercial responsibilities. Those that survive necessarily must change to meet them.

Productive change will require resolution of conflict between traditional and innovative management philosophies. Managers must come to accept the fact that organizations are essentially political entities; that member involvement is prerequisite to commitment. They must become, in Ozley's words, working-with rather than working-for organizations.

Most of all, success will require leadership rather than management and a willingness to accept the concepts itemized by Drucker: accountability for quality of work life; entrepreneurial innovation; the obligation to make knowledge more productive; acceptance of management as a humanity as well as a science, and responsibility for economic and social development.

ADDITIONAL READING

Ackerman, Robert W. "How Companies Respond to Social Demands," *Harvard Business Review,* July–August 1973, pp. 88–98.

Beale, Calvin L. "Six Demographic Surprises of the 1970s," in *U.S. Population: Where We Are; Where We're Going.* Washington, DC: Population Reference Bureau, 1982.

Cooper, M. R., et al. "Changing Employee Values: Deepening Discontent? *Harvard Business Review,* January–February 1979, pp. 117–125.

Diebold, John. *Making the Future Work: Unleashing Our Powers of Innovation for the Decades Ahead.* New York: Simon & Schuster, 1984.

Drucker, Peter F. "Management's New Role," *Harvard Business Review,* November-December 1968, pp. 49–54.

Gooding, Judson. *The Job Revolution.* New York: Walker, 1972.

Greenwald, Mathew. "Beyond the Baby Boom: How Will the Baby Bust Be Different?" Speech to the American Demographics Institute, New York City, June 1986.

Hall, E. K. "A Plea for the Man in the Ranks," in Ernest C. Miller, ed., *Human Resources Management: The Past is Prologue.* New York: AMACOM, 1979.

Harrison, Roger. "Understanding Your Organization's Character," *Harvard Business Review,* May-June, 1972.

Herzberg, Frederick. "The Human Need for Work," in *How to Be a Better Leader.* Cleveland: Penton, 1983.

Longman, Richard. "Richer or Poorer: Will the Baby Boom Live Better Than Their Parents?" Speech to the American Demographics Institute, New York City, June 1986.

Mintzberg, Henry. "Who Should Control the Corporation," *California Management Review* 27, No. 1, Fall 1984, pp. 90–113.

Naisbitt, John, and Patricia Aburdene. *Reinventing the Corporation.* New York: Warner Books, 1985.

Ozley, Lee M. "Falling Prey to a Management Fallacy," in *How to Be a Better Leader,* Cleveland: Penton, 1983.

Pascarella, Perry. *The New Achievers: Creating a Modern Work Ethic.* New York: Free Press, 1984.

Thurow, Lester. *Zero Sum Solution.* New York: Simon & Schuster, 1985.

Tuleja, Thaddeus F. *Beyond the Bottom Line: How Business Leaders Are Turning Principles into Profits.* New York: Facts on File, 1985.

Viola, Richard H. *Organizations in a Changing Society: Administration and Human Values.* Philadelphia: Saunders, 1977.

4
MANAGEMENT AND LEADERSHIP

Accelerating change is endemic in varying degrees in contemporary society. Products and services are changing at an unprecedented pace. Their "life cycles," to use a marketing term, are growing ever shorter. Workplaces also are changing in several ways, but at a somewhat slower rate. Computers and robotics are being introduced in some industries, while others, as in the case of the steel industry's "mini-mills," are being totally redesigned. In values, life-styles, and demographics, workers are changing with equal if less obvious speed. With few exceptions, however, management remains tradition bound and organizations suffer as a result, as was perhaps best described by Thomas L. Brown in *Industry Week:*

One mid-level design chief for a major clothing accessories manufacturer recently told me that he had observed innumerable differences in managerial and employee priorities at his plant. In fact, he said with a shrug, people in the plant didn't seem to agree on many key operational points. The senior managers, he felt, were "the most out of touch" with the people on the plant floor—and with their subordinates as well.

I asked how he managed to deal with these conflicts. He replied: "There is *nothing* that can be done. The junior managers will just have to wait until they get promoted—after the senior guys pass on. These conflicts will be solved *funeral by funeral.*"

CHANGE AND CONFLICT

Generational change resolves some conflicts, but usually creates others. The World War II generation inevitably will yield its senior management positions to the baby boomers, who ultimately will be supplanted by members of the baby-bust generation. These changes, however, appear less and less likely to occur at a pace adequate to resolve contemporary and emerging organizational problems.

Mortality and morbidity rates have been improving and mandatory retirement was abolished by the Congress in 1986, which will lengthen the working lifetimes of senior managers and exacerbate intergenerational differences. Organizations are placed at risk in an era in which many executives already appear to be managing their organizations and industries into economic decline.

Contemporary Problems

Apparently contemporary management principles may cause rather than cure poor performance. General Motors Corporation's experience with H. Ross Perot's Electronic Data Systems arguably is a case in point. In the mid-1980s GM acquired and attempted to assimilate EDS. GM Chairman Roger Smith hailed the acquisition as a leap forward in technology and management. Perot's pragmatic management techniques, he said, were to help GM create a more productive organization. At that time the auto manufacturer was also proclaiming a "great leap forward" with its Saturn project, designed to produce "new" motor vehicles that would recapture GM's automotive world leadership.

After months of private and public prodding by Perot to bring GM into the twentieth century, the automaker reversed course. Perot's stock was repurchased by GM, and he was removed from the GM board. The Saturn project had been radically reduced in scope. The company was closing plants and furloughing workers. General Motors' traditional management style apparently had prevailed, and its decline appeared to be continuing.

Cause or Cure?

Modern management techniques appear to be the cause of less than satisfactory economic performance, rather than a cure. They tend to produce short-term efficiency at the expense of long-term results. This point was underscored by Harvard Professors Robert H. Hayes and William J. Abernathy in a discussion of organizational productivity. Their comments were at least equally applicable to human-resources management.

Our managers still earn generally high marks for their skill in improving short-term efficiency, but their counterparts in Europe and Japan have started to question America's entrepreneurial imagination and willingness to make risky, long-term competitive investments. As one such observer remarked to us: "The U.S. companies in my industry act like banks. All they are interested in is return on investment and getting their money back. Sometimes they act as though they are more interested in buying other companies than they are in selling products to customers.

The behavioral pattern Hayes and Abernathy described is paralleled in the human resources sector. In traditional organizations, which constitute an overwhelming majority, long-term productivity—and perhaps even survival—are being sacrificed for short-term gain. These organizations are encountering radical qualitative and quantitative change in the work force, yet they persist in treating employees as disposable components of production, rather than resources to be developed.

The key to long term success—even survival—in business, [Hayes and Abernathy concluded], is what it always has been: to invest, to innovate, to lead, to create value where none existed before. Such determination, such striving to excel, requires leaders—not *just* controllers, market analysts and portfolio managers. In our preoccupation with the braking systems and exterior trim, we may have neglected the drive trains of our corporations.

Leadership versus Management

Leadership and management are the central concepts in the discussion above. The extent to which they differ from one another is critical. A manager, by definition, is one who directs and controls; a person who manipulates resources and expenditures. A leader, in contrast, is one who leads—the guiding and directing head of an organization. The differences between the definitions are control and manipulation on the one hand, guidance on the other.

Control and manipulation have long been characteristics of traditional organizations, but traditional structures are inadequate for today's complex organization. So, too, are traditional approaches to human-resources management. Workers are amenable to leadership, but increasingly resistant to control and manipulation. Contemporary organizations require a blending of leader and manager, identified more than two decades ago by Stephen B. Miles, Jr. as "the management politician."

THE MANAGEMENT POLITICIAN

Politics and politician over the years have undeservedly acquired pejorative connotations. Politics is defined primarily by Webster as the "science of civil government." Only after citing the primary definition does Webster define politician as "one addicted to, or actively engaged in, politics as managed by parties; often, one primarily interested in political offices or the profits from them as a source of private gain."

The second definition somehow has been popularized in the United States. The first has become associated with a more dignified term: statesman. Even more curious are still-prevalent U.S. perceptions and expectations of political and governmental leaderships. Politicians are assumed to be self-serving and are held suspect in keeping with Webster's second definition. Leaders, on the other hand, are expected to be self-sacrificing and adhere to exemplary standards of conduct. These stereotypes persist in the face of a system under which today's politician can become tomorrow's statesman.

Concurrent character change is unlikely in the absence of heavenly intervention.

Transitions from manager to politician—or management politician—hopefully are more readily accomplished. A blending of the primary attributes of the two roles is essential to success in contemporary workplaces. As Miles puts it,

> The very essence of the business leader, in business as well as government, is that he blends politics and statesmanship.... The ability to govern is dependent on the ability to gain power and keep it. Power is seldom, perhaps never, given away. It must be worked for, or bought and paid for, in some way.... In the United Nations, in a municipal legislature, or, for that matter, in any other type of organization, those who seek to lead or manage must necessarily be politicians in both senses.... The manager in a business enterprise who must work with people to keep "the possible" in constant alignment with what he finds to be "the desirable" is, to that extent, a politician.

Politicians and managers are organizational servants, accepting the values, morals, and ambitions of their organizations. Many would be proud to call themselves organization men or women, yet they fail to recognize the essentially political nature of their roles. They try to prove that management is an honorable, ethical, and highly specialized profession akin to medicine, law, or engineering. They seek the prescriptive authority of the expert, rather than the earned authority of the leader.

Prescriptive authority, unfortunately for would-be expert prescribers, is becoming progressively less valued in U.S. society. Professionals more and more are held accountable for their failures, in the courts and otherwise. Second opinions are becoming a way of life in many professions. Thus, the only recourse of managers is to political authority; to power granted by the governed—a commodity earned through performance rather than awarded by organizations or licensure.

The leaders or political managers of today and tomorrow have a great deal at stake as they seek to perfect new skills. If they fail in their political roles, if they persist in managing rather than leading, they may find themselves without personnel, without production, and perhaps without organizations.

The role of leader is akin to that of the drum major in a parade. Resplendently dressed, he prances ahead, setting the pace, a dominant figure commanding respect. Should the parade turn left while he continues alone, that impression would quickly change. Rather than being admired, he would become a subject of ridicule or worse.

Contemporary conditions require that managers adopt new and different roles in their organizations. They must become integrators and synthesizers, rather than experts and commanders. They must embrace rather than resist accelerating change. As George Cabot Lodge put it," the manager must form a certain attitude of mind, a willingness to confront manifold change openly and with breadth of vision, not with the heels dug in and the old blinders on."

Successful leaders must also have considerable knowledge of organizations and the ways in which they function. A number of schools of thought exist as to the nature of organizations, the nature of management, and the elements of leadership.

LEADERS, MANAGERS, AND ORGANIZATIONS

Most management theorists view contemporary organizations from one of four perspectives: human resources, systems, teamwork, and cultural. Advocates of the human resources approach emphasize human development to enhance organizational productivity. The systems perspective is based on general systems theory, which posits the interdependence of organizational components and emphasizes the role of communication in achieving optimum results. The teamwork approach incorporates human resources principles, but concentrates on team rather than individual performance. The cultural school focuses on shared organizational values and their role in inducing employee behavior. Managers usually approach their work from one of these perspectives. Leaders, in contrast, tend to apply them as circumstances require.

The Human Resources Approach

Participative decision making and strong employee–employer relationships are the focal points of the human resources approach to organizations. McGregor, Likert, Miles, and others are among its leading exponents.

Their models are founded on the belief that individuals want to contribute to organizational success and are capable of so doing. They view workers as underutilized resources and envision managers' primary challenge as developing and applying their abilities toward mutually beneficial ends.

The human resources school emphasizes upward communication. Downward communication is designed to provide current organizational information, convey instructions and behavioral guidelines, and stimulate upward communication to which management must respond.

The Systems Approach

General systems theory is based on the premise that the whole is greater than the sum of its interdependent parts. Organizations are viewed as social systems. External environments are considered suprasystems, and internal components are seen as subsystems.

Systems theorists embrace equally human relations perspectives and such classical concepts as organizational structure, hierarchy, and span of control.

Systems advocates such as Daniel Katz and Robert Kahn categorize organizations as either open or closed. The former are perceived as responsive to their environments, dynamic and ever-changing. The latter are nonresponsive, static, and predictable.

While the extent of environmental interaction varies, it is considered essential to survival. "No organization can be viewed in isolation," according to Andrews and Baird, "for each is as much a product of its environment as a contributor to it."

The Teamwork Approach

Teamwork theorists such as William Ouchi assign a greater value to lateral communication than to the vertical variety. Lateral communication, they contend, fosters the development of work teams such as those in Japanese organizations.

Their concept is reminiscent of the human relations approach, although employees are viewed as team subsystems rather than groups of individuals. The teamwork school emphasizes problem solving at the lowest possible organizational level and, at least in this respect, goes contrary to traditional chain-of-command practices.

The Cultural Approach

Advocates of the cultural school emphasize organizational value systems, norms, and behaviors as controlling productivity. Successful organizations, they contend, emphasize expeditious decision making, productivity achieved through motivated personnel, and person-to-person communication.

Success or failure, according to cultural advocates, can be understood by examining organizational value systems, norms, and behaviors. Employees are viewed as behaving in keeping with organizational expectations and in anticipation of rewards. Values and norms, they contend, create those expectations.

None of the concepts described briefly above can be considered either right or wrong. All are noteworthy in that they create alternative views of organizations. Careful analysis of any given organization is apt to uncover elements of several models of which managers should be aware.

MANAGEMENT SKILLS

While contemporary theoretical constructs tend to emphasize the need for communication skills, they are but one component of managerial success.

Three sets of skills are essential: technical, conceptual, and communication or human resources. They are not uniformly applied across individual careers. Communication and human resources skills are more consistently required, but all skills are used in varying degree.

Technical Skills

Managers with technical expertise are knowledgeable concerning the content of their jobs. They are able to perform required tasks and serve as resource persons for their juniors or subordinates.

Technical expertise is a perishable commodity. The half-life of knowledge today is estimated at five years. Virtually everything college graduates take with them from the academic world presumably will have become obsolete in a decade. Although the need for technical skill tends to decline as careers progress, most technically successful managers continuously update their skills through formal or informal means.

Those who rise through organizational ranks may successfully delegate significant portions of their technical work. Those who would command the continuing respect of their peers, however, tend to maintain technical competence regardless of hierarchical position.

Conceptual Skills

Conceptual skills include the ability to think creatively, comprehend internal and external interrelationships, and understand the organization's role in society. While applicable throughout the manager's career, the conceptual skills vary in application with managerial level.

At lower managerial levels, for example, individuals must understand interrelationships between their jobs and those of others. At unit, departmental, or divisional levels, the focus shifts accordingly. At the corporate level, senior executives are concerned with the position of organizations in their industries and in context with other external environments. Managerial need for conceptual expertise thus tends to increase as careers progress.

Communication Skills

Human relations or communication skills include the ability to interact and function successfully in one-on-one, small-group, and public communication. They also encompass the ability to understand and motivate employees.

Unlike the need for technical expertise, which tends to decline over a career, and the need for for conceptual ability, which tends to increase, communication skills are consistently required. They are very important during managers' early years and equally important in the twilight of their careers. At the outset they may be primarily concerned with subordinates. Later, senior executives and board members may become primary communication targets. Although different, these situations are equally demanding. They are almost as demanding, in fact, as the requirements of successful leadership.

LEADERSHIP

Management and leadership, as indicated earlier, are not one and the same. Many can manage. Few can successfully lead. With rare exceptions, contemporary theory has done little to separate management from leadership and to deal with the two as distinct concepts. Other than in terms of communication, all but one prevalent theory deals with management to the exclusion of leadership. In addition, according to Andrews and Baird, "they examine existing leadership styles and employee needs without acknowledging the inevitability of some change, as well as the potential for growth."

The one exceptional theory is advanced by Paul Hersey and Kenneth Blanchard, who view leadership styles in context with the characteristics of those being led. They define four leadership behavior categories, which vary in applicability with the maturity of employees addressed:

1. High task/low relationship, in which leaders define roles and then tell group members how and when to accomplish specific tasks

2. High task/high relationship, in which leaders remain directive but encourage joint two-way communication and joint problem solving

3. High relationship/low task, in which leaders serve as facilitators rather than directors, using two-way communication and joint problem solving

4. Low relationship/low task, in which workers perform with little leadership input.

Styles Applied

High-task/low-relationship leadership is most appropriate where employees are low in job and psychological maturity. Where job maturity is low but psychological maturity is high, high-task/low-relationship behavior produces best results. Where workers are low in psychological but high in job maturity, high-relationship/low-task behavior is preferable. Low-relationship/low-task behavior is used where employees are high in psychological and job maturity.

The study of leadership has been approached from varying perspectives and with varying degrees of success. Over the years, several researchers have attempted to isolate the traits and styles exhibited by leaders. Others have examined the circumstances in which leadership is exercised and variations among those who exercise leadership.

Leadership Traits

Early investigators of leadership sought to identify inherent traits of successful leaders. Several, including technical, intellectual, and leadership-effectiveness qualities, paralleled the management-skill clusters discussed above. Others included willingness to share responsibility, emotional balance and control, ethical conduct, integrity, and communication ability. The value of such traits varies, however, with the situations in which leaders find themselves. They may also vary with leaders' positions in organizational hierarchies.

More recent investigations have focused more on leaders' communication behavior, with only moderate success. As Andrews and Baird pointed out, "it is unlikely that any investigation will ever reveal an unvarying set of leadership traits that are completely free of environmental, task and socio-emotional conditions within and surrounding the group or organization."

Leadership Styles

Results of research in leadership styles can be summarized as not unlike those obtained in context with leadership traits: While the process has become better known as a result, there appears little likelihood that a single style will ever be found that is generally superior to others in all contexts. Situational factors again were found of considerable importance.

Democratic leadership styles were found superior in several situations. Participative styles were favored in others.

Situational Approaches

Research efforts over some 15 years led theorist Frederick Fiedler to identify three factors that determine the relative effectiveness of leadership styles: the power of the leader's position, the structure of the task at hand, and the social relationships between the leader and group members.

He found authoritarian leadership most effective where power is high, tasks are clearly structured, and sound social relationships can be maintained. He also found the authoritarian approach best at the opposite extreme, where leaders have little power, tasks are not clearly structured, and social relationships are poor. Between the extremes, Fiedler found democratic styles more appropriate.

Functional Approaches

The functional approach to leadership involves a different concept. It suggests that leadership is exercised by any group member who promotes achievement of group goals. Since more than one group member may per-

form leadership functions, all members of the group conceivably may contribute to reaching specified objectives. Each, however, may be capable of
leadership in specific circumstances.

How, then, should those who would be effective leaders behave? Andrews
and Baird advanced several practical guidelines worthy of universal application:

1. Good managers regularly examine their attitudes toward fellow workers.
2. They are good listeners.
3. They encourage others to express dissenting views.
4. They create a supportive organizational climate and are likely to be
   a. Descriptive rather than evaluative—nonjudgmental, slow to question others'
      standards and values, willing to seek additional information
   b. Problem oriented—interested in defining mutual problems and cooperatively
      seeking solutions rather than in identifying individuals who can be blamed
   c. Spontaneous—straightforward, honest, and tactfully direct, unwilling to deal
      with others in manipulative ways
   d. Respectful—interacting as equals, demonstrating and seeking mutual trust and
      respect, encouraging participative planning while deemphasizing status,
      power, and formal role relationships
   e. Empathic—attempting to see issues and problems from others' perspectives,
      identifying others' needs, interests, and values
   f. Provisional—willing to admit that one could be wrong, open to new ways of
      doing things, tentative in one's views.
5. They are ethical.

Leaders necessarily respect the human dignity and thoughts of workers.
Only in this manner can they earn their participation in the improvement
process. Those who offer ideas bare their egos to assault. They risk being
stripped of their dignity by cruel or unthinking superiors. Successful managers understand their roles as listeners and helpers in these circumstances.

Nevertheless, they will have difficulty dealing with changing workers.
Technological advances in recent years have been changing attitudes toward
work. People, particularly young people, view their jobs far differently than
once was the case. They take a fundamentally different view of why they
work and what they should obtain as a reward for working.

The pressures that once made them work uncomplainingly are virtually
gone. They will totally disappear with the impending human resources
shortage. While relatively few view work as a burden to be avoided, younger
workers seek more than pay checks. They want opportunity for advancement, and more.

They are more mobile and harder to retain. They think nothing of moving from city to city for new opportunities. They consider jobs something to be kept only as long as they are satisfying.

They want to be listened to; to be informed in advance of organizational plans; to be "part of the action." While fewer managers today are totally disregarding the people in their organizations, too many continue to apply behavioral science to manipulate.

These conditions are intolerable in an era in which organizations are struggling to survive. They can be reversed, however, only where managers seek to empower others rather than gain more power for themselves.

The shift in values will not be easily accomplished. Traditional autocratic techniques relabeled as participative management can only compound organizational problems. Managers must adapt themselves and their systems to the realities of today's workers. Any effort to perpetuate traditional manipulative approaches can lead only to disaster.

PROBLEMS AHEAD

Multiple barriers stand between contemporary managers and the management politician or leadership role. They are in part personal, in part organizational. Personally, they involve the generation gap described earlier and the impact of traditional educational systems. Organizationally, they include traditional motivational mechanisms, accountability systems, performance evaluation techniques, and communication systems. Nevertheless, a considerable amount can be accomplished.

Educational Systems

Typical holders of master's degrees in business administration are woefully ill equipped to succeed in tomorrow's workplace. Other than for the relatively few who have elected to specialize in human-resources management, their studies have dealt primarily with economics, accounting, marketing, and related business disciplines. Their backgrounds in the humanities and social sciences are so limited as to be virtually nonexistent.

Restricted curricula. Inadequate educational backgrounds are produced by the highly restrictive academic curricula prescribed by accrediting bodies and blindly followed by academic administrators arguably more concerned with peer approval than product quality. Their attitudes are supported by academics and businessmen who for different reasons are equally resistant to change. Traditionalist postsecondary educational institutions are governed through collegial systems that render them also resistant to change. Membership in these organizations is limited to those who have completed predetermined rites of passage symbolized by graduate degrees. Members tend to cling to what might be called an "I did it; therefore you must do it" philosophy.

The same sort of rationale arises in the business community. Those who hire graduates tend to prefer mirror images of themselves—for example, those who have master's degrees in business administration, whether or not they remain appropriate in a changing society.

Outcomes, however, are more important than techniques. Business-school graduates are less well equipped than others to cope with the human component of the organizations they serve. Even a concerted effort to change the educational system, of which little evidence now exists, would require many years to complete. Organizations will thus be forced to cope with emerging human resources problems without substantive academic assistance. They will have to rely on organizational systems that too frequently are ill designed to cope with new realities.

Organizational responses. In some instances, responses are already taking shape. Individual companies and entire industries are taking matters into their own hands. For example, in 1986 the hospitality industry launched a national campaign to convince workers that theirs is an industry of opportunity for workers (Associated Press, New York, October 18, 1986).

A month earlier, *Industry Week* published a report on industry's efforts to better educate workers. Entitled "Corporate Colleges Come of Age: Filling Voids in the Educational System," the article recounted the development of the Wang Institute of Graduate Studies in Massachusetts. Also mentioned was the National Technological University at Ft. Collins, Colorado, whose sponsors include General Dynamics and Hewlett-Packard.

A listing of 18 corporate colleges accompanied the article. As many were managerially oriented as were technically oriented, and their graduates may provide considerable assistance to organizations seeking solutions to leadership and motivational problems.

Motivational Systems

Contemporary motivational systems are of little assistance to managers seeking to make workers a part of their organizations. Traditional approaches provide no method through which organizations can share the product of their efforts other than through job holding, a system that tends to be counterproductive.

Compensation systems based on hourly wage rates are common in business and industry. In aggressive expense-cutting programs launched in the mid-1980s, some organizations went so far as to link benefits to numbers of hours worked.

While organizations espouse productivity, their compensation systems thus tell workers that it is the number of hours they spend on the job, rather than what they accomplish, that is most important. This concept is driven home through disciplinary systems that consider a multitude of other sins more onerous than failure to produce.

"Low production as a cause for discharge or discipline of workers is only fourth on the list of causes, behind misconduct, insubordination, and absenteeism, accounting for only 11 percent of such action," David Macarov pointed out. Earlier studies showed 90 percent of those who lost jobs did so because of poor health, poor personalities or dispositions, too much talking, carelessness, untidiness, intemperance, and lack of reliability. In addition, few workers are free to depart upon fulfilling production quotas, and flextime workers are required to put in predetermined numbers of hours.

Similar contradictions have arisen in so-called quality-of-work-life or QWL programs. The concept is relatively new. Few follow-up studies have been undertaken to validate results, yet one significant weakness has appeared. Most deal with with what Frederick Herzberg called hygienic factors or dissatisfiers. They have dealt primarily with relationships between workers and between workers and supervisors, rather than with work itself. They were oriented toward reducing dissatisfaction, rather than inducing satisfaction.

The Jackass Fallacy

Consultant Harry Levinson calls attention to a "fundamental unconscious management attitude that is responsible for most contemporary management–labor problems." He calls it "the great jackass fallacy" and blames it in part on weaknesses in personal and educational backgrounds.

Some...pursue executive careers to obtain power over others as a way of compensating for real or fancied personal inadequacies, or as a reaction to an unconscious sense of helplessness. They are neurotically driven, and their single-minded, perpetual pursuit of control blinds them to their own subtle feelings and those of others. Furthermore, many executives have engineering, scientific, legal, or financial backgrounds. Each of these fields places a heavy emphasis on cognitive rationality and measurable or verifiable facts. People who enter them usually are trained from childhood to suppress their feelings, to maintain a competitive, aggressive, non-emotional front. They are taught to be highly logical, and they seek to impose that kind of rationality on organizations.

As a result, they simply do not understand the power of people's feelings, and all too often they are incapable of sensing such feelings in everyday practice without considerable help. They are like tone-deaf people who, attending an opera, can understand the lyrics but cannot hear the music.

Carrot and Stick. The conditions described above contribute to the carrot-and-stick reward-and-punishment philosophy, Levinson says. He describes asking executives to visualize that philosophy and describe the central image involved. Most often, he says, the central figure is a jackass. The characteristics of a jackass are stubbornness, stupidity, willfulness, and unwillingness to go where someone is driving him. These, by interesting coincidence, are also the characteristics of the unmotivated employee. Thus it becomes vividly clear that the underlying assumption which managers make about motivation leads to a self-fulfilling prophecy. People inevitably respond to the carrot-and-stick by trying to get more of the carrot while protecting themselves against the stick. This predictable phenomenon has led to the formation of unions, the frequent sabotage of management's motivation efforts, and the characteristic employee suspicion of management's motivational (manipulative) techniques.

Employee perceptions of such systems produce predictable responses. They attempt to protect themselves against manipulation and accompanying feelings of helplessness. This process is rendered more damaging by typical bureaucratic structures, which tend to magnify those feelings and reinforce the jackass fallacy. Techniques such as job enrichment and group dynamics are futile in these circumstances. "Despite whatever practices the organization implements, people will avoid, evade, escape, deny, and reject both the jackass fallacy and the military-style hierarchy."

Deeper problems. In many if not most organizations, the problem is deeper still. It is rooted in near-total absence of managerial credibility. Management is not only suspect but assumed to be deceitful as well as manipulative. Few employees in any organization have not experienced disillusionment at the hands of personnel directors, supervisors, or managers, who promised—or were believed to have promised—raises, promotions, or long-term careers. A great deal of effort, considerable time, and consistent contrary performance are essential to reverse such conditions.

Any effort to create a new organizational reality must deal with motivational factors, positive and negative. These are most clearly seen in the summary results of 12 studies conducted by Frederick Herzberg (see Figure 4.1). They suggest a dual approach to concurrently eliminate dissatisfaction and enhance satisfaction. The Herzberg approach assumes a commitment to human resources development through fair and equitable dealings with employees.

As in the educational sector, organizations are striving for improvement in this area. General Electric, Borg-Warner, and Honda of America are, in the words of a *Business Week* headline (September 15, 1986), "Letting Workers Help Handle Workers' Gripes." While the operational scope of the peer-review panels has been limited, they appear to warrant and receive greater employee support than predecessor mechanisms.

Reorganized systems. Some organizations are becoming more human-resource sensitive in other areas. Shenandoah Life Insurance Co., for example, has reorganized work systems to accommodate new technology. The Shenandoah success was detailed by *Business Week* in an article entitled "Management Discovers the Human Side of Automation: Companies Are Finding That Workers Are the Key to Making Technology Pay Off" (Sep-

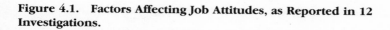

Figure 4.1. Factors Affecting Job Attitudes, as Reported in 12 Investigations.

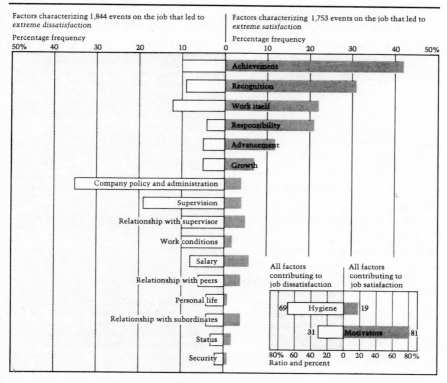

Source: Reprinted by permission of the *Harvard Business Review*. Exhibit from "One More Time, How Do You Motivate Employees" by Frederick Herzberg (January/February 1968). Copyright © 1968 by the President and Fellows of Harvard College; all rights reserved.

tember 29, 1986). In an accompanying box the magazine defined changing approaches to organizing work (see Figure 4.2).

These developments suggest that organizations may indeed be turning to what Professor Herzberg called "the dynamics of caring." They have a responsibility to attend to people's animal needs, he suggested, without expecting a quid pro quo. "Too often, managers try to manipulate people's animal needs as a way to get more work out of them," Herzberg wrote. "Tend to these needs, but expect no reciprocity—no motivation in return for caring."

What else does it take to lead a winning team? Harvard Business School Professors Wickham Skinner and W. Earl Sasser offer four "lessons from high achievers":

Figure 4.2.   The Changing Approach to Organizing Work.

What Management Assumes About Workers

Old Way. Worker wants nothing from the job except pay, avoids responsibility, and must be controlled and coerced.

New Way. Worker desires challenging job and will seek responsibility and autonomy if management permits.

How the Job is Designed

Old Way. Work is fragmented and deskilled. Worker is confined to narrow job. Doing and thinking are separated.

New Way. Work is multiskilled and performed by teamwork where possible. Worker can upgrade whole system. Doing and thinking are combined.

Management's Organization and Style

Old Way. Top-down military command with worker at bottom of many supervisory layers; worker is expected to obey orders and has no power.

New Way. Relatively flat structure with fewer layers; worker makes suggestions and has power to implement changes.

Job Training and Security

Old Way. Worker is regarded as a replaceable part and is given little initial training or retraining for new jobs. Layoffs are routine when business declines.

New Way. Worker is considered a valuable resource and is constantly retrained in new skills. Layoffs are avoided if possible in a downturn.

How Wages Are Determined

Old Way. Pay is geared to the job, not the person, and is determined by evaluation and job classification systems.

New Way. Pay is linked to skills acquired. Group incentive and profit-sharing plans are used to enhance commitment.

Labor Relations

Old Way. Labor and management interests are considered incompatible. Conflict arises on the shop floor and in bargaining.

New Way. Mutual interests are emphasized. Management shares information about the business. Labor shares responsibility for making it succeed.

Source: From "The Changing Approach to Organizing Work." Reprinted from the September 29, 1986 issue of *Business Week* by special permission; © 1986 by McGraw-Hill.

1. They employ the practice of analysis with great effect.
2. They succeed in motivating subordinates and satisfying superiors.
3. They manage themselves.
4. They focus on one task of prime importance at a time. Organizations' contemporary human-resources problems constitute such a task.

SUMMARY

Changes in the management of products, services, and workplaces are accelerating in the United States. People are changing as well, but human-resources management techniques remain essentially unchanged. In an era in which leadership has become an essential to organizational success, executives continue their efforts to manage the human component of their organizations.

The circumstances require leaders or management politicians—individuals who can blend politics and statesmanship to create organizational leadership. Successful management of the contemporary organization, in other words, demands a new manager to address the era's new needs.

To a greater extent than ever has been the case before, communication skills are essential to the manager. Need for technical and conceptual skills vary as managerial careers progress, but skill in communicating is necessary at every level.

Leadership styles may vary with the nature of tasks to be undertaken and leader relationships with subordinates. Traits required in leaders, nevertheless, remain constant. In addition to the skills itemized above, they include willingness to share responsibility, emotional balance and control, ethical conduct, and integrity.

Even when equipped with all of these, contemporary managers must overcome several barriers. They include traditional motivational mechanisms, accountability systems, performance-evaluation techniques, and communication systems. Considerable time and no little effort are required to produce necessary changes.

Barriers to change arise in contemporary educational systems, which limit curricula. These are being overcome in part by innovative organizations that have established systems of their own. Others have concentrated early efforts on changing internal systems to better meet organizational needs. While change has not come rapidly, it is occurring and will continue as organizations adapt to new circumstances.

ADDITIONAL READING

Andrews, Patricia H., and John E. Baird, Jr. *Communication for Business and the Professions.* Dubuque, IA: Brown, 1986.

Brown, Thomas L. "Bridging the Value Gap: Recognizing Differences Is a Start. But How Can Managers Reconcile Them?" *Industry Week,* August 4, 1986.

Drucker, Peter F. "New Templates for Today's Organizations," *Harvard Business Review,* January-February 1974.

Gooding, Judson. *The Job Revolution.* New York: Walker, 1972.

Harrington, H. James. *The Improvement Process: How America's Leading Companies Improve Quality.* New York: McGraw-Hill, 1987.

Hayes, Robert H., and William J. Abernathy. "Managing Our Way to Economic Decline," *Harvard Business Review,* July-August 1980.

Herzberg, Frederick. "The Dynamics of Caring," in *How to be a Better Leader.* Cleveland: Penton, 1983.

————. "One More Time: How Do You Motivate Employees?" *Harvard Business Review,* January-February 1968.

Katz, Robert L. "Skills of an Effective Administrator," *Harvard Business Review,* September-October 1974.

Levinson, Harry. "Asinine Attitudes Toward Motivation," *Harvard Business Review,* January-February 1973.

Lodge, George Cabot. "Business and the Changing Society," *Harvard Business Review,* March-April 1974.

McClenahen, John S. "Corporate Colleges Come of Age: Filling Voids in the Educational Spectrum," *Industry Week,* September 29, 1986, pp. 45–46.

Miles, Stephen B., Jr. "The Management Politician," *Harvard Business Review,* January-February 1961.

Ouchi, William G. *Theory Z: How American Business Can Meet the Japanese Challenge.* Reading, MA: Addison-Wesley, 1981.

Pascarella, Perry. *The New Achievers: Creating a Modern Work Ethic.* New York: Free Press, 1984.

Skinner, Wickham, and W. Earl Sasser. "Managers with Impact: Versatile and Inconsistent," *Harvard Business Review,* November-December 1977.

5

DECEIT, DUPLICITY AND DISCONTENT

The light at the end of the tunnel is a freight train. Today's human resources problems can only grow worse in the remainder of the 1980s and little improvement is likely in the ensuing decade. Many organizations' survival beyond the turn of the century may be a function of willingness and ability to meet this challenge.

More farsighted organizations are already at work. Those that succeed will be tomorrow's winners. Their competitors for scarce human resources inevitably will be losers. The most successful of the winners will be those prepared to create a reality to which they already are paying lip service. It need consist in most cases of little more than fair and equitable treatment of all personnel. Such conditions exist in few organizations today and are perceived to exist in fewer still.

THE CREDIBILITY GAP

The problem arises out of perception as well as reality. Human beings' perceptions are their realities—when they believe they are ill treated, they behave accordingly, even where reality is quite different. Today's reality, unfortunately, most frequently supports workers' feelings of ill treatment and skepticism about their employers. The facts by now should be apparent to every manager. Those of relatively recent vintage include

Plants that have closed subsequent to union give-backs, which managements promised would prevent such action;

Tens of thousands of middle managers who had been given every indication that theirs were "career" positions now among the unemployed;

Employers seeking to escape their commitments to provide benefits to their retired employees;

Other employers extracting money from accounts set up to fund employees' retirement benefits;

More and more jobs being "exported" to Southeast Asia, Mexico, and elsewhere;

Entire industries in circumstances ranging from recession to collapse in the nation's
"Rust Bowls."

Illusions Destroyed

Any U.S. worker who harbored any illusions concerning job security and
employer loyalty almost inevitably lost them during the early 1980s. During
this period of "downsizing," hundreds of thousands lost their jobs—three
million in the Fortune 500 alone. A greater number of jobs was created
during the same period, but most were lower paying and less prestigious.
Their creation was little comfort to the many dislocated workers who had
assumed themselves safe in career positions.

Bureau of Labor Statistics data show that more than 11 million workers
over the age of 20 lost jobs between 1979 and 1984. During the same
period, of more than a half million discharged professional and managerial
employees, only half managed to find similar jobs.

At mid-decade the end was not in sight. AT&T Information Systems was
planning on reducing its managerial and professional ranks 30 percent by
the end of 1986. General Motors was planning to cut its salaried work force
25 percent by 1990. Chrysler laid off almost half its salaried employees
between 1978 and 1986.

A LITANY OF LIES

These and other events have demonstrated repeatedly to almost every
worker that managers' casual promises are all but meaningless. Far too many
Americans have been too often told, "Do a good job and large raises come
quickly"; "this is a career position"; "we always promote from within";
"we're committed to fairness and equity."

The list could go on for pages. And these, as employees view them, are
only the sins of those who do the hiring. They are compounded by virtually
every other individual in a position of organizational responsibility, from
the chief executive officer to the first line supervisor. Wittingly or unwit-
tingly, they almost invariably create what appear to employees to be a litany
of lies.

The lies begin during preemployment interviews. They are continued by
immediate superiors. They are compounded and recompounded by organizations' conflicting statements in multiple media and to multiple audiences. They can and often do occur during each of ten occasions in
organizational life for planned interpersonal communication, as listed by
John B. Miner:

1. The selection process
2. Orientation of new employees

3. Obtaining information
4. Appraising employee performance
5. Handling disciplinary problems
6. Counseling employees
7. Explaining new policies and procedures and problem solving
8. Training and instructing
9. Dealing with employee complaints and dissatisfaction
10. Separation interviews.

Deception can occur in any one of these situations. With the exception of the separation interview, it probably is present more often than not.

BEGINNINGS OF DECEIT

The employment interviewer's casual comments are but a small part of the deluge of half-truths and falsehoods to which typical organizations subject personnel. More than a few usually are—or have been—contained in what many call the "employee handbook" or "personnel manual." They are perhaps fewer now than was the case before the nation's courts started interpreting these documents as contracts, but they nevertheless persist.

Before the Interview

While the first of the major deceits employees experience usually occur during one or more interviews, the process begins earlier with "Positions Available" advertising. A single copy of almost any metropolitan daily newspaper provides an abundance of examples.

"Excellent opportunity."

"Excellent benefits and opportunities for advancement."

"Excellent salary and company benefit plan."

"Excellent compensation plan. Full benefits program."

"This could be your opportunity to join one of the fastest growing industries today."

"We offer an excellent opportunity with growth potential."

"Nobody, but nobody, offers you all these goodies. We train if experienced or nonexperienced."

Good Jobs? Were it not for the fact that wording in advertising of this sort has been essentially unchanged for more than a decade, one might assume that these messages come from companies hard-pressed to fill key positions. They appear instead in ads for jobs of the sort that offer little potential—for truck drivers, pest control personnel, clerks, typists, and the like.

Deceptive terminology in many cases extends beyond generalities into specifics. Many an advertisement for a public relations position includes such tell-tale phrases as "meet the public" and "60 words per minute." The advertisers were looking for receptionist-typists, but honesty was sacrificed in the interests of attracting more ambitious candidates.

Applicant expectations are thus expanded beyond the limits of the jobs they seek before their applications are filed. The deception tends to continue in many personnel or human-resources departments.

Here the objective is to fill the job as rapidly as possible with the best candidate available. What should be fact-finding interviews on both sides often become sales presentations by company representatives, who frequently feel pressure from superiors to get the job filled. The problem almost invariably is magnified by absence of accountability. Organizations' senior managers seldom hold human resources departments accountable for turnover rates, although such performance standards might discourage "overselling" jobs to applicants.

Employment Interviews

Employment processes in most organizations involve multiple interviews. Candidates are preliminarily screened by human resources personnel, and the best two or three are then interviewed by prospective superiors. Where management positions are involved, there may be several postscreening interviews, sometimes with several members of the organization.

As superior candidates move through the interviews, the potential for their being misled compounds. The "selling of the company" proceeds at an accelerating pace. The career of every stock clerk or secretary who progressed to the rank of assistant manager is recounted in glowing detail. Each and every organizational benefit is displayed as if through a magnifying glass, whether or not it is truly exemplary of what too often is termed "the best in the industry."

The Orientation Process

After an applicant is hired, during the orientation process the interviewers' overstatements are often further compounded, especially through some of the sections of the employee handbook or personnel manual. The first compounding frequently occurs in the chief executive officer's introductory statement. Others are apt to be found in descriptions of disciplinary policies, performance-review systems, and compensation mechanisms.

Introductory statement. Handbook introductory statements traditionally contain all the usual platitudes concerning organizational commitments to personnel. In the absence of the sort of oversight that the Securities and Exchange Commission provides for corporate annual reports, they tend to extol the virtues of the organization in glowing terms. Fairness and equity are two of the more popular values that chief executives delight in promising.

The reality often is far different. Favoritism and discrimination are frequently found in working environments. Inept and untrained technicians, who often come to positions of power through politics rather than performance, quickly demonstrate how "the system" really works.

Due process and discipline. Many if not most personnel handbooks superficially assure employees of "fair and equitable treatment." Those who consider using the established system to resolve inequities, however, often find themselves frustrated by a Catch 22 appeal policy, under which all employee complaints first must be taken to immediate superiors.

Employees' perceptions are that even if they win, they lose. The supervisor's decision may be overturned, but the employee remains under his or her supervision. Few have the temerity to avail themselves of such a system. Inequity and unfairness thus are systemically condoned. Discontent festers. Workers involved in such a situation become marginally productive, at best. At worst, they may be counterproductive, as in the case of Detroit auto workers who reportedly created product defects to vent their ill feelings.

Performance review. Frustration can also arise in context with the best of worker-evaluation systems. Many are predestined to failure by their design. These are systems that consider such factors as "attitude," "cooperation," and "willingness to work" in determining the value of employee performance. Neither these nor similarly ambiguous characteristics can be quantitatively or qualitatively measured. Since such criteria seldom bear any discernible relationship to productivity, measurement would be inappropriate in any event.

The best of performance-evaluation systems can be counterproductive, unless evaluators are held accountable for their application. This seldom is the case in the best of circumstances, where supervisors are reasonably unbiased and relatively well trained, for the reason that no one enjoys confrontation, which almost inevitably arises where performance-appraisal systems are applied as intended. "Satisfactory" or "above average" ratings are distributed indiscriminately to all involved, and the system fails.

Reward mechanisms. Although authors of employee handbooks often especially extol variable reward mechanisms that enable supervisors to reward exceptional performance, typical reward systems seldom produce the desired results.

Supervisors who are not accountable for the administration of reward systems almost invariably misuse them. "About the same for everyone" is the least damaging and most frequently used approach. The same rationale that governs performance appraisal applies here. Where one employee's reward is significantly greater than another's, the less-rewarded employee is apt to protest. Supervisors then must justify their decisions and expose themselves to unpleasantness.

Some will risk confrontation to reward favorites and punish those they dislike. From a management standpoint the mechanism then becomes destructive rather than merely ineffective. It is destructive, in fact, in several ways. While discouraging productivity, it creates continuing deterioration in organizational capability. Again, the reason is simple: Employees faced with such circumstances tend to seek jobs elsewhere. The best qualified among them necessarily can most readily find other employment. When the better leave and the worse remain, the organization deteriorates.

SUPERVISORY PROBLEMS

Perhaps the greatest source of employee discontent in any organization is the behavior of first-line supervisors. With rare exceptions they are selected on the basis of seniority or technical skill. Their educational backgrounds most often provide virtually none of the knowledge or skills necessary in management or leadership.

Organizations compound these weaknesses by providing little or no orientation or training. This morning's rank-and-file worker readily becomes this afternoon's supervisor. A manager's handshake often is the sum and substance of supervisors' preparation for positions that disproportionately influence the welfare of the organization.

Employee Perspectives

From the standpoint of employees, supervisors and managers *are* the organization. They hold the power of economic life and death. Younger employees, especially, tend to view their superiors as omnipotent. What the supervisor says and does is taken as reflective of senior management's policies or—at the minimum—of what senior management knowingly tolerates.

If supervisors are intolerant, the organization is intolerant. If supervisors behave unfairly, the organization is unfair. Perhaps even more potentially damaging from management's standpoint, immediate supervisors—skilled or unskilled—tend to become role models for their subordinates.

Where supervisors permit favored employees to sleep on the job, such behavior automatically becomes acceptable in the eyes of every employee. If supervisors neglect to enforce organizational policy, it becomes nonexistent to their subordinates.

Variation in supervisory behavior across unit or departmental lines tends to be even more damaging. Such conduct inevitably becomes common knowledge in any organization. It is taken as incontrovertible evidence that management is unfair or uncaring. Any potential for real employee commitment to the organization is lost in the process.

Management Failures

Behavior of the sort described above exists only where management is inept or uncaring. Managers who maintain the health of their organization, however, follow the advice of Peter F. Drucker:

1. If I put a person into a job and he or she does not perform, I have made a mistake. I have no business blaming that person, no business invoking the "Peter Principle," no business complaining. I have made a mistake.
2. "The soldier has a right to competent command" was already an old maxim at the time of Julius Caesar. It is the duty of managers to make sure that responsible people in their organizations perform.
3. Of all the decisions an executive makes, none is as important as the decisions about people because they determine the performance capacity of the organization. Therefore, I'd better make these decisions well.
4. The one "don't": Don't give new people new major assignments, for doing so only compounds the risks. Give this sort of assignment to someone whose behavior and habits you know and who has earned trust and credibility within your organization. Put a high-level newcomer into an established position where the expectations are known and help is available.

Changing roles. When organizations attempt to meet the needs of the contemporary employee without heeding Drucker's admonitions, problems tend to compound. They arise out of another factor noted by Drucker: change in the work place.

The jobs and roles of workers and supervisors are changing. Supervisors are faced with especially dramatic changes for which they are ill prepared. As factory workers become programmers rather than operators, they need assistants rather than supervisors; information and training rather than oversight. Experience to date suggests that such change may be difficult to achieve.

Anticipated blue-collar resistance to such innovations as quality circles, for example, has proven unfounded. Considerable resistance to them has been encountered, however, from supervisors concerned over loss of authority. Such programs not only eliminate the need for supervision but enable workers to communicate directly with organizational staff members, destroying supervisory control of this process.

Impediment to productivity. "It can be argued," Drucker pointed out, "that the traditional supervisor is an anachronism and an impediment to productivity." He almost inevitably becomes so in organizations that seek to motivate and reward the contemporary worker. Mechanisms through which these objectives can be achieved produce a self-motivated, self-directed worker who requires no supervisor in the traditional sense. Where supervisors remain, they must at least be reeducated and retrained. No organization can afford their existence in traditional models.

Further Frustration

Problems that supervisors inflict on their employees and organizations are a small portion of those that employees encounter in traditional organizations. All are compounded by internal inconsistencies, which arise from variation in policy interpretation and application among supervisory personnel. The variation serves as one of several persistent reminders of problems internal to each operating unit.

Difficulties are further complicated by frequent contradictions between proclaimed policy and workplace reality. They occur equally in potentially litigious areas, such as equal employment opportunity, and less sensitive areas, such as quality control. They are especially prevalent where official proclamations conflict with the realities of day-to-day procedure in the office or on the shop floor.

CONFLICTING MESSAGES

Conflict in organizational messages often is management's most pervasive problem. As others have pointed out at length, organizations consistently ask for productivity, but reward attendance. In fact, the problem goes far beyond this obvious dichotomy. Workers persistently receive conflicting messages. Some originate with immediate supervisors, but the more damaging among them are created by senior managers. They are especially prevalent in communication intended for the financial community and for consumers of the organization's products or services.

Financial Messages

Organizations' formal financial messages, for the most part, are contained in quarterly and annual reports. Some are also "packaged" in senior executives' presentations to financial analysts. Still others are the result of interviews with the mass media—especially the business press.

Management's objective in conveying these messages is to enhance perceptions of the organization among primary financial constituencies—shareholders, financial analysts, and others, whose behaviors influence the market for the organization's securities. To achieve this objective, good news tends to be overemphasized and bad news minimized.

Conflict. The messages involved often come into conflict with others designed for employees. While the financial community may be told of minor problems in a specific operational area, for example, they may be pictured to members of the organization as a threat to economic survival.

This is not an unusual phenomenon. In their most moderate form, senior managers' messages tend to be magnified by subordinates. A standing joke in the newsroom of a large southern newspaper, for example, once involved staff members' ability to tell by reading each morning's edition which street the editor had used when driving to work the prior day. He would often pause at the city desk en route to his office to inquire of the city editor as to when a particular street was to be repaired. The city editor interpreted such inquiries as royal commands and appropriate articles duly appeared in the next day's newspaper.

Results are less humorous where, for example, a mildly put instruction to closely monitor expenses is magnified at succeeding levels of the organization to produce a disproportionate response at the worker level. A full-scale cost-cutting campaign, perhaps involving an end to all overtime and layoffs for some workers is viewed with skepticism where senior managers' perquisites are not similarly curtailed.

Contradictory moves. Economy campaigns with curbs on rank-and-file wage increases can produce similarly negative results when large bonuses are announced for top officers. While superficially of minor import, such actions produce considerable deterioration in credibility. Organizational credibility has been especially strained in recent years as jobs have disappeared, eroding loyalty as well as trust and confidence.

In a 1986 survey of middle managers conducted for *Business Week,* Louis Harris and Associates found that 56 percent had assumed, on taking their current jobs, that they would be able to retain them as long as their work was satisfactory. Only 44 percent believed that that was still the case. Forty-six percent expected employers to cut back on salaried work forces in the next few years. And 65 percent thought salaried employees were less loyal to employers than had been the case ten years earlier.

Such perceptions will not rapidly change. Apparent contradictions in organizational messages can only compound the problem. Where the financial community is given glowing accounts of organizational success, for example, workers cannot be expected to accept a concurrent call for austerity. Organizational credibility suffers in similar fashion where promotional materials make exaggerated claims.

Commercial Exaggeration

Marketing and advertising managers logically seek to "position" their products and services to attract favorable customer attention. Their efforts frequently produce further credibility problems.

Consider, for example, the small manufacturer who elects to emphasize customer service in sales messages in order to offset the market dominance of larger organizations. Such an approach is not only logical but justifiable where there is a real commitment to service, but only under those circumstances.

Where members of sales, shipping, and customer-service units are aware that performance falls short of claims, conflict arises. The issue involved may not be quite as significant to employees as those described earlier, but the conflict renders management less credible than ever. If managers mislead customers, workers reason, they are apt to be deceiving employees as well.

Quality claims. The same problem arises where advertising stresses product quality, while employees know quality control systems are lackadaisical at best. It may be encountered again when promotional materials stress support services that employees know are quantitatively or qualitatively lacking.

Potentially most ludicrous from employees' viewpoints, and most destructive of credibility, are claims of superior products or services from an organization of high-caliber personnel. Workers are better able than managers or supervisors to judge their peers. Where management internally condones ineptitude, while externally claiming expert capabilities, the organization becomes a laughing stock in employee eyes.

COMMUNICATION CONFLICT

Personnel may laugh at conflicting messages organizationally directed to diverse constituencies. They tend, however, to take senior management's traditional communication efforts more personally, and rightfully so. All too often they perceive management messages directed to them as assuming them to be gullible if not mentally underequipped. Roger M. D'Aprix described the situation well a decade ago.

If an organization has substantial employee problems...and if it is publishing a glossy magazine that never acknowledges that there is a single problem in the organization...it is clear that people will begin to ask questions.

They will question the sanity and the intelligence of the people who publish such stuff, and they will certainly compare their everyday experience with the picture presented in the magazine. When these two things are inconsistent with one another, people will be both confused and angry. And they will certainly long for someone to tell them the truth.

Message Problems

The typical organizational publication, whether it be a mimeographed newsletter or a glossy magazine, conveys little information of interest to employees. It produces recognition for outstanding performance, informs personnel of staff and policy changes, and avoids material that might tend to mislead them. At best, it is largely ignored. At worst, it produces resentment.

Perennial exhortations in the form of posters, pay-envelope inserts, and other materials of the same sort induce much the same response if they produce a response at all. The communication manager of a large hospital once advanced a theory the author has found to be of considerable merit. The effectiveness of an employee communications program, he said, can be readily measured by the condition of the parking lot on the day employee newsletters are distributed. If it's littered with discarded newsletters, the program is in trouble.

Mechanical Problems

Employee communication failures arise out of multiple problems. Where one exists, others often arise as well. Most common among them are the assumptions of senior managers as well as those involved in message preparation and delivery.

Both groups tend to fall victim to a snare that entangles many communicators. It can best be expressed in a simple sentence: "If I understand it, everyone will understand." While average educational levels in the United States are increasing, the assumption is simply untrue.

Educational level. Today's senior managers usually have graduate degrees. Their immediate subordinates for the most part are college graduates. Few organizations are largely composed of such individuals. Only one in four people in the United States has completed a college education. Workers' vocabularies are poorer than those of executives, and their ability to comprehend messages probably is deteriorating rather than improving. The rapidly growing Hispanic population of the United States assures that this is or soon will be the case. Resistance to cultural assimilation, in fact, may be one of the major issues of the next decade.

Packaging. Employee publications in most organizations also suggest another tenuous assumption, that the attractiveness of the package assures digestion of content. Packaging rationally can be assumed to play a role in message delivery only with regard to text/illustration mix. The less literate — and there are many in the contemporary organization — tend to assimilate illustrated information better.

In too many organizations communication managers would be better served by electronic rather than print media in meeting the informational needs of employees of varying educational background. Instead, they fall victim to the assumption that "slicker" is better.

Recipient control. The bulk of communicators' problems, however, probably arises out of still another assumption, that messages prepared and transmitted necessarily are received, understood, and acted upon. They fail to understand that the communication process is controlled by the receiver rather than the sender. Where messages are not received, understood, or acted upon, the most skillful preparation and dissemination become exercises in futility.

Even where messages are received, results may be less than satisfactory. Recipient values and attitudes — not those of senders — determine how they will be received and interpreted, and whether they will be acted upon. Any communicator whose messages are not adjusted for value and life-style changes that have occurred in recent years is at considerable risk.

Origins of Motivation

Communicators must also recognize, as the Massachusetts Institute of Technology's Leo D. Moore pointed out, that "motivation arises from mutuality of interest and little else in our industrial environment."

The greatest jobs of management have been accomplished where managers were close to their people, in regular communication with them, and gave continuous evidence of understanding their interests and the relation of these interests to those of the manager. This is the essence of good communications. It does not mean bigger and better bulletin boards or company newspapers. It is a striving for mutuality of interests based on an understanding that goes deeper than the obvious, that rests on the depths of man's make-up — his aims, hopes and desires. It accepts a man for what he is and permits him to become a better man for all of it. This is management *with* others.

"For example," says D'Aprix, "the management that simply assumes that it has the respect and loyalty of its people, that the people will give their allegiance because they believe management knows best and will do what is right for them is crazy. I can think of no other adjective to describe that management's state of mind."

Message failure. Management messages self-destruct, in other words, where they can be taken by employees as symptomatic of their being talked *at* rather than talked *with.* "Adults employed by any organization," D'Aprix said, "should be treated as adults and . . . their personal stake in that organization — no matter how large or small that stake may seem — should be respected. In short, they should be recognized as *members* of the organization."

Many managers communicate as if the reverse were true. Their attitudes suggest that employees can accept their dictates or quit and go elsewhere. They pretend to care about people, but persist in manipulating, dehumanizing, and brutalizing them—actions that speak far louder than any words.

Organizations no longer can afford the luxury of treating workers as consumable or disposable resources. The supply is becoming far too small. Workers inevitably will gravitate toward organizations where their human as well as economic needs are met. Other organizations quickly will find their very survival threatened.

Managers who accept this premise have taken the first step toward leadership. The second can then be taken with relative ease: recognizing that employees are as important to the welfare of the organization as shareholders, customers, and regulators. Other than in wartime, when many organizations have found themselves at the mercy of vendors, they have been most sensitive to the requirements of the former groups. War produced manpower shortages, of course, but emergency legislation froze many workers in their jobs. Wages were frozen as well, and relatively little competition for human resources developed.

Employee shortage. The shoe now is in process of moving to the other foot. Human resources will be more scarce than dollars. New customers and stockholders will be more readily found than new employees. As Drucker said,

We face a growing mismatch between jobs and available labor supply. Both are changing, but in different, often opposite directions. As a result, the job openings increasingly do not fit the available people. In turn, qualifications, expectations, and values of people available for employment are changing to the point where they no longer fit the jobs offered.... employers increasingly will have to change what they mean by "labor market." Increasingly it will be the job seeker who is the "customer" with job opportunities and job characteristics having to satisfy the job seeker. Traditionally employers have seen the labor market as homogenous, divided only by very broad lines: age and sex, for example, or manual workers, clerical workers, and managerial and professional workers. But increasingly the available work force is segmented into a fairly large number of different markets, with considerable freedom for the individual to switch from one to another. Increasingly, therefore, employers will have to learn that jobs are products that have to be designed for specific buyers and both marketed and sold to them.

Interdependency. Organizations that accept Drucker's admonition will, by implication, have taken the third necessary step. They will have acknowledged a level of interdependency consistent with that long ago accepted as to shareholders, customers, and regulators. By implication they will have recognized the necessity for raising human-resources and communication functions to the same level as marketing and sales.

They will have committed themselves to monitoring the interests, needs, and preferences of existing and prospective employees with the same diligence devoted to customers and prospective customers. They will create equally hospitable environments for them. They will require that all members of the organization treat employees with dignity and respect. They will communicate with them openly, truthfully, and on the employees' own terms.

The transition involved will not be an easy one, but it must be accom-

plished. Those unwilling or unable to accept the necessity for new relationships between organizations and their employees — existing or prospective — will quickly become liabilities that organizations can no longer
afford. Senior executives, middle managers, and first-echelon supervisors all
will be faced with the same circumstances.

Accepting change. Logic suggests that all will accept contemporary reality.
The circumstances will be little different from those that existed when civil
rights, occupational safety and health, and other principles became part of
organizational life. Only when this point has been reached — and not before
— can managers begin bringing workers together into effective, efficient
teams. The task is not easily accomplished. The goal can be achieved, however, where truth and honesty prevail and the interests of all parties are
considered.

ORGANIZATIONAL PURPOSE

A great deal has been written in recent years concerning organizational
"culture." A better word might be "purpose." Most accept the fact that too
many workers today are permitted to drift purposelessly through their daily
tasks. Reversal of these conditions, however, does not require charismatic
leadership or high purpose. "Not all business corporations," as Perry Pascarella has pointed out, "can make their mission that of service to some
lofty social purposes, but all can define some human end toward which
their product or service contributes.

Leaders do not create organizational purposes. They find them by communicating with others; by determining what the group wants to achieve
and then pointing out the direction in which they can work toward common
purposes. A successful leader brings people together in common purpose,
Pascarella says, "when they are aware they are free to choose not to commit
to that purpose." He brings their values to the surface and articulates a
vision or purpose toward which all can strive. He helps them see the difference between what is and what can be.

The basic issue, as Ozley suggested, is "whether an organization will be
a 'working for' organization or a 'working with' organization." The latter
are characterized by several attributes. They respect the human dignity of
all workers. They emphasize rewards to productive personnel rather than
punitive measures toward nonperformers. Their policies are clearly written,
consistently implemented, and continually reviewed. They maintain fair
wage/benefit structures supported by functional performance-appraisal programs. They attach accountability to authority to insure appropriate behaviors at all organizational levels. And they support all of these elements with
an effective communication program.

What constitutes an effective communication program? Accurate information, communicated honestly and in keeping with audience character-

istics on a timely basis. These elements are more complex than they appear, as Fred Carvell and many others have pointed out. Methods by which they can be designed and made operational are discussed in the remaining chapters of this book.

SUMMARY

Organizations bent on survival beyond the turn of the century must bridge a credibility gap of near cosmic proportions between employees and managers. While varying with organizations, the problem exists in most of them as a result of considerable deceit. It begins in classified advertising for personnel and continues through interview, hiring, and orientation processes.

The most damaging elements involved are contained in the typical organization's employee handbook. They include due-process provisions of disciplinary policies that are predestined to failure. Performance review and reward mechanisms are similarly flawed, primarily through the absence of user accountability

Employees completing the orientation process then are turned over to first-line supervisors who necessarily are the organization's least well trained middle managers. Senior management too often forgets that these individuals, from the standpoint of their subordinates, literally are the organization.

In organizations seeking to meet contemporary economic problems, potential for difficulty is especially great. Workers and workplaces are changing. These changes require accompanying change on the part of managers and supervisors, especially the latter. When they fail to change, they can readily become barriers to rather than expediters of productivity.

Problems among supervisors and managers are compounded by conflicting messages that employees receive from multiple sources. Proclaimed policy and workplace reality frequently are in conflict, especially where managers and supervisors are not accountable for results. Further conflicts are found between messages designed for employees and those fashioned for shareholders and customers.

The problem is rendered inordinately complex where organizations adhere to traditional employee communication patterns. While their mechanical designs have tended to improve in recent years, their content continues to leave employee readers unimpressed. Communicators too often assume that readers are as well educated as themselves and, more critically, that senders rather than receivers control the communication process.

They must recognize instead that motivation arises out of community of interest. Their challenge increasingly will be to educate and inform employees in this context, establishing premises from which community of interest will be accepted and acted upon. Employees must be talked with rather than at. They must *be* members of the organization to consider themselves members of the organization.

The contemporary organization increasingly will be as dependent upon its employees as any vendor, shareholder, or customer group. Long-term success will be a function of ability to adapt to this new reality, to become a working with rather than a working for organization.

ADDITIONAL READING

Carvell, Fred H. *Human Relations in Business,* 3rd ed. New York: Macmillan, 1980.

D'Aprix, Roger M. *The Believable Corporation,* New York: AMACOM, 1977.

Drucker, Peter F. *The Frontiers of Management.* New York: Dutton, 1986.

Miner, John B. *People Problems: The Executive Answer Book.* New York: Random House Business Division, 1985.

Moore, Leo B. "How to Manage Improvement," *Harvard Business Review,* July-August 1958.

Nussbaum, Bruce, et al. "The End of Corporate Loyalty?" *Business Week*, August 4, 1986.

Ozley, Lee M. "Falling Prey to a Management Fallacy," in *How to be a Better Leader.* Cleveland, Penton, 1983.

Pascarella, Perry. *The New Achievers: Creating a Modern Work Ethic.* New York: The Free Press, 1984.

Sanderson, Susan R., and Lawrence Schein. "Sizing up the Down-Sizing Era," *Across the Board,* November 1986.

6

A MATTER OF COMMITMENT

Organizational success through the remainder of the century will require ethics, morality, and commitment; a real belief in equality of obligation to all stakeholder groups; and the will to see that the obligation is discharged. Committed leadership will be the most important element. The nature of humans and of the organizations they have created requires that tremendous inertia be overcome. Leaders will not succeed by merely issuing orders. They must take any and every step necessary to ensure that directives are carried out in spirit and letter.

In essence, organizations and their managers can be what many in the United States perceive them to be, or they can be something more. Fifty-six percent of the U.S. population consider corporate executives dishonest, believing that they commit white-collar crime to make a profit for themselves and their companies. And 67 percent are dissatisfied with contemporary ethics and standards of behavior. Not a pretty record, perhaps, but the figures nevertheless reflect people's perceptions, as reported by *Public Opinion* in late 1986.

Such perceptions influence the welfare of organizations. Whether they improve or deteriorate will be determined by managers. Organizational success or failure, as University of Southern California Professor James O'Toole wrote, may be in the balance.

Management is basically a moral undertaking. Am I saying that viewing business as a moral undertaking will guarantee success, or that failure to do so will cause a good company to go bad? Sorry, life isn't that simple. I'm merely asserting that no company has ever gotten into financial hot water by taking the high road. No company has ever produced red ink because it behaved ethically, because it invested for the long term, because it treated employees with respect, or because it put something back into its community. Of course, companies that do none of those things succeed, too. Yet the low road is fraught with risk. For it is often the case that corporations that play fast and loose end up alienating their customers, their vendors, their employees and their stockholders. . . .

All I am claiming is that managers have a choice. As there are no rules that free managers from the terrible responsibility of choosing what products to market and what strategies to pursue, managers must also choose whether to treat employees well or treat them poorly, and whether to produce safe, high-quality goods or shoddy ones.

Managers in the past have been led to believe that success is realized only by those who "take the low road," O'Toole wrote, "but there is now evidence that managers are free to make a choice that few had thought open to them: They can choose to conduct their work lives by the same high principles with which they conduct their private lives."

The companies I have studied — including Motorola, Dayton Hudson, Deere, Herman Miller, and W. T. Gore — dispel the myth that the only way to succeed in business is at the expense of employees, customers and society. The high road these companies follow is not one of altruism, it is not pious or trendy "social responsibility," and it is not do-goodism. Much as an individual can lead a moral life, without being a social worker or a Mother Teresa, a corporation can behave morally by leading a principled existence — what Aristotle called a "good life" in the individual context.

THE GOOD LIFE

What does the good life require of organizations? Four steps appear essential. First, the traditionally categorical approach to organization and motivation must be set aside. Second, organizational assumptions as to human behavior must be established. Third, the organization must make a commitment to morality. Finally, systems conducive to moral and ethical conduct must be established.

Organizational Concepts

Hundreds if not thousands of theories of organizational structure and employee motivation have been propounded in recent years. They generally can be grouped into four categories: meritocratic, egalitarian, behaviorist, and humanist. Each theory in each category involves one or more assumptions, stated or unstated, and each appeals to a particular set of managerial beliefs.

Meritocratic. Meritocracy implies distribution of rewards in keeping with individual productivity. The theory is consonant with free-enterprise economic principles and thus frequently has been embraced in principle by organizational managers. It has proven successful in the relatively few organizations in which merit has been successfully measured and rewarded.

Egalitarian. Egalitarianists consider meritocracies unfair in that "survival of the fittest" overly penalizes the unfit. They prefer organizations that create a broad range of entitlements for all workers and limit managerial discretion. Their ranks are peopled by unionists and those of a socialist bent. Egalitarian organizations tend to favor employees among stakeholder groups and to be less than optimally productive as a result.

Behaviorist. The behaviorist philosophy places the group ahead of the individual. Behaviorists are committed to environmental conditioning as a control mechanism. Employee monitoring and regulation, coupled with a variety of incentive schemes are employed to produce desired results.

Humanist. Quality of life is the primary focus of the humanistically oriented. They emphasize policies designed to enhance individual growth and development and to give employees a major decision-making role.

Vanguard Companies

Managers tend to favor the meritocratic approach, while union officials prefer egalitarianism, and students are inclined toward humanism, but successful organizations — what O'Toole calls "Vanguard companies" — adopt a balanced approach designed to achieve all of the specified objectives.

The leaders of Vanguard companies believe that their corporations will not be viewed as legitimate by employees if they are organized to maximize only one goal or value. They also believe that all four values are necessary if a corporation is to be productive in the long term.

The task of management . . . is to find ways to simultaneously satisfy these four competing, but equally legitimate, objectives. . . . there is no one best place to be on the managerial quadrant, and . . . "getting as much of all four desirable outcomes as possible" does not mean being in the geographical middle of each quadrant, in a state of compromise, offering a little of each. It actually means breaking through the trade-off barrier by creatively designing work systems which permit the simultaneous realization of all four *necessary* objectives.

The key to success, O'Toole says, requires a close look at underlying assumptions. He compared those of traditional managers with those he perceived in a Vanguard company (see Figure 6.1).

Commitment to Morality

There are no prerequisites to a commitment to organizational morality. Managerial fiat will suffice, and no substantive resistance will be encountered, provided one condition is met: All involved in the organization must be accountable for results.

"Substantive resistance" and organizational inertia are not one and the same. The former implies conscious decision making; the latter may be a product of resistance to change. It occurs more often where ill-advised executives have a reputation for erratic behavior; where priorities change from day to day and managers have learned "this, too, will pass."

Vested interests. Substantive resistance arises where managers or super-

Figure 6.1. Alternative Assumptions about Employees.

Traditional Organizations	Vanguard Organizations
1. Workers are paid to do, not think.	1. Behavior is a consequence of how employees are treated.
2. Workers have little to contribute in terms of ideas that will improve productivity.	2. Employees are intelligent, curious and responsible.
3. The sole reason people work is to make money.	3. Employees need a rational work world in which they know what is expected of them and why.
4. Workers are all alike.	4. Employees need to know how their jobs relate to the jobs of others and to company goals.
5. There is one best way to manage workers.	5. There is only one class of employees, not a creative management group and a group of others who carry out orders.
6. The function of managers is to manage; the function of workers is to carry out orders.	6. There is no one best way to manage change.
7. Employees do not want to accept responsibility for the quantity or quality of their own work.	7. No one knows how to do his or her job better than the person on the job.
8. Capital and management are the major sources of increased productivity.	8. Employees want to have pride in their work.
9. Worker participation, profit sharing, stock ownership, and the like are soft-headed at best, socialistic at worst.	9. Employees want to be involved in decisions that affect their own work.
10. Given any opportunity, workers will goof off; the role of the supervisor is that of a policeman to keep workers in line.	10. The responsibility of every manager is to draw out the ideas and abilities of workers in a shared effort of addressing business problems and opportunities.

Source: Adapted from James O'Toole, *Vanguard Management: Redesigning the Corporate Future*. New York: Doubleday, 1985. Copyright © 1985 by James O'Toole. Reprinted by permission of Doubleday.

visors have a vested interest in the status quo. Appropriate accountability systems negate any tendency to protect such interests. Reward systems must support rather than detract from organizational objectives. Where this is not the case, senior managers in practical terms are sending mixed signals to subordinates.

Mixed signals at best create confusion and delay response. At worst, they encourage recipients to do nothing until messages are adequately clarified. Clear direction is essential to organizational response. Where it is given, and where it is supported by necessary systemic changes, desired results usually are achieved.

Changing standards. Where countervailing philosophies have been the norm, a clear statement of new organizational standards is virtually essential. Management is asking, in effect, for a change in institutionalized behavior. Unequivocal presentation of new standards is vital to induce what O'Toole considers essential: deeds as opposed to words.

It is what a company does — and not necessarily what it says — that ultimately makes the difference between organizational effectiveness and ineffectiveness. Important, it is not simply in their constitutions that the Vanguard treat their employees as stakeholders; the Vanguard manifest their commitment to employee rights and responsibilities in all aspects of management.

This approach to human-resources management is essential if organizations are to create a community of purpose with their employees. Where organizations' primary commitments are to profit, the effort may well be an exercise in futility. Neither employees nor middle managers will be prone to accept such an approach.

Pascarella makes essentially the same point.

Management fights an uphill battle when it tries to build a feeling of unity and mutual dependence while confining corporate purpose to economic objectives. Unless the organization's members can envision some human, nonquantifiable values and purpose, they feel they are selling themselves out by committing to the corporate goals. They want something more enduring — more fulfilling to their full range of human needs....

Self-respect or self-esteem must have an ethical basis. When that basis does not exist, people must be manipulated into working, but when the company cares, employees will care. When they perceive the company as being unfair to them or to others, they will not respond with responsible work behavior. Workers in "don't care" companies don't mind calling in sick since they feel their absence won't hurt the system; in fact, they may be happy if it does. People who are participating in a humanistic setting, on the other hand, realize the burden they put on fellow workers and the possible economic harm their absence will cause. They realize, too, that they are undermining the respect that others have paid them. Their decision to come to work or stay home becomes an ethical one. It then becomes not simply a matter of being fired for unsatisfactory conduct but the possible pain of no longer

being a part of things. The humanistic organization, therefore, runs on ethical behavior because it begins with individuals' respect for themselves, their colleagues,
and others they serve. Ethics, not rule books, set the standards for behavior.

Few would argue the desirability of the circumstances Pascarella describes. They do not, however, spring into being instantaneously and alone.

Systemic Imperatives

Stakeholder status for employees is frequently accompanied by other ele
ments, including employee stock ownership, a measure of job security,
lifelong training, flexible benefits, participation in decision making, freedom
of expression and incentive compensation systems. All are significant. On
close examination, however, they all but necessarily arise out of the stakeholder concept.

Given organizational commitment to equitable treatment of all stakeholders, other necessary organizational attributes logically develop. O'Toole
described those of the Weyerhauser Company:

In a free-enterprise society, a company's only assurance of its future is its ability to
earn a profit. At Weyerhauser, we believe that *how* that profit is earned is critical
to the Company's continued success. For this reason, we commit the Company to
the following values and principles.

Integrity
Integrity in all dealings, internal and external.

Stewardship
Long-term, responsible stewardship of land and timber.

Fairness as an Employer
Fair, considerate treatment of employees in a work climate that encourages full
utilization of their abilities.

Balance
Decision making that reflects an appropriate balance between short and long-term
perspectives.

Management decisions that balance the legitimate interests of shareholders, bondholders, employees, customers, and of the communities in which the Company is
a major employer.

To whom does Weyerhauser management have a special obligation?

Employees
Employment that contributes to economic security, personal development, personal
dignity and pride.

Shareholders
A return on investment consistent with the risk and with competitive opportunities.

Bondholders

Protection of their underlying interest through a sound, conservative capital structure.

Customers

Conduct of our business in a manner that fosters long-term preferred-customer/preferred-supplier relationships.

Communities

Management of the Company in a financially prudent manner, pursuing stability and continuity of operation, in order to be a good corporate citizen.

The Weyerhauser concept implies a good deal more than is apparent. Included are the moral and ethical underpinnings previously discussed, total understanding of the stakeholder concept by all involved, a structure adequate to ensure that the organization's commitments will be fulfilled at all organizational levels, and a communication system sufficient to the needs of all involved.

Organizational Cultures

The organizational attributes described above in a sense also express Weyerhauser's values or, if you prefer, "culture." They are more readily reduced to writing than rendered in reality. Not a few organizations caught up in the "corporate culture" boom of the early 1980s attempted to establish values by managerial fiat. Most of these efforts were predestined to failure.

A culture grows out of what an organization is rather than what someone or some group says it is. Where a culture exists, it may beneficially be expressed in writing for the sake of newcomers who otherwise would have to assimilate it more slowly. What is put on paper, however, must be reflective of reality. Any conflict between words and deeds readily becomes apparent and credibility suffers as a result. When major organizational problems arise, as cultural anthropologist Peter C. Reynolds found at Falcon Computer Company (not the company's real name), such credibility gaps can be especially destructive.

Shared models. "Cultures are shared models of social relations and almost everyone knew that the operative values at Falcon were hierarchy, secrecy and expediency, regardless of what the official culture said...," Reynolds wrote.

Clearly, a model of the culture must be close enough to the truth that it can be referred to without eliciting smirks, but this is not to say that ideal models of social relations are irrelevant to day-to-day life, or that cultural ideals are generally treated with skepticism by a society's participants. Human beings, in corporations as elsewhere, live in a moral universe, and the most interesting thing about the official Falcon culture is how little credence it gave to the moral standards already operative in the company.

At Falcon...the overall corporate culture was most clearly revealed in the disparity between the official and the actual, in the mismatch between the real and ideal cultures. Although probably all societies have a disparity between idealistic and realistic models of social relations, because people are ethical animals and the world is imperfect, at Falcon the falsification of realistic models was sanctioned and encouraged by the social organization. Falcon culture was expressed not by the ethical ideals presented in the values meetings, but by the greater intercultural disparity between the ideal and the real.[1]

Price of Deceit?

Falcon Computer became one of Silicon Valley's better-known financial disasters. Reynolds wondered whether the Falcon Values document was "an idealistic program that went wrong or a cynical use of rhetoric by people who communicated to their subordinates a far different model of acceptable behavior." He offered no conclusions, but provided a caution worthy of note by any who seek to establish or remodel organizational values.

Reynold's description of Falcon Computer should be considered with care by any organizational executive tempted to "establish a new culture" to enhance productivity. The process is difficult and time consuming in the best of circumstances. Total and honest commitment is essential. Failure can be costly and disastrous where cynical leaderships attempt to use the process for manipulative ends.

SCOPE OF COMMITMENT

The scope of the commitment necessary to render today's organization productive in tomorrow's world is difficult to comprehend. While focused on human resources, it involves considerably more. Organizations must cope with an economy rapidly becoming global in scope. Accelerating technological change can remake companies in a matter of months. And change in values and life-styles should be an organizational concern not only in terms of employees but consumers and others as well.

The commitment necessary to change or establish a new reality in the typical organization need not be time consuming. It literally can be established by managerial fiat, provided all involved in implementation are held accountable for outcomes.

Bridging the chasm that exists between management and labor is another matter. It takes time. It involves considerable frustration. Yet it can be done. Indeed, for survival's sake, it must be done.

---

[1]From Peter C. Reynolds, "Corporate Culture on the Rocks," *Across the Board,* October 1986. Copyright (c) 1986, The Conference Board.

Areas of Change

Commitment to moral and ethical management is the first, the shortest, and by far the easiest step in the necessary process of organizational change. Awakening personnel to the fact that the change is real and permanent rather than superficial and transient is another matter. It is the most difficult, complex, and time consuming of those required.

Most of the others are mechanical or technical in nature. They can be separated into two groups. The first involves reexamining existing process and procedures. The second consists of modifying them appropriately to conform to the new reality. As these processes are completed and communicated to employees, their perspectives will change accordingly. Processes and procedures that require reexamination include

1. Personnel policies, especially those dealing with disciplinary matters
2. Job descriptions
3. Performance-appraisal procedures
4. Reward mechanisms
5. Benefit programs.

Disciplinary Matters

Organizational executives, managers, and legal counsel spend inordinate amounts of time, effort, and money in devising personnel policy and procedure manuals. Superficially, they are intended for the guidance of all employees. Pragmatically, they are exercises in anticipating misbehavior. Their focus is the small percentage of prospective policy/procedure abusers, rather than the much larger group that generally conforms to rational policy directives.

Time allocation. Organizations thus pay considerably greater attention to members who misbehave than to those who conform to accepted norms. Managers seldom pause to consider this anomaly. Does the organization devote the greatest amount of time, attention, and recognition—positive or negative—to dedicated, productive team players? To managers and supervisors who most effectively discharge their obligations to the organization and their subordinates? Or to those who are are chronically absent or tardy, over budget, or otherwise causing problems?

Are problem generators being "rewarded" with more supervisory and managerial attention, while problem solvers are largely ignored? While counterproductive behavior can be neither tolerated nor ignored, far greater organizational benefits would accrue, were greater attention paid to productive personnel.

A better way. Those responsible well might ponder allocation of their time to employees categorized in three groups: the relatively small numbers who at one extreme excel and at the other underperform, and the large group between the extremes. Attention to underperformers creates no incentive for the majority. Were comparable time devoted to those who excel, the reverse would tend to be true.

Compensation Systems

Much the same circumstances exist in many if not most organizations with regard to compensation mechanisms. They are skewed to the benefit of marginal rather than superior workers. With few exceptions, these systems tend to overreward personnel who barely meet minimum acceptable performance standards. At the same time, they make no provision for adequately rewarding the overperformer.

Fairness and equity, in other words, are sacrificed for uniformity. This is the case despite the fact that compensation, more than any other factor, tells employees precisely what the organization thinks of them. The results range from counterproductive to highly destructive.

Counterproductive outcomes occur as workers capable of superior performance limit their efforts in keeping with reward potential. Destructive results develop as superior personnel elect to take their talents and capabilities to organizations that offer better reward systems.

Perceptions of fairness and equity in compensation are based on two factors. First is the method by which rate changes are calculated. Second is employee understanding of the system and, especially, any safeguards it contains to prevent inequity.

No secrecy should attach to these elements. Every effort should be made to see that workers are thoroughly conversant with all aspects of compensation systems, short of colleagues' salaries or wage rates. Where systems produce equitable rewards—and only there—will they have employee support.

Performance Appraisal

Equity is also central to what only infrequently can accurately be called performance appraisal. The term "merit review" is more appropriate in many organizations. The difference? Merit is difficult if not impossible to measure. This is especially so where merit encompasses such factors as attitude and willingness to work. Merit review is thus unlikely to produce equitable results. Where it leads to adjustments in compensation level, these are apt to be inappropriately distributed as well.

Performance appraisal, on the other hand, will produce salutary results if several prerequisites are met. First, performance standards must be known to workers in advance and expressed in measurable quantitative and qualitative terms. Second, and perhaps more important, the system must be equitably applied.

Equity essential. Equitable application is not easily achieved in the absence of appraiser accountability. Where there is neither incentive to make performance appraisal systems work nor disincentives to discourage their abuse, they become significantly less productive than otherwise would be the case. The reason is a function of human nature. Virtually no individual enjoys confrontation. No supervisor wants to explain to angry employees why their evaluations were less favorable than those of coworkers, or why their raises consequently were smaller.

Avoidance of confrontation then becomes one of the governing elements of the system. It tends to produce generally comparable appraisals and relatively uniform wage increases within each appraiser's operating unit.

Further problems. Were this the only unanticipated outcome, the resultant situation might be marginally tolerable. It becomes wholly intolerable when the day arrives on which a layoff is necessary, or on which a marginal employee "crosses the line" and deserves to be terminated. Performance appraisal records then will fail to support the appropriate personnel action, and the organization suffers as a result.

Job Descriptions

Performance appraisal and compensation mechanisms are often influenced by job descriptions, which frequently fall short of functional standards. Job descriptions are generic documents. They are designed to encompass all tasks that under any circumstances might be assigned to any individual in the job category involved.

Thus, job descriptions seldom describe what individual employees are called upon to accomplish. The set of tasks assigned to the individual might better be termed a position description for the sake of differentiation. It consists of those responsibilities assigned to individual workers by their immediate superiors.

In the hands of proficient managers and supervisors, position descriptions are productive tools. They enable employees to be assigned those tasks at which they excel. The result is greater productivity and more employee satisfaction. With appropriate specificity in quantitative and qualitative areas, the position description thus becomes a better basis for performance evaluation.

Employee Benefits

Benefits are a significant but less volatile component of the employee satisfaction formula. They are significant because they are one of the factors considered by prospective employees in determining whether to preliminarily consider any job vacancy. They are less volatile because their administration is less susceptible to inequity.

Benefit programs nevertheless deserve careful development and periodic review by employers. Special attention to the so-called flexible or cafeteria benefit concept is especially appropriate. It first came into vogue in the late 1970s and early 1980s, as traditional systems came under pressure due to rising costs and changing life-styles.

Demographic and life-style changes then started to reduce the number of traditional, nuclear, single-wage-earner families. Employers found uniform benefit programs less appropriate as a result. Employees in households with two wage earners suffered through unnecessary duplication of benefits. Employers "lost" as well, in that the attractiveness of their benefit packages to existing and prospective employees declined accordingly.

In response, employers started adding more and more optional benefits to their programs. Workers received uniform benefit credits and were permitted to use them for the benefits they preferred. In some cases, they were permitted to elect additional benefits in lieu of cash compensation. In a relative few, benefits could be converted to cash as well.

The Critical Element

None of the factors discussed above is unusually difficult to manage. Each can be designed to complement an effective human-resources system. The best intentions of senior management, nevertheless, often go awry in program implementation. In virtually every case, difficulties arise from one source: first-line managers and supervisors.

Ineffectiveness at the lowest management echelon is a product of several factors. Those involved, despite their critical roles in organizations, are often underequipped by education or training for managerial positions. They are frequently thrust into these roles with little or no preparation on the part of the organization. Most important, they are seldom held accountable for the results of their actions.

Where supervisors and managers are accountable for results, all-important performance appraisal, compensation, and disciplinary systems tend to function well. Where those involved are not held accountable, the reverse tends to be true.

Organizational commitments to moral and ethical conduct thus must be accompanied by total-accountability systems, which must apply equally to middle managers, supervisors, and rank-and-file personnel.

FURTHER COMMITMENTS

Organizations committed to moral and ethical management must embrace two further elements common to successful organizations—education and training. Each is necessary to organizational growth and development and essential in human-resources management.

Personnel Education

Many if not most individuals come into the job market today relatively well equipped technologically, but without the breadth of background necessary. This is especially the case in terms of economics.

If employees are to accept and support organizations' needs to equitably serve stakeholder groups, they must understand basic economic principles. They must be able to differentiate the roles of management, ownership, and labor. They must comprehend the changing concept of social responsibility.

Too few colleges and universities today require economics courses other than in their business curricula. Disproportionate numbers of graduates remain economically ignorant. Conditions are worse among those who do not complete college educations. Only a miniscule number of high schools offer economics courses and they almost invariably are electives.

Managerial Education

Equally important from an organizational standpoint are the skill and knowledge levels of managers and supervisors—especially those first-line managers and supervisors who almost invariably direct the activities of new employees. They disproportionately influence—for better or worse—the long-term behavioral patterns of their subordinates.

Too often, results are far worse than might have been the case. The principle of the self-fulfilling prophecy is usually at the root of the problem. It suggests that workers will live up to the expectations of their managers or supervisors in much the same way that children tend to reflect the behavioral expectations of their parents. Those who expect the best get the best. Those who expect the worst find it.

Some managers treat their subordinates in a way that leads to superior performance, but most treat them in a manner that creates performance levels poorer than those of which workers are capable. Reasons for such behavior are unclear, but research suggests that workers are most influenced by their superiors' expectations. High expectations appear to produce high productivity, while the reverse appears equally true. Managerial and supervisory expectations thus may function as self-fulfilling prophecies.

This phenomenon is especially significant where entry-level workers are involved. Their personal standards are apt to be established in their first jobs. When their superiors fail to challenge them, these standards will be unnecessarily low and self-image may be impaired as well. In the alternative, the worker may quickly seek more encouraging pastures.

Most organizations have not developed effective first-line managers and supervisors rapidly enough to meet their human-resources-development needs. In consequence, they are underdeveloping their most valuable resource and incurring heavy attrition costs. These circumstances will become less and less tolerable as available entry-level personnel become fewer in number. A new breed of managers will emerge as a result. Over time, they may well redesign the organization as well as its now archaic perspectives on human-resources management.

THE NEW MANAGERS

Managers, like workers, invariably are shaped by employer philosophy and standards. An accurate profile of the new manager is difficult to predict in an era of organizational change. Some of the changes themselves offer insight into what may be required of managers.

Organizations that survive contemporary challenges will necessarily have been oriented to the future rather than the present. They will have focused on human resources, and on the consumer market rather than the stock market. They will have applied emerging technologies to enhance their performance and will emphasize quality in all areas.

Developmental Strategy

These will be organizations that have taken the lead in meeting the needs of all stakeholders. They will have changed organizational values, as well as compensation, reward, and incentive systems, in keeping with contemporary circumstances. In sum, they will follow developmental strategies espoused by O'Toole, Peters and Waterman in 1982, and Peters in 1985. They will

develop a bias for action rather than analysis

listen to customers and meet their needs

encourage internal entrepreneurship

obtain productivity by cultivating people

adopt hands-on, value-driven management techniques

maintain lean, simply structured organizations

build employee autonomy around core values

New Systems

Organizations that meet these criteria almost inevitably will require new management systems and managers. Philip R. Harris, president of Harris International, Ltd., a management consultant firm, suggests that they will:

be more professionally competent and self-actualized;

be oriented toward talent utilization, participation, collaboration, wellness, and enhanced personal life;

seek meaningful and personalized work experiences, allowing for more control over life and work space as well as a more relaxed and informal work environment;

desire opportunities to exercise creativity and responsibility while expecting generous entitlements;

engage in negotiations as leaders of semi-autonomous units for managerial and economic arrangements within a corporate context concerned about mutual interests of both colleagues and the firm;

transmit organizational culture to teams or work units in which their function is to be both facilitator and model of high-performance behavior;

work intensely for profit while also pursuing diverse leisure and fitness activity that is recreative;

place high priority on career development, colleagueship, networking, research and computer skills and continuous learning;

believe in corporate social responsibility, environmental and consumer protections, earned equality, and quality service that is profitable;

practice synergy and collaborativeness, circular organizational communications, risk taking, and especially innovation.

Such managers will be in marked contrast to those of the contemporary organization, as Harris shows in Figure 6.2.

An organization led (rather than managed) by individuals who meet Harris's characterization will differ considerably from most of those in existence today. Where his almost ideal set of characteristics are met, and especially where they are accompanied by appropriate organizational communication systems, organizations almost inevitably will succeed.

SUMMARY

Organizations that survive the trials of the 1990s will have become far different from those that predominated a decade earlier. They will have met the standards implicit in a new set of social values and life-styles adopted by a new generation of workers. They will behave morally and ethically in their dealings with all stakeholders.

The change retrospectively will appear to have been most radical within survivor organizations. They will have made the transition from traditionalistic models to become what O'Toole described as "Vanguard companies," changing not only their perspectives of human-resources management but their underlying assumptions.

Senior managers in such companies will have established rigorous moral and ethical standards by fiat. They will have enforced them, however, by

Figure 6.2.   Contrasting Attitudes and Styles of Managers.

Traditional Manager of the Disappearing Industrial Work Culture	*Transformational Manager of the Emerging Metaindustrial Work Culture*
• Stodgy/Rigid: staid, slow to act; closed-minded to new ideas and approaches	• Dynamic/Flexible: forcefully acts in response to people/situations/markets; open-minded
• Past Oriented: concerned for "how we always did it" and maintenance of status quo	• Anticipative/Future Oriented: concerned for planning change, forecasting tomorrow
• Short-term Oriented: considers immediate impact, profits, markets, and issues	• Long-term Oriented: considers down-the-line implications of present actions and strategies
• Quantity/Product Oriented: culture-bound to "our way and what's good for us" in terms of numbers, goods, and things that produce profits; meets the bottom-line considerations only	• Quality/Service Oriented: culture-sensitive to customer/consumer needs that results in profitable performance; exercises corporate social responsibility
• Institutional/Hierarchical Oriented: loyal to organization, accomplishment of tasks, and following chain of command or orders	• Individual/Team Oriented: concerned for people, group loyalties, and process, using informal networks and relationships; participative
• Competitive/Combatative: plays fiercely as in sports for game's sake and winning only; sometimes arrogant and manipulative in pursuit of the prize	• Cooperative/Facilitative: seeks synergy and enjoyment in business/professional life; consults and collaborates with others for win/win experiences
• Pack Thinking: plays it safe and goes along with the crowd; blends in like the organization man; does what everybody else does	• Vanguard Thinking: stays informed and on the cutting edge; innovates and takes responsible risks even if it means being a creative deviant
• Conformity/Re-enforces Dependency: big daddy knows best; does what he's told; believes in power for the few elite at top, being an organization man	• Initiative/Autonomy: encourages creative thought and action; interdependence; self-help, awareness, and responsibility; power sharing and networking
• Pragmatic/Mechanistic: concerned for the practical and quantifiable; for getting things done at any cost; number counter/cruncher	• Conceptualizer/Synthesizer: concerned for concepts, models, and paradigms that fit ideas and things together for action purposes; links together pieces and parts into a whole
• Environmentally Amoral: exploitative and conquering approach toward nature; concern is for economic security and welfare only	• Environmentally/Ecologically Sensitive: partner with nature on Spaceship Earth; preserves and conserves where feasible; enhances quality of life on planet earth
• Average Performance: concerned for unit production and organizational standards or for quantity called for in union contracts	• Competent Performance: sets high personal and professional standards for self and others; concerned with self-development and actualization

Source: From Philip R. Harris, *Management in Transition: Transforming Managerial Practices and Organizational Strategies for a New Work Culture*. San Francisco: Jossey-Bass, 1985. Reprinted with permission.

developing new behavioral standards for their organizations. These will accommodate to the economics and technology as well as the values and life-styles of the new century. They will include appropriate personnel policies, performance-appraisal procedures, reward mechanisms, and benefit programs. Each will have been designed to insure equitable application and all will be reinforced with an appropriate accountability mechanism to assure managerial and supervisory compliance.

Education and training will be a part of every successful organization's ongoing programs. Such efforts will extend from new employees to the most senior executive. They will be essential where management is committed to developing a "new organization" to match the needs of the new worker and the new society.

ADDITIONAL READING

Harris, Philip R. *Management in Transition: Transforming Managerial Practices and Organizational Strategies for a New Work Culture.* San Francisco: Jossey-Bass, 1985.

Lipset, Seymour M., and Ben J. Wattenberg, eds. "An Erosion of Ethics?" *Public Opinion,* November/December 1986.

Livingston, J. Sterling. "Pygmalion in Management," *Harvard Business Review,* July-August 1969.

O'Toole, James. *Vanguard Management: Redesigning the Corporate Future.* New York: Doubleday, 1985.

———. "Sic Transit Excellence," *Across the Board,* October 1986.

Pascarella, Perry. *The New Achievers: Creating a Modern Work Ethic.* New York: The Free Press, 1984.

———. "Making Change a Way of Life," *Industry Week,* April 14, 1986.

Peters, Thomas J., and Waterman, Robert H. Jr. *In Search of Excellence.* New York: Harper & Row, 1982.

Peters, Thomas J. *A Passion for Excellence.* New York: Random House, 1985.

Reynolds, Peter C. "Corporate Culture on the Rocks," *Across the Board,* October 1986.

7

REMOVING THE BARRIERS

Commitment to fair, equitable treatment of employees as well as other stakeholders is the first step on a long road. Management's accompanying statements, viewed against a backdrop of past performance, usually first produce responses ranging from skepticism to outright disbelief. They are accepted and matched by employee commitments only when performance follows promises. Performance usually requires little more than compliance with earlier promises—implicit and implied. They include

1. Compensation in keeping with productivity
2. A productivity-oriented performance-appraisal system
3. Disciplinary policies designed to induce compliance rather than produce punishment
4. Human-resources-development programs to enable all personnel to realize their potential
5. Accountability for results at every organizational level to ensure that systems function as intended.

Developing the first four elements requires concentrated organizational effort. The fifth usually is created in support of the first four. These and other changes in human resources management are creating a new emphasis in this component of the business system. As *Business Week* reported in late 1985, "human resources managers aren't corporate nobodies anymore." Their skills are becoming vital in creating systems appropriate to the new organizations.

COMPENSATION SYSTEMS

The structure of contemporary compensation systems in most organizations tends to discourage achievement of management's proclaimed primary objective: productivity. While calling for enhanced individual and organizational performance, most organizations compensate personnel for attendance. Rather than encouraging productivity, they induce personnel to perform at no better than minimally acceptable levels.

Two systemic difficulties lead to these conditions. First, rewards are not perceived by employees as being linked to performance. Second, reality in large part matches their perceptions. Where it does not, reward systems are so cumbersome and misunderstood as to range in efficiency from unproductive to counterproductive.

"Important rewards must be perceived," said Edward E. Lawler, III, "to be tied in a timely fashion to effective performance."

In short, organizations get the kind of behavior that leads to the rewards their employees value. This occurs because people have their own needs and mental maps of what the world is like. They use these maps to choose those behaviors that lead to outcomes that satisfy their needs. Therefore they are inherently neither motivated nor unmotivated to perform effectively; performance motivation depends on the situation, how it is perceived, and the needs of people.

Michael LeBoeuf put the problem more succinctly:

People withhold their best efforts when they see little or no relationship between what they do and how they are rewarded. And that's a common problem for over 75 percent of the American labor force. As one middle manager put it: "I learned a few years ago that the difference between busting my gut and taking it easy is about $2,000 a year before taxes. So now, instead of aiming for the maximum possible, I shoot for the minimum acceptable."

Systemic Prerequisites

Successful compensation systems must be designed to meet multiple wage criteria. They include adequacy, equity, balance, cost effectiveness, incentive, and security. Balance refers to the total reward package of wages and benefits. Cost effectiveness requires compensation levels satisfactory to employees and within employers' means. Security requires they be adequate to meet employee needs.

Comparability of wages. Equity in compensation levels is a product of comparability. Wages for any given position should be comparable to those earned in similar jobs in other organizations, in different jobs in the same organization, and in the same job within the same organization.

Such comparisons are not always possible. Smaller organizations may have only one individual in a given role. Others may reward seniority. Still others may adopt compensation strategies that go contrary to comparability.

Those in the latter group intentionally pay more or less than comparable wages. Organizations that pay more assume they will attract and retain more proficient personnel. In those that pay less, managements may be seeking higher short-term profits. They necessarily risk long-term problems in the process.

Inherent weaknesses. Neither of the latter strategies is apt to prove successful over time. The low-pay approach will quickly become dysfunctional as supplies of entry-level employees diminish. The high-pay alternative will prove productive only to the extent that organizations meet other employee needs. Systems more sophisticated than the traditional will be necessary in any case.

Many compensation systems are also flawed in that they are designed for management's convenience rather than for motivational value. They almost inevitably ignore the fact, for example, that rewards should follow desired performance as promptly as disciplinary action follows unacceptable behavior. This factor is especially critical in terms of individuals' "horizons." Younger, less well educated workers tend to respond more favorably to smaller, more frequent rewards. The older and better educated will respond as well and perhaps better where rewards are of greater size and less frequent.

Compensation Systems

Compensation systems in the United States traditionally have been developed on the basis of job requirements. Education, skill, effort, responsibility, and job conditions have been primary criteria in organizational efforts to establish appropriate wage structures. One of four basic evaluation systems then, has customarily been used in establishing wage rates.

Ranking. Job-comparison or ranking systems are most often used in smaller organizations. They permit employers to rank order jobs, but provide no insight into relative content or difficulty of tasks assigned. They also are weak in that they generate no data to support managerial decisions.

Grading. Grade-description systems are slightly more sophisticated than ranking systems. Fixed written scales are employed to evaluate jobs, which then are sorted into grades, as in the case of the U.S. Civil Service System. These systems provide somewhat more supporting information, but are weakened by necessarily imprecise grade descriptions, in that the system provides no criteria by which users can weight factors involved in each job.

Points. The weighting-factor problem is eliminated in point systems, which usually involve 8 to 12 job-related factors. Each is evaluated on a point scale to produce a point total indicative of job value. Were experience a factor, for example, one point might be given for each year's service up to a predetermined maximum. Point systems are relatively precise and yield substantial documentation. Installation and maintenance, however, are difficult, time consuming, and costly.

Factors. Factor-comparison systems combine ranking and point systems. They are more analytical than point systems and produce point totals that can be converted directly into dollars. Results are usually applied in context with preexisting wage rates. Subsequent job-content changes are prone to produce inequities.

Systemic Assumptions

All of the systems described above were once amenable to successful application. Each produced satisfactory results where organizations consisted of members of the baby-boom and earlier generations. Human beings then could be safely considered disposable resources. Productivity was increasing so rapidly that waste was tolerable in almost any form.

These conditions no longer exist, nor are they likely to exist again. Contemporary organizations find waste intolerable. They require optimum productivity of every employee. And as replacements become more and more difficult to find, they no longer will be able to consider employees a disposable resource.

A new definition of "compensation" and a new distribution mechanism now are essential. They must be based on a new approach to work and workers. Traditional systems were concerned with work rather than workers. Almost without exception, they assumed equal capability and productivity among workers. New systems, to achieve optimum results, must assume inequality and be structured to produce compensation accordingly.

"In order to retain good performers," Lawler pointed out, "they must be paid more than poorer performers. Failure to do this is likely to lead to a situation in an organization where the poorer performers are retained by the system and the good performers leave because they know they will receive better rewards elsewhere." Such circumstances are intolerable in the face of the impending manpower problem. Compensation mechanisms thus demand reexamination.

Redefining Compensation

Compensation has traditionally been defined in the United States as consisting largely of wages and salaries. Commissions and bonuses are not uncommon, but for the most part are confined to the sales field. Only in selling has variation in human productivity been accepted and accommodated through performance-based compensation. Some organizations have gone so far as to vary sales-commission rates, raising compensation levels for exceptional achievement.

While successful sales personnel have thus been rewarded in proportion to their productivity, most of the population has been burdened with regressive compensation mechanisms. Superior performance seldom produces a pat on the back. Rewards rarely are proportionate to performance, even where productivity has been recognized. Other than among senior managers, disproportionately small shares of enhanced organizational output have instead been allocated to those who produced improvement.

A new approach. A new concept of compensation is necessary, if only to correct past injustice. It is essential if employers are to convince personnel that "the system" is equitable and productivity will be rewarded. The extent to which it should be rewarded will doubtless be argued at length in almost every organization, but adequate measurement techniques already exist.

Virtually everything man produces can be measured quantitatively and/ or qualitatively, directly or indirectly. More important, potential organizational savings arising out of qualitative improvement and added earnings resulting from quantitative improvement are readily calculated. Savings generated through employee compliance with organizational policy and procedure are also amenable to reduction to mathematical form.

Managers can attach precise dollar values to increased hourly production of widgets, to reductions in defect rates, to improvement in employee attendance, and to other components of productivity. They should be more than willing to commit themselves in advance to put a portion of those savings into the pockets of individuals who generate them.

A key question. Once having set aside the blinders that accompany traditional compensation techniques, managers need respond to only one question to establish the basis for new compensation mechanisms: How much am I willing to pay for every additional dollar of gross profit the system produces?

Several aspects of the question deserve elaboration. First, performance-based compensation systems generally do not apply to every unit of production. They deal instead with production beyond that which already exists. Second, they require only a contingent commitment on the part of management. Additional compensation is granted only after productivity has improved and, presumably, resultant profits are already in the bank. Third, other than as to raw materials in manufacturing operations, revenues created through enhanced productivity consist for the most part of net profit.

Disproportionate profits. Productivity increases without additional investment in plant or labor add considerably more to "the bottom line" than otherwise is the case. Reduced defect rates are similarly productive. Improved employee attendance factors produce even greater profits. Contemporary benefit systems ensure that personnel in most cases will be paid, whether or not they work. Expense continues whether or not they are productive.

Management's compensation decisions should be difficult only as to amounts involved and the manner in which they should be allocated. How much of the added profits should go into workers' pockets and what distribution mechanisms should be used? Wage-incentive plans succeed where three conditions are fulfilled. First, they must permit earnings in excess of base rates. Second, they must produce benefits to both organization and employee. Third, they must be readily understandable.

Simplicity is important in several respects. While group rather than individual incentives at times may be appropriate, they should be limited to relatively small groups. Workers' response to incentives is directly proportional to their perceptions of their ability to control outcomes. Perceived ability to control varies inversely with work group size. Annual profit-sharing bonuses based on overall organizational productivity thus have little individual incentive value, except in small organizations.

From the Top Down

There is, furthermore, significant potential for improvement in the administration of reward systems. Workers inevitably know their jobs better than anyone else. Supervisors and managers necessarily know their subordinates better than anyone else. These facts suggest a logical approach to compensation that can be practically applied throughout every organization.

"Throughout" is the key word in the concept. Performance-based compensation literally can and should be applied from the board or governance level downward in every organization. Senior management incentives are quite common in contemporary organizations. They were created, as *Industry Week's* Michael A. Verespej points out, because otherwise little incentive for executive action exists "when companies are neither doing well nor experiencing major problems." Middle managers occasionally participate as well. The rewards involved in every case are functions of organizational performance.

The same principle should be used throughout the organization. Boards and senior managers already have calculated prospective additional profits based on improved performance. They need only allocate portions of those profits "down the organization," enabling middle managers and supervisors to reward subordinates who contribute to their successes.

The Accountability Factor

In establishing performance-based compensation mechanisms, organizations create two other elements essential to success: accountability and responsibility. The latter is produced by the former. Essentially, managers and supervisors rewarded on the basis of productivity are being held accountable for results. In these circumstances, they diligently exercise responsibilities that earlier tended to be neglected or ignored.

Their responsiveness in the human resources sector is most significant in context with long-term organizational needs. Managers and supervisors dependent on worker performance become more responsive to their needs.

They become more concerned over absenteeism and tardiness, more interested in seeing organizational policy and procedure equitably administered.

They concurrently become more responsive to their superiors and to new demands imposed by the system at every managerial and supervisory level. Most involve increased need for knowledge and skill in the administration of human resources management systems. Those that require the greatest attention are the performance-based compensation and performance-appraisal systems through which rewards are allocated.

Compensation Alternatives

A broad range of factors can be considered in designing performance-based compensation systems. Most organizations first employ one of the several alternative approaches described above to create a hierarchy of jobs. Hierarchies are based for the most part on job demands and required personnel qualifications. They also involve applying a new concept: minimum acceptable performance. (MAP)

MAP defined. Minimum acceptable performance is that level of accomplishment below which an employee would be terminated. It might be alternatively defined as that level of productivity adequate to justify entry-level wage rates. Compensation increments beyond MAP may include several granted on the basis of seniority. They usually are limited to the first 18 to 24 months of employment, during which most workers approach the peaks of learning curves relative to their positions. Performance-based systems thereafter usually provide wage increments in only two forms. The first consists of percentage adjustments granted to all personnel with changing cost-of-living indexes. The second consists of performance-based bonuses in keeping with individual employee productivity beyond MAP. Such bonuses may be granted to individuals or groups and at varying intervals.

Individual versus group incentives. Decisions as to use of individual and group incentives should be left to individual managers. A combination of the two usually proves most effective. Individual incentives induce optimum productivity. Group incentives produce a self-policing effect. They also discourage behavior that may be productive for individual employees, but that may negatively impact others.

The self-policing effect occurs where a majority of personnel in a functional unit are committed to obtaining a given bonus. Any laggards find themselves under increasing pressure to perform. Social ostracism is the ultimate penalty and a more painful punishment than any manager can impose.

Highly productive workers engaged in manufacturing on occasion can generate difficulties for those "down the line" and "up the line" by setting too rapid a pace. Group incentives based on qualitative rather than quantitative standards in these circumstances can serve as a deterrent and enhance overall productivity.

Bonus intervals. Frequency of bonuses, like types of bonuses, are best left to well-trained managers and supervisors. Frequency should be more a function of the employee group involved than of any other factor. Larger, less frequent bonuses best motivate those in upper socioeconomic groups. Smaller and more frequent rewards better serve worker groups lower on this scale.

Bonus size and frequency is less important in encouraging productivity than the performance-appraisal systems by which employees are governed. They are simple in concept but demanding in application. Although substantial training in their use is usually required, self-interest renders managers and supervisors more than usually interested in acquiring the necessary knowledge and skill. Their interests and those of every member of the organization, from board member to janitor, essentially are caught up in the interplay between compensation on the one hand and attitudes and behaviors on the other. Lawler summarized the factors involved as follows:

1. Satisfaction with rewards, such as pay, is a function of how much is received, how much others are perceived to receive, and perceptions of what should be rewarded.
2. Satisfaction with rewards can influence overall job satisfaction as well as absenteeism, recruitment, and turnover.
3. Rewards will motivate whatever behavior is seen to lead to their reception if, and only if, they are important to the individual.
4. Under certain conditions, participation in pay decisions can lead to better decisions and to higher commitment to decisions.
5. Depending on how it is treated, the pay system can be a positive or a negative force in organizational change efforts.

Employers who would enhance employee performance must supply answers to three critical questions with which employees are most concerned. First, and most important among them is, What's in it for me?; second, How hard will I have to work to earn the reward?; and third, Can I really be certain that the reward will be forthcoming? Individuals will expend the necessary effort, according to Andrew J. DuBrin, under the following circumstances:

Hard work leads to favorable performance.

Favorable performance leads to a reward.

Reward satisfies an important need.

Need satisfaction is intense enough to make effort seem worthwhile.

Subjective probability is high that effort will lead to favorable performance and that favorable performance will lead to reward.

If probability of reward is low, payoff must be big.

These factors become especially positive forces when linked directly to effective performance-appraisal systems.

PERFORMANCE APPRAISAL

Performance appraisal is a relatively new concept that has evolved in recent years in response to inherent weakness in merit review. The latter process produced generally unsatisfactory results in three areas. First, merit proved impossible to measure. Second, review alone produces no behavioral change; further response is essential to induce improved performance. Finally, the merit review process was episodic rather than ongoing and bore little relationship to the day-to-day activities of employees involved.

Performance appraisal, in contrast, is an ongoing process that begins during employees' first days on the job and continues throughout their careers. From the outset, it differs significantly from merit review.

The process is not without pitfalls, which originate primarily in appraiser weaknesses. Yet the process arguably remains the best available tool. A major potential pitfall in the system arises out of economic considerations. Good performance-appraisal ratings produce expectations of reward, but many systems are structured in a manner that denies adequate resources to provide those rewards. This and other problems are avoidable, however, and potential for organizational improvement is significant. Organizational allocation of predetermined portions of increased profits to individuals involved eliminates structural problems.

The essence of the system is a design that accepts and minimizes the fact that personal judgments, subjective values, and human perceptions are involved. Designs should create understanding and thereby dampen any tendency toward bias and error. They improve morale and performance by enhancing the probability that desired behaviors will be rewarded and poor performance corrected.

A Matter of Understanding

Any potential for satisfactory worker performance in the absence of a clear understanding of job requirements is virtually nonexistent. Such understanding is seldom achieved in the context of traditional review systems. Although employees are usually told what to do, they are generally left to their own devices in determining how much of it is necessary and at what quality level it must be performed to achieve minimum acceptable performance.

Job descriptions. New employees are often given copies of job descriptions during interview or orientation processes, but these documents seldom adequately describe employers' expectations. They usually are generic documents enumerating every task that may ever be required of any individual in the job category in question.

Employees on the job are assigned certain sets of tasks, specified by what might better be termed "position descriptions" than job descriptions, and consisting of those duties required by immediate superiors. In one respect, however, the descriptions usually are no better than job descriptions. Quantitative and qualitative standards are seldom mentioned. Instead, employees are left to obtain such information by observation or from peers.

Employee understanding. The result is a near total lack of understanding of minimum acceptable performance. Supervisors and managers leave themselves open to the most damning of responses to criticism during subsequent merit reviews—"but you never told me."

The nature of the accountability system and the performance-appraisal process demand a different introduction to a new job. Supervisors and managers accountable for unit performance begin on-the-job orientation with the equivalent of an abbreviated performance review. The process involves enumerating tasks to be performed and specifying qualitative and quantitative standards for each. It ideally is undertaken with the instrument that will be used in subsequent performance appraisals.

Appraisal Instruments

Successful appraisal processes require prior mutual understanding of performance standards. In large organizations they may be standardized to some extent. Managers and supervisors more often find an individualized approach more productive. This practice permits developing position descriptions that best conform to the knowledge, skills, and preferences of individuals involved.

Why should managers render the process so complex? Because individuals almost invariably are most productive in work for which they are well equipped. They do more of it, and they do it better. Managers and supervisors accountable for unit productivity find it in their interests as well as those of their employees to capitalize on this principle.

Total responsibility. Another principle of near equal value is total responsibility. As defined by former IBM executive Clair F. Vough, it involves dividing work so that individuals can be assigned total jobs rather than parts of jobs. They can thus be better held accountable, he says, and tend to perform better, because they can more readily see the results of their efforts.

Any manager or supervisor can handle these processes well with a few basic tools. They include an appropriate appraisal instrument, perhaps a bit of basic human relations training, and a clear understanding of their superiors' expectations. The latter component, as in the case of their subordinates, is critical. It is equally important, of course, from the standpoint of their superiors. Mutual understanding, accountability for results, and incentives to produce those results must interlock at all levels of the organization.

Other points. Vital to the process at all levels is a simple concept: That which is rewarded gets done. Where systems produce problems, managers need only look to what is being rewarded in order to find solutions. What should be rewarded? Michael LeBoeuf suggested managers should reward

Solid solutions instead of quick fixes

Risk taking rather than risk avoiding

Applied creativity instead of mindless conformity

Decisive action rather than paralysis by analysis

Smart work instead of busy work

Simplification rather than needless complication

Quietly effective behavior instead of squeaking joints

Quality work instead of fast work

Loyalty rather than turnover

Working together instead of working against.

Each of these elements can be rendered in measurable terms and made part of the performance-appraisal process.

Appraisal Processes

Job orientation and all subsequent performance-appraisal processes are most effectively undertaken with the organization's appraisal instrument. Performance-appraisal instruments can be uniform to the extent that jobs in a given unit are similar. In small- to medium-sized organizations, they tend to resemble blank sheets of paper (see Figure 7.1).

The form permits supervisors to proceed through a logical series of steps to create mutual understanding of tasks to be performed. Copies of completed forms should be given to employees for reference. Originals are then used in succeeding performance-appraisal processes.

Form requirements. The first column of the form requires clear statements of tasks to be performed. The second and third columns require specifying quantitative and qualitative standards. Succeeding columns provide space for clear statements of any improvement that may be necessary and for any interim review dates that the appraiser may require.

Routine performance appraisals are best undertaken annually or semiannually. They should be scheduled on the basis of employee anniversary dates in order to ease supervisory/managerial work loads and ensure ade-

Figure 7.1. Part of Federal Express Corporation's Performance Appraisal Form.

STEP III: **PERFORMANCE PLANNER**

_____
NAME

In this section of the Individual Progress Discussion Review, you are to work with your staff member in order to provide a developmental plan which is designed to improve areas of performance concern noted in your description of the staff member's performance (Step II). Areas of greatest concern would be those you rated as "regular parts of the job" in which the employee rated three or below. In addition, you will want to alert your staff member to areas you feel would be important in preparing this employee for future career opportunities.

Performance areas where improvement is needed (you may wish to consider only those categories where importance exceeds 3 and performance is rated less than Satisfactory).	Knowledge, skills or abilities that must be developed to result in the improvement.	Developmental Activities/ Assignments. These are activities you and the staff member plan to address the area of needed experience.	Projected Implementa- tion date (month/ year).	Projected Completion date (month/ year).

Source: Courtesy of Federal Express Corporation.

quate time for this critical process. Rewards should come immediately afterward to reinforce performance-evaluation outcomes.

Mixed blessings. The absence of uniform reward dates other than for general cost-of-living adjustments is a mixed blessing. It renders budgeting processes more complex. Departmental or other compensation requirements for a given year are more difficult to calculate. On the positive side, it minimizes complaints arising from employees who compare the size of performance-based compensation increases.

Distractions induced by tendencies to compare are also minimized where compensation beyond cost-of-living adjustments occurs in the form of bonuses. These necessarily are nonrecurring in the absence of continued superior performance. The process thus shifts employee attention from reward to performance. With improved performance, reward follows all but automatically.

Accrual mechanisms. This desirable tendency is reinforced where operational units literally earn bonus dollars by performance. Budgets are necessarily projections. Employees can and should understand that funds for tomorrow's bonuses are created by today's performance. Senior management's budgeting system ideally should make funds available to middle managers and supervisors at regular intervals throughout the year.

Mechanisms of this sort bind managers and supervisors inextricably to their subordinates. They win or lose together; they become a team. The self-policing mechanism mentioned earlier tends to become a strong force in operational units.

Other salutary benefits accrue as well. For example, workers find it emotionally unacceptable to take a sick day for personal business when they have strong loyalties to peers and superiors.

Finally, the nature of the appraisal instrument renders organizations more responsive. Necessary changes are specified, together with target dates for individual employees. Managers and supervisors, in addition, can modify standards in keeping with changes in organizational direction.

System responsiveness. Performance appraisal and compensation systems together thus induce greater employee responsiveness to the organization, superiors and peers. Responsiveness levels are further improved where disciplinary systems are inherently fair, equitable, and administered accordingly.

Disciplinary systems usually meet these standards in the hands of accountable managers and supervisors, who quickly recognize that improprieties on their part tend to destroy unit cohesiveness and productivity. The system itself, however, must be equally supportive of equitable administration.

DISCIPLINARY SYSTEMS

Successful disciplinary systems are not created to facilitate punitive action. They are designed to produce compliance, which implies willing cooperation on the part of those governed by the system. It is forthcoming only where systems are equitably and fairly administered. Equity can be achieved through the efforts of managers and supervisors. Fairness is a function of the system itself.

Systemic Weaknesses

Fairness, like beauty, is in the eye of the beholder. What appears fair to one may seem unfair to another. Historically, perceived unfairness has arisen where disciplinary systems have appeared unduly harsh and inflexible or where they have unnecessarily penalized usually loyal and productive employees.

These conditions develop where the policy appears to punish every conceivable offense rather than encourage compliance. Punishment-oriented policies traditionally consist of lengthy lists of offenses. Lists tend to grow over time as unforeseen circumstances develop or new problems arise. They often grow so lengthy as to require recasting into multiple lists, which are frequently given categorical labels akin to misdemeanors, felonies, and capital-punishment offenses.

Employee intimidation. Merely the extent of lists of offenses and the ominous, legalistic phraseology with which they are intoned intimidate employees. They often specify verbal warnings for first offenses, written warnings for second infractions, and terminations for third violations. Worse, they imply that management views personnel with suspicion; that the organization is populated with assorted miscreants.

Employees reading such policies could easily assume that lists of offenses were created to ensure that there would always exist some pretext for disciplinary action. Traditional circumstances, from their perspective, are much like those student pilots encounter in hundreds of pages of Federal Aviation Administration regulations. It is virtually impossible, instructors are fond of telling students, to pilot an airplane without technically breaching one or more of them.

Unnecessary oppressiveness. Disciplinary policies, overall, tend to conjure up an impression of "big brother" just waiting to pounce. Resulting circumstances might give rise to "gallows humor" were they not so oppressive, unnecessary, and impractical.

Traditional policies requiring verbal and written warnings prior to termination tend to be ineffective for several reasons. In the long run, they also become counterproductive. First, verbal warnings by their nature produce no documentation. Today's legalistic society demands appropriate records. Second, they encourage overuse of verbal remonstrances because they are less burdensome to managers and supervisors. Written warnings are relatively cumbersome and time consuming. They also may be viewed by managers and supervisors as too serious a penalty for such offenses as absenteeism and tardiness. Systemic weaknesses thus tend to create either nonfunctional or dysfunctional policy enforcement.

Policies often are not enforced by a majority of managers and supervisors. Gross inequity results when those who are especially conscientious seek to enforce them. Morale deteriorates, and the organization is placed in an untenable legal position. Terminated employees who can cite comparable cases that did not result in like punishment are apt to be ordered reinstated and compensated by courts of appropriate jurisdiction.

Alternative Approaches

Superior disciplinary policies that protect organizations as well as employees can be developed along less legalistic lines. They also can be rendered more practical in application and more equitable in results. Such policies proceed on the assumption that most organizational personnel are well meaning. They provide adequate safeguards against major offenders, with adequate protection and due process for all.

Policy components. Disciplinary policies are administered most effectively where managers and supervisors are held accountable for results. Such a system tends to bind managers and their subordinates into functional teams, minimizing the potential for punishable offenses. Discipline, then, is viewed as a last resort and/or as a tool toward helping operational units and their members achieve mutual objectives.

More effective disciplinary policies developed in recent years have several commonalities. First, they eliminate verbal warnings as disciplinary devices and substitute written reprimands. These are usually administered through short forms requiring nothing more than the date, the employee's name, and the nature of the offense.

Second, the policies are designed to be forgiving rather than punitive. A predetermined number of written warnings within a specified time span triggers a suspension, often with pay. The latter practice, as Laurie Baum pointed out in a *Business Week* article, produces surprisingly beneficial results. A further offense, again within the specified time frame, produces termination. Such systems create multiple advantages.

1. Passage of time clears employee records. Reprimand copies become inapplicable to a suspension or termination when the predetermined number of days or weeks after date of issue has elapsed. Employees who encounter domestic difficulties that result in short-term attendance problems, for example, can easily clear their records through subsequent compliance. When problems persist, they may find it necessary to take leaves of absence to avoid further penalties.

2. Reprimands, because of their short-term applicability, are more acceptable to managers and supervisors as well as employees. This is especially the case where

the forgiving nature of the system and the organization's need for protection
against chronic abusers are understood.

3. Reprimands are more readily given, because managers and supervisors seldom
   are aware of individual employees' standing in the context of the disciplinary
   policy. Suspension or termination can result, but these actions are automatic
   rather than specified by manager or supervisor.

Other penalties. The reprimand is not adequate in all circumstances. Most
organizations using reprimand-based policies maintain short lists of "capital
offenses" requiring immediate termination. Virtually every other offense is
handled by reprimand. The only exceptions are criminal accusations that
have a direct bearing on the employee's work. Then, suspensions without
pay are most frequently applied. Were a hospital employee who has access
to narcotics charged with narcotics trafficking, for example, an automatic
suspension would be in order. Equity requires that employees not be terminated until a judicial decision has been made, yet patients must be pro-
tected.

The greatest benefit in such systems is not in their relative simplicity and
ease of applicability. It is generated by employee perception that the system
is fair and equitable. It engenders trust in organizations and their senior
managements, which can be significantly reinforced through comparable
due-process policies.

Due Process

Courts in recent years have increasingly limited employers' right to terminate employees at will. Due process now is prerequisite to discharge.
Organizations' due-process procedures, however, can go far in meeting
employee perceptions of equity and fairness as well as legal requirements.

'Skip-step' appeals. At least two factors are advisable in the legal context.
One is a so-called skip-step appeal procedure, which enables employees to
take problems to individuals other than their superiors. Immediate superiors
too often are party to problems at hand. Employees required to first consult
their superiors view themselves as being in lose-lose situations. Even if
appeals are upheld, they must continue to work with supervisors perceived
as potentially having been prejudiced against them in the process.

Employers using such systems are often lulled into a false sense of security
by the absence of significant numbers of appeals. They view such a condition
as indicating that their organizations are relatively problem-free, when the
reverse may be the case. Where the nature of appeal systems discourage
their use, one of two ultimately destructive outcomes is likely: In one,
employees involved may become marginally productive; in the extreme,
they may create major problems. In the other, they may resign. Either result
is expensive to the organization.

Executive appeals. The second factor advisable in appeal procedures is a "court of last resort" in one of several forms. Some form of arbitration is most convincing of management sincerity. Appropriate panels can readily be drawn from within the organization. A typical formula permits each party to select one member. The two then agree on a third, and the panel's decision is binding on both parties.

Where management is perceived as credible, appeals to chief executive officers also may be employed with satisfactory results. In Federal Express Corporation, for example, employees who have exhausted all steps in the organization's formal appeal process may have their cases reviewed by a panel chaired by Board Chairman Frederick Smith. Such processes serve two purposes. First, they are reassuring to employees. Second, they induce caution on the part of chief executives' subordinates, none of whom want poor decisions reversed on appeal.

DEVELOPMENTAL SYSTEMS

Employee growth and development has seldom been a major organizational concern—an undesirable attitude, but understandable. Personnel have traditionally been considered disposable components of production. Ample replacements have always been available, and managements have been preoccupied with other problems perceived to be more pressing. These circumstances no longer exist. With the manpower pool declining in size, organizations' human resources are becoming less readily replaceable and, consequently, more precious. *Fortune* editor Judson Gooding put the problem rather succinctly.

Where employees were often taken for granted in the past, it is now becoming apparent to more and more executives that this attitude is no longer valid. Workers today have a degree of personal and economic freedom never before known. Managers are going to have to pay more attention to the investment made in finding workers, hiring them, training them, developing them. They are going to have to become more aware of the costs of losing them, whether by day-at-a-time absenteeism of the sort suffered by the auto plants, or by higher turnover, as occurred with some telephone jobs, and as happens with junior managers who dislike their jobs or their companies.

Techniques through which personnel can be retained are thus gaining increasing attention. Generally categorized as growth and development programs, they are designed to meet the traditional needs of organizational personnel and more.

Career Ladders

Almost without exception, organizations have become more sensitive to their need for so-called career ladders, which are little more than well-defined pathways through which employees can move "up the organization" as their skill and knowledge levels improve.

Parallel tracks. Alternative "ladders" are also becoming increasingly common to accommodate professional and technical personnel who prefer to practice their basic skills, rather than become managers. These have developed most rapidly in advertising and public relations firms and similar organizations, which traditionally have offered no alternative to management positions for upwardly mobile employees. Parallel tracks, as they have come to be called, now are being made available. They lead to senior professional status rather than management, but afford comparable levels of compensation and responsibility.

Organizational needs. Development programs are also being tailored to meet organizational needs in several ways. Most common among them are inducements to middle managers to facilitate the development of their subordinates. Managerial proficiency in a growing number of organizations is judged in part on the extent to which managers encourage subordinates to prepare for promotion. In some few cases, reward systems are designed to recognize those who thus assist the organization in developing new generations of leadership.

Employees are increasingly amenable to enhancing their knowledge and skill levels to further their careers. So prevalent has the process become that the *Christian Science Monitor* in late 1986 dedicated a special section to the subject. Entitled "Going Back: Why Adults Are Lining up for Classes," it dealt with every aspect of continuing education. Formal degree programs, self-help courses, and others were featured in comprehensive discussions of what educators have come to call "lifelong learning." It is increasingly necessary as the whole body of knowledge expands, but must be recognized as well as encouraged in the organization.

The latter point is especially applicable where managers otherwise might be tempted to retain highly productive employees rather than see them promoted. Unit productivity may benefit, but the organization is penalized.

Other Tools

The developmental process is increasingly facilitated through educational programs ranging from in-house seminars to company-paid degree programs. In a few instances, large corporations have gone so far as to establish their own degree-granting institutions.

While techniques may vary with organizations, the continuing decline in the entry-level manpower pool is making such efforts increasingly common.

Personal and career growth appear to be ranking ever higher on individual priority lists and organizations have little alternative but to respond.

In approaching these and other benefit programs, however, employers must remain sensitive to employee skepticism and cynicism. Employer withdrawal of benefits in multiple situations during the mid-1980s compounded this problem. Trust will have to be reestablished before organizations can achieve a reasonable return on benefit investments. As Robert M. McCaffery put it, "employees must believe that benefit plans are sound and secure, and that they will do what the company claims they will do."

SUMMARY

Attracting and retaining qualified personnel in the 1990s and beyond will require more than verbal commitment. Promises must be followed by performance. Organizations must function in the mutual interests of all stakeholders, and employees must be accepted as equal to owners, managers, customers, and others.

Equality requires more than gross economic commitment. Rewards must be equitably shared on the basis of productivity. Control policies must be recast to emphasize compliance rather than discipline. Appropriate career ladders must be created for all personnel. Finally, all of these organizational components must function as designed.

Productivity-based compensation systems are readily designed and implemented. They require only that minimum acceptable performance be defined for each individual in the organization. This process is most easily accomplished by each individual's immediate superior.

Definition of minimum acceptable performance requires specifying qualitative and quantitative criteria for each major task assigned to the individual. These, in turn, can become measures of productivity. Allocation of rewards can then be safely delegated to managers and supervisors, provided they are held accountable for results. The overall result is an integrated system in which success and reward for one produce success and reward for all.

Organizational commitments of sufficient resources to provide systemic rewards are readily made where minimum acceptable performance has been prescribed. Performance at above-minimum levels, in keeping with specified criteria, necessarily enhances productivity. Management need only commit itself in advance to allocate predetermined portions of resultant earnings and/or savings to those involved.

Productivity-based reward systems in and of themselves contribute to creating desired behavioral objectives. Such additional control mechanisms as may be necessary can then be incorporated into "forgiving" systems, designed to produce compliance with policy and procedure rather than punishment for misbehavior.

Further incentives for conformity to performance standards can be made

Communicating for Survival

a part of the organization's human resources development program. Programs must encourage individual growth beneficial to organizations and employees. The system also must encourage managerial and supervisory contribution to individual growth through direct or indirect rewards.

With necessary accountability components specified at every level, organizations become more productive, to the benefit of all stakeholder groups.

ADDITIONAL READING

Baum, Laurie. "Punishing Workers with a Day Off," *Business Week,* June 16, 1986.
Bennis, Warren G. "Chairman Mac in Perspective," *Harvard Business Review,* September-October, 1972.
DuBrin, Andrew J. *Human Relations: A Job-Oriented Approach.* Reston, VA: Reston, 1981.
Gooding, Judson. *The Job Revolution.* New York: Walker, 1972.
Hoerr, John. "Human Resources Managers Aren't Corporate Nobodies Anymore," *Business Week,* December 2, 1985.
Irwin, Victoria, et al. "Going Back: Why Adults are Lining up for Classes," *Christian Science Monitor,* October 24, 1986.
Lawler, Edward E., III. *Pay and Organization Development.* Reading, MA: Addison-Wesley, 1983.
LeBoeuf, Michael. *The Greatest Management Principles in the World.* New York: Putnam, 1985.
McCaffery, Robert M. *Managing the Employee Benefit Program.* New York: AMACOM, 1972.
McGregor, Douglas. "An Uneasy Look at Performance Appraisal," *Harvard Business Review,* September-October 1972.
Noble, Kenneth B. "When Walking Papers Lead to Court," *New York Times,* October 13, 1985.
Oberg, Winston. "Make Performance Appraisal Relevant," *Harvard Business Review,* January-February 1972.
Von Kaas, H. K. *Making Wage Incentives Work.* New York: AMACOM, 1971.
Vough, Clair F. *Tapping the Human Resource: A Strategy for Productivity.* New York: AMACOM, 1975.

8

FINDING THE FORMULA

The ultimate objective of communication is behavioral change. There may be intermediate steps along the way and the communication may be direct or indirect, but the objective remains the same. With few exceptions, even the philanthropic activities of individuals and organizations are oriented, at least in part, toward behavioral objectives. Those well thought of in their communities gain small but significant advantages in competitive situations.

Success in inducing behavioral change requires a knowledge of the existing attitudes, opinions, and behaviors of those involved. In the absence of such information, communicators' problems are like those of giving directions without knowing a traveler's starting point. Simplistically put, getting from point A to point B requires knowledge of both points. Without it the effort at best is apt to be wasteful and at worst fruitless.

The research process is designed to accomplish several objectives:

1. Determining basic attitudes of employees so messages can be appropriately designed
2. Measuring group opinion to avoid reliance on subjective information of questionable value
3. Identifying existing and prospective trouble spots that require early attention
4. Reducing ultimate program costs through use of better-focused messages
5. Determining the relative potential of available channels of communication
6. Identifying employee interests and concerns
7. Establishing baseline data through which programmatic progress can subsequently be monitored.

SOURCES OF INFORMATION

Information concerning any population or group of individuals is available from multiple sources. Most can be categorized as demographic or psychographic in nature. The former category deals with such basics as age, race, income, educational level, and the like. The latter encompasses social values, life-styles, and similar attributes. In organizations, further information can be obtained from personnel records, through survey research, and otherwise. All are important in establishing valid bases for organizational communication programs.

The several forms of research are especially beneficial when undertaken in sequence to produce optimum results. Demographic and psychographic research are the first logical steps, which should be followed by informal fact-finding processes before survey research is undertaken. The objective is as complete a valid statistical picture of the employee group as possible.

Demographic Data

Perhaps the most often used source of demographic data in the United States is the records of the Bureau of the Census, which provide considerable information concerning age, race, marital status, income, and educational levels. Other sources include college or university libraries, industrial development offices, and similar organizations. The Bureau of the Census, a component of the Department of Commerce in Washington, regularly publishes catalogs of information available in printed or electronic form.

Starting point. The logical starting point of demographic research in employee populations consists of determining where members of the organization reside. They can most easily be sorted in most cases through U.S. Postal Service zip codes, which employees must specify on tax-withholding statements.

Bureau of the Census information is available by zip-code designation. In addition to the data itemized above, the bureau categorizes individuals by occupation, home ownership, and a host of other factors of value in characterizing the organization's employee population.

Organizing data. Organizational communicators may find it advisable to analyze census data in detail. In larger organizations, for example, individual operational units may be of sufficient size to justify analyses of members as organizational subgroups. This process is especially worthwhile in organizations that are geographically diverse, with multiple plants or divisional offices.

Communicators thus proceed in much the same manner used by political campaign managers and analysts, who seek as much information as possible concerning the electorate in every area in which the candidate is interested. When all available demographic data have been catalogued, the research effort can then turn to the psychographic sector.

Psychographic Data

Large amounts of so-called psychographic data are available to organizational communicators. Most apply exclusively to the national population. A great deal may be available, however, for regions, states, and major metropolitan areas.

By psychographic data is meant such information as population distribution in terms of values and life-styles (VALS), a typology created by the Stanford Research Institute. They are described in Arnold Mitchell's *The Nine American Lifestyles; Where We Are & Where We Are Going.* Other similar information on a national scale is provided by Richard Louv *(America II)* and Oxford Analytica's *America in Perspective.*

These volumes provide little that can be directly extrapolated to neighborhood, state, or regional areas. They do, however, offer considerable insight into the beliefs of workers. They can be supplemented by information readily available on a day-to-day basis in the *New York Times,* the *Wall Street Journal,* the *Christian Science Monitor,* and other publications.

This information collectively provides insight into emerging and developing trends and life-styles which necessarily influence contemporary work forces. It may not be amenable to summary in statistical form, but can be valuable to communicators preparing for necessary survey research.

Fact Finding

At least three types of information are available to those contemplating organizational communication programs. Anecdotal or experiential information is the least reliable, since it may be a product of organizational mythology or managerial/supervisory experience. It may be worthy of collection as indicative of organizational culture, but must be treated with skepticism.

No organization is without its tales of legendary employee behavior. Although occasionally entertaining, they tend to be so exaggerated as to be worse than valueless for planning purposes. Experiential reports are little better. They assume that reporters have been exposed over an adequate period of time to a cross-section of the employee population—conditions that are virtually never fulfilled.

Managers and supervisors are usually less than candid, even when knowledgeable concerning internal problems. They perceive—and rightly so—that subordinate behavior is in part reflective of management and/or leadership quality. When confronted with statistical evidence, however, most will reluctantly concede that problems indeed exist.

Organizational records. Some valuable although superficial data concerning employee attitude and opinion can be drawn from existing organizational records. Absenteeism and tardiness rates, product quality data, disciplinary records, employee turnover rates, customer complaints, and other documented information can be helpful.

This is especially the case where data have been compiled periodically over extended periods of time. Period-to-period deterioration in any of these areas can safely be taken as evidence of deterioration in loyalty or morale. It may also signal decline in employee perceptions of organizations and/or their managerial and supervisory personnel.

Defining problems. More precise definition of problems can occasionally be achieved by recasting data by shift, department, or other organizational subdivision. Problems arising out of managerial or supervisory ineptitude are often readily identified by comparing data across these subdivisions.

Senior managers prone to deny managerial or supervisory weakness in their organizations often become more forthright when faced with such information. A typical comment: "I could have told you where the problems were."

All of this information is helpful in determining "where we are." When available over extended periods, the data are also indicative of organizational direction. Employee attitude and opinion tend to improve or deteriorate. Stability is relatively rare, other than at the extremes.

Other data. Examinations of personnel records should also be oriented to provide as much demographic data as can be extracted from this source. Age, educational level, seniority, number of dependents, and other elements that might influence individuals' perceptions of the world, the organization, and their jobs should be of special interest.

Information once readily available from personnel records, such as marital status and ages of dependents, may no longer be available from this source. Equal employment opportunity legislation has made such information "off limits" insofar as application forms and other records are concerned. Much of it can be obtained, however, through survey research.

Survey Research

Demographic and psychographic analyses of employee groups are a prerequisite to survey research. Analyses of other organizational records should also be conducted before survey efforts begin, since information gained in this manner helps guide questionnaire development.

Data adequate to plan a communication program predestined to success can be obtained only through survey research conducted by qualified and experienced personnel. The latter terms imply more than is apparent. "Qualified" in this instance means adequately educated and trained in appropriate research techniques. Data gathering and analysis must be conducted with considerable care to produce dependable results. "Experienced" means equipped with significant field practice in applying pertinent knowledge and training. Given the criticality of organizational human resources management today, anything less represents too great a risk.

The risk is compounded by the fact that researchers will be dealing with the most volatile component of the organization, its personnel. Their skepticism and distrust of management constitute a barrier that must be surmounted if candid responses—and accurate data—are to be obtained.

Organizational Audits

Organizational research can take several forms, among them attitude surveys, communication audits, awareness surveys, and readership surveys. A relatively comprehensive audit is a logical point of departure for organizations attempting to establish or enhance organizational communication programs.

Audits are among the most productive devices in contemporary use. They can be designed to generate data of the sort more commonly elicited through other research techniques. They involve more detail than traditional attitude/opinion studies. One of the best suited to organizational application is the ICA (International Communication Association) Communication Audit, developed through the combined efforts of more than 100 communication professionals during a period of more than five years.

The ICA Audit process includes a questionnaire survey, interviews, network analysis, communication experience data, and maintenance of communication diaries by organization members. Resultant data provide a comprehensive picture of organizational communication systems.

Audit data define existing practices and behaviors in organizations and help predict communication program outcomes. They enable planners to act rather than react to meet organizational communication needs by permitting relatively precise definition of organizational alternatives. Communication programs can be tested and monitored. Information flows can be charted. Cost factors can be more precisely specified, and programs in general can be better oriented to solve specific problems.

INFORMATIONAL NEEDS

Research and communication programs produce the best results when carried out in keeping with well-conceived and adequately designed plans. Research planning must address a number of critical factors if necessary information is to be obtained. Early in the planning phase, planners must respond to such questions as, What information is needed? How will it be analyzed? How will results be used?

Informational needs

Communication audits must necessarily examine the informational needs of the audience involved. Are they receiving the information they require? In what areas do informational shortfalls exist? Is information disseminated by the organization being received? Is it being understood and acted upon?

Audits can and should accomplish a great deal in organizational settings. What are employees' perceptions of the organization? What do they think of its products or services? How do they perceive their immediate superiors, subordinates, and peers? Are they satisfied with the organization's performance-evaluation system? With the compensation system? With their fringe benefits?

The audit, in other words, should be used as an organizational-development as well as a communication tool. Results should improve management's knowledge of employees' perceptions and relative values. They should enhance understanding to a point at which organizations can respond with deeds as well as words.

Minimum Data Needs

While organizational audits can provide a great deal of information, practical limitations require that they focus on primary communicator needs. Foremost among these are data that will provide a sound foundation for the communication program. This necessarily includes information on several specific topics.

Most obvious among the topics is prevalent attitude and opinion. What do employees think of their working environment and its component parts? Less obvious but of equal importance are data concerning the manner in which employees receive information and the degree to which they are amenable to receiving it. Survey data should permit existing and prospective communication channels, which might be used in the anticipated program, to be assessed.

Preliminary insight into the relative efficacy of communication channels can be obtained through analysis of personnel records. Employee ages and educational levels usually are valid indicators. Orientation toward print media is generally stronger in older generations. Younger people who grew up with television and videocassette recorders are usually predisposed toward electronic delivery systems. Educational level is also a valid indicator of affinity for printed rather than electronically delivered information. The more years of formal education individuals have completed, the more comfortable they tend to be with the printed word.

The extent to which existing organizational communication channels are accessed is worthy of note. This should not, however, be taken as an indicator of potential use. The content of traditional organizations' employee communication media is often far from attractive to employees. A change in content format in these circumstances may be all that is necessary to induce attention and assimilation of content.

Information necessary in selecting communication vehicles can best be obtained from employees' answers to two questions. The first, regarding current sources of information, might be posed as shown in the format pictured here.

```
How much information are you currently receiving about
the organization and your job from each of the following
channels?
```

	Very Little	Little	Some	Great	Very Great
Employee newspaper	1	2	3	4	5
Bulletin Boards	1	2	3	4	5
Payroll Stuffers	1	2	3	4	5
Staff Meetings	1	2	3	4	5
Memoranda	1	2	3	4	5
Supervisor	1	2	3	4	5
Fellow Workers	1	2	3	4	5
Grapevine	1	2	3	4	5

Any other formal communication devices currently in use should be added to the list.

The second question should concern sources from which respondents would *prefer* to receive information concerning their organization and their jobs. It should include all channels of communication listed in the first question, as well as others that would be practical. The latter group might include periodic meetings with senior managers, videotaped presentations on subjects of special interest, telephone "hot lines" by which employees can quickly obtain information on pressing issues, and so on. Questionnaire designers should include every conceivable medium amenable to practical application in their organizations.

Available data suggest that worker communication channel preferences may differ significantly from those in use. Employees in a 1982 study conducted by the International Association of Business Communicators and Towers, Perrin, Forster, and Crosby support this contention (see Figure 8.1).

Informational Needs

As in the case of channels of communication, questionnaire designers should not assume that employees are receiving all the information they want. A

Figure 8.1.   Employee Preferences for Sources of Information.

Preferred Ranking	Sources of Information	Current Ranking
1	My immediate supervisor	1
2	Small group meetings	4
3	Top executives	11
4	Employee handbook/other brochures	3
5	Local employee publication	8
6	Orientation program	12
7	Organization-wide employee publication	6
8	Annual state-of-the-business report	7
9	Bulletin boards	5
10	Upward communication program	14
11	The union	9
12	Mass meetings	10
13	Audiovisual programs	15
14	Mass media	13
15	The grapevine	2

Source: From Roy G. Foltz, "Communication in Contemporary Organizations." From *Inside Organizational Communication* 2E, edited by Carol Reuss and Donn Silvis. Copyright © 1985 by Longman. All rights reserved.

logical set of questions to elicit employee preferences might be constructed in the manner illustrated above. The first question should deal with information currently being transmitted by management; the second with other subjects in which employees might be interested. In the alternative, a list of subjects might be presented with two response scales on which employees can indicate both the amount of information they want and the amount they now receive.

Dangerous assumptions. Assumptions by managers and communicators about employee informational needs are dangerous. Personnel in any organization are influenced by external as well as internal events, which can produce significant change in their interests. While valid data are lacking, it appears logical, for example, to assume that employees are more interested today in employers' economic circumstances than they were formerly. Plant closings, business failures, and mergers have made layoffs and staff reductions commonplace occurrences in recent years. Employee confidence in long-term employment has demonstrably declined as a result. Interest in companies' economic health, product lines, and responses to external pressures, such as imports, has doubtless increased.

Educational potential. These conditions suggest a far greater potential receptivity to economic information on the part of most workers. Research conducted by the International Association of Business Communicators and Towers, Perrin, Forster, and Crosby supports this viewpoint (see Figure

Figure 8.2.   Employee Preferences for Types of Information.

Rank	Subject	Combined "very interested" and "interested" responses
1	Organizational plans for the future	95.3%
2	Productivity improvement	90.3%
3	Personnel policies and practices	89.8%
4	Job-related information	89.2%
5	Job advancement opportunities	87.9%
6	Effect of external events on my job	87.8%
7	How my job fits into the organization	85.4%
8	Operations outside of my department or division	85.1%
9	How we're doing vs. the competition	83.0%
10	Personnel changes and promotions	81.4%
11	Organizational community involvement	81.3%
12	Organizational stand on current issues	79.5%
13	How the organization uses its profits	78.4%
14	Advertising/promotional plans	77.2%
15	Financial results	76.4%
16	Human interest stories about other employees	70.4%
17	Personal news (birthdays, anniversaries, etc.)	57.0%

Source: From Roy G. Foltz, "Communication in Contemporary Organizations." From *Inside Organizational Communication* 2E, edited by Carol Reuss and Donn Silvis. Copyright © 1985 by Longman. All rights reserved.

8.2). Organizations should capitalize on this opportunity. Workers economically educated in the businesses of employers are better able to present organizational perspectives of contemporary issues to family, friends, and acquaintances. Employers who fail to capitalize on the disproportionately strong influence that workers exercise do themselves a disservice.

Educational tasks can be undertaken to a limited extent in the course of the audit, through questions designed to measure employee knowledge in specific subject areas. Using such questions, however, implies willingness on the part of employers to remedy deficiencies. The same principle applies in other areas as well, and caution is advisable.

Action Imperative

Organizational communication audits are not casual undertakings. They should be a product of a management commitment to improved performance through human relationships enhanced by action as well as communication.

The nature and content of audits implies willingness to meet employee needs, and the implications will be taken as commitments to action by audit participants. Subsequent failure to carry through on implied commitments will compound any preexisting employee relations problems.

Management decisions to inquire into areas of potential investigation should thus be made with care. No aspect of the organization should be addressed that senior management is not prepared to defend or modify. Willingness to correct perceptual problems alone is inadequate — commitment to appropriate action is necessary as well. As Roger D'Aprix has pointed out, proactive rather than reactive communication benefits employers by

1. Identifying organizational priorities and concerns
2. Focusing on the significance of events rather than their mere occurrence
3. Providing perspective and sense of order
4. Anticipating and justifying change
5. Linking events with the organization and fostering a greater sense of meaning in work
6. Encouraging leaders to match words with actions
7. Encouraging hope and optimism.

Conducting an organizational audit ultimately produces improvement or deterioration in employee relationships. Problems are resolved where management responds. They are made worse in the absence of appropriate response. Hungry dogs should be awakened only by those prepared to feed them.

Information Analysis

Survey information can be analyzed in several ways, the least tedious and most productive being analysis by computer. Computers are simultaneously advantageous and demanding. Advantages arise in that information can be subjected to multiple analyses—by department, by respondent age, by position, by income level, by seniority, and so forth. Using a computer to conduct such analyses requires, however, that data be entered in numerical form. Verbal responses do not lend themselves to computer manipulation.

Computer applications. Sophisticated computer programs permit users to quickly identify key words in interview transcripts. Sorting such responses by category is tedious, however, and subsequent analyses are time consuming. More important, verbal comments cannot be ranked numerically.

The ability to rank data numerically is especially helpful where organizational audits are planned on a regular basis. Only rarely have survey questionnaires been tested so extensively as to permit development of statistical norms to which results can be compared. (Goldhaber and Roger's ICA Communication Audit is one of these.) Repetitive audits, preferably conducted on at least an annual basis, are thus highly advisable.

Comparable data. Initial audits permit statistical analysis of results across departments, age groups, income levels, and so on. Subsequent audits enable analysts to determine the extent of improvement or deterioration in employee attitude and opinion. Since comparable data are necessary to reflect change over time, care in the construction of initial survey questionnaires becomes doubly important.

RESEARCH ALTERNATIVES

Information can be obtained from employees orally or in writing. Oral information gathering can be accomplished through in-person interviews or telephone interviews. Written information can be obtained in person or by mail. None of these techniques is perfect. All have strengths and weaknesses, some of which are inherent in the processes, while others involve individuals. Both must be minimized to obtain results at reasonable cost.

Research Questionnaires

Questionnaires are necessary regardless of the manner in which research is to be conducted. Their design varies with the information-gathering procedure. A number of potential pitfalls, however, exist in the preparation of questions—a process requiring considerable precision. Four of the more common are especially important: bias in questions, double-barreled questions, "courtesy bias," and response scales.

Question bias. The manner in which questions are posed can bias responses. Asking respondents, for example, whether they consider something to be good (or bad) suggests that they reply accordingly. This problem is most easily avoided by forming questions in the form of absolute statements and asking respondents to indicate the extent to which they agree or disagree.

Double-barreled questions. The double-barreled question poses two inquiries in the same sentence. For example, "Do you think beer and wine sales should be barred on Sundays" is a question that for some respondents will defy yes or no answers. It refers to two different forms of alcohol. Respondents may agree as to one or both. Resultant data would be unreliable.

"Courtesy bias." Questions involving "courtesy bias" tend to occur often in employee surveys. They produce inaccurate responses because they invite "correct" answers. They are most troublesome where used in in-person or telephone surveys. Questions concerning organizational policy, for ex-

ample, almost inevitably would produce biased responses in these circumstances. Respondent anonymity is necessary to avoid this problem.

Answer categories. Responses can also be distorted by inappropriate answer categories. "Very often," "occasionally" and "never," for example, would produce less accurate responses than "very often," "frequently," "occasionally," and "never." Perceived distance between "very often" and "occasionally" is greater than that between "occasionally" and "never."

Alternative Designs

Over the years, question design and construction has produced a broad range of potential approaches. Two of the best are contained in the ICA Communication Audit designed by Goldhaber and Rogers. One consists of a set of absolute statements. Respondents are asked to indicate the extent to which they agree or disagree with each one on a five-point scale (see Figure 8.3). The second is an especially effective bipolar design, in which respondents are asked to indicate (a) the amount of information they receive and (b) the amount they need on identical scales (see Figure 8.4). Researchers thus obtain both comparative data as to areas of information in which respondents are most interested and data as to any information gaps that may exist.

Survey Techniques

There is a greater range of choices in administering employee surveys than exists with other groups. Organizational personnel are a more accessible audience. Their names and addresses are known, and most appear more or less regularly on organizational premises.

The latter factor permits on-site as well as telephone or mail surveys. Considerable care must be taken, however, to avoid response bias where on-site techniques are used. This is especially true where morale is low or where employee relations problems have existed.

On-site surveys. Significant levels of employee skepticism or suspicion of management are apt to distort on-site survey responses, unless exceptional care is taken to assure confidentiality. Use of outside research organizations is advisable in most cases. Trained survey personnel, perceived as more objective than organizational staff members, tend to minimize suspicion and encourage respondent candor.

Where suspicion is high, written questionnaires administered in privacy are generally preferable to interviews. Respondent anonymity can be demonstrated by excluding managers and supervisors from the survey area. Outsiders should supervise the process, and locked containers should be provided for completed questionnaires. Data tabulation and analysis should be done off the employer's premises.

Figure 8.3.   Organizational Communication Relationships, Assessed through a Segment of the ICA Communication Audit.

Sources of Information

Instructions for Questions 51 through 68

You *not only* receive various kinds of information, but can receive such information from *various sources* within the organization. For each source listed below, mark your response on the answer sheet that best indicates: (1) the amount of information you *are* receiving from that source and (2) the amount of information you *need* to receive from that source in order to do your job.

Sources of Information	This is the amount of information I receive now					This is the amount of information I need to receive				
	Very Little	Little	Some	Great	Very Great	Very Little	Little	Some	Great	Very Great
Subordinates (if applicable)	51. 1	2	3	4	5	52. 1	2	3	4	5
Co-workers in my own unit or department	53. 1	2	3	4	5	54. 1	2	3	4	5
Individuals in *other* units, department in my organization	55. 1	2	3	4	5	56. 1	2	3	4	5
Immediate supervisor	57. 1	2	3	4	5	58. 1	2	3	4	5
Department meetings	59. 1	2	3	4	5	60. 1	2	3	4	5
Middle Management	61. 1	2	3	4	5	62. 1	2	3	4	5
Formal management presentations	63. 1	2	3	4	5	64. 1	2	3	4	5
Top management	65. 1	2	3	4	5	66. 1	2	3	4	5
The "grapevine"	67. 1	2	3	4	5	68. 1	2	3	4	5

Source: From Gerald M. Goldhaber and Donald P. Rogers, *Auditing Organizational Communication Systems: The ICA Communication Audit.* Copyright © 1979 by Kendall-Hunt Publishing Company. Reprinted with permission.

Employees should be asked to go in groups to the survey site to complete questionnaires, in order to assure optimum participation. Response rates decline where employees are permitted to do so individually at their own convenience. They further deteriorate if surveys are completed at home and mailed to the research organization.

Off-site surveys. Off-site surveys are tantamount to mailing survey forms and asking they be completed and returned by mail. Response rates tend to be low, although the process usually is less expensive than on-site procedures. Postage and mailing costs are more than offset by the labor costs involved in on-site research.

Figure 8.4.   Preferences for Specific Communication Channels and the Extent to Which They Are Used, Examined in a Segment of the ICA Communication Audit, Using a Bipolar Scale.

Channels of Communication

Instructions for Questions 107 through 122

The following questions list a variety of channels through which information is transmitted to employees. Please mark your response on the answer sheet which best indicates: (1) the amount of information you *are* receiving through that channel and (2) the amount of information you *need* to receive through that channel.

Channel:		*This is the amount of information I receive now*						*This is the amount of information I need to receive*				
		Very Little	Little	Some	Great	Very Great		Very Little	Little	Some	Great	Very Great
Face-to-face contact between two people	107.	1	2	3	4	5	108.	1	2	3	4	5
Face-to-face contact among more than two people	109.	1	2	3	4	5	110.	1	2	3	4	5
Telephone	111.	1	2	3	4	5	112.	1	2	3	4	5
Written (memos, letters)	113.	1	2	3	4	5	114.	1	2	3	4	5
Bulletin Boards	115.	1	2	3	4	5	116.	1	2	3	4	5
Internal Publications (newsletter, magazine)	117.	1	2	3	4	5	118.	1	2	3	4	5
Internal Audio-Visual Media Videotape, Films, Slides)	119.	1	2	3	4	5	120.	1	2	3	4	5
External Media (TV, Radio, Newspapers)	121.	1	2	3	4	5	122.	1	2	3	4	5

Source: From Gerald M. Goldhaber and Donald P. Rogers, *Auditing Organizational Communication Systems: The ICA Communication Audit.* Copyright © 1979 by Kendall-Hunt Publishing Company. Reprinted with permission.

Off-site surveys can also be conducted by researcher visits to employee homes or by telephone. Both approaches are relatively costly, and neither is apt to produce a high response level. Telephone surveyors often find as many as 50 percent of their calls unanswered. Response rates are similar where surveyors go door to door. Call-backs by telephone or in person rapidly escalate costs.

Types of Surveys

One of two basic types of survey can be administered with reasonable certainty that results will be valid: a sample survey or a population survey.

Population surveys include all individuals within subject groups—in the present case, all employees. Sample surveys involve administering questionnaires to representative groups or samples selected at random from populations.

Survey applications. Each type of survey has a place in traditional scientific research. Sample surveys are used where populations are so large as to make population surveys impractical or overly expensive. This seldom is the case with employee populations. Population studies are advisable for employee groups, because they create a sense of involvement with the organization. Individuals tend to be flattered when their opinions are asked.

Sample selection is critical where sample surveys are used. A random sample is essential. Drawing a random sample requires a selection process in which every member of the population has an equal opportunity to be selected. This can be handled in several ways. Many computer programs will generate lists of predetermined size from existing master lists, a process that is usually practical in organizations of a size that would recommend random sampling. Random-number tables printed in statistics texts can also be used to generate lists of participants. Finally, the sample can be taken by selecting at random a starting point in a complete list of employees and then using every third, fifth, tenth, or nth name on the list.

Stratified sampling. A similar technique called random stratified sampling can be used where researchers want to analyze responses of employees in subgroups or insure that subgroups are proportionately represented in the sample. These circumstances often arise when plants, departments, or other operational units are of disparate size. Lists of employees are first subdivided by group where random stratified sampling is used. One of the random selection processes described above is then applied to each group.

ALTERNATIVE TECHNIQUES

Several other information-gathering techniques may be applied to obtain supplemental information. Most helpful among them are so-called focus group sessions which bring knowledgeable individuals together to discuss specific topics, and interviews with individual managers. They are applied in that order in most cases.

Focus Groups

Focus-group discussions are appropriate in several situations. One occurs where effective management and communication strategies have eliminated any semblance of skepticism or distrust on the part of personnel. Focus groups then may be used to identify problem areas, which survey questionnaires can then address. This approach is advisable where audits are to be conducted for the first time.

Survey follow-up. Focus interviews can also be used subsequent to surveys. When survey data have been tabulated and analyzed, questions inevitably arise. Most have to do with employee perceptions concerning specific issues or channels of communication. The questions can often be resolved through focus group interviews which allow detailed discussion. Well-timed focus group interviews can also provide immediate feedback as to prospective steps that management may take to meet employee concerns.

Opportunities. Open-ended questions, sometimes appended to multiple-choice questionnaires and requesting "any additional comments or suggestions" from employees, often call management attention to minor, readily solvable problems. Immediate organizational response can go far toward convincing personnel that management does, indeed, intend to address their concerns.

Prompt response. Significant improvement in morale has often been produced by prompt response—for example, where organizations have improved parking lot lighting for night employees, or seen to it that coffee was available throughout their shifts. Similar reactions have occurred where human resources offices were kept open one evening and one night a month to answer employee questions.

Individual Interviews

Interviews with individual managers usually are best delayed until after surveys are complete. Preferably, they are scheduled subsequent to focus-group interviews as well.

Individual interviews are most helpful where detailed information is required concerning specific problems in small work groups. Statistical data yielded by surveys is more subject to distortion where groups are small. Focus group approaches may or may not be helpful. Considerable participant reticence can occur where parties to problems at hand are inadvertently invited to participate.

Individual interviews then may be advisable. They should be employed with discretion, however, in that they, like focus-group sessions, are relatively costly.

Follow-Up Devices

Communication audits, as indicated earlier, preferably should be undertaken at approximately annual intervals. Between these major efforts a number of devices can be used to track employee attitude and opinion—among them, "hot-line" telephone systems and suggestion systems in any of several forms.

Hot lines are telephones answered by recording devices through which employees can pose questions and receive prompt responses. Most organizations promise answers within 24 to 48 hours. Some compound the value of the hot lines by keeping permanent records of inquiry subjects. They are valid indicators of the ebb and flow of employee interests.

Suggestion systems often offer similar potential. They tend to attract anonymous negative comments as well as serious suggestions. Analyzing anonymous items can provide insight into "how well we're doing" in employee relations at any given moment.

Some organizations encourage informal suggestions through employee publications, such as a newsletter. These "Good Idea" programs, as they're often called, are designed to attract ideas and comments through regularly published suggestion coupons. When suggestions are adopted, small rewards—usually no more than $50 to $100— go to the originators. The objective, as with more formal communication systems, is to enhance information flows to the benefit of all involved.

SUMMARY

Success in organizational communication is a function of communicators' knowledge of employee groups. It can best be obtained through a series of formal and informal research efforts. Included are demographic, psychographic, and survey research, as well as a number of other information-gathering techniques.

Demography deals with data of the sort most commonly acquired from the Bureau of the Census. Available by Postal Service zip code as well as by census tract, the data include resident profiles by age, sex, income, occupational level, and a host of other characteristics.

Demographic data are best interpreted in context with psychographic factors such as the values and life-styles categories designed by the Stanford Research Institute. These, in turn, can be elaborated through analysis of contemporary trends, as described in popular publications and otherwise.

With demographic and psychographic data in hand, informal inquiries are in order to assess information available from organizational records. Of special significance are those such as age, occupational level, income level, and other factors which become more meaningful in the light of previously acquired information.

Other organizational records are also helpful. Absenteeism and tardiness data, for example, usually are valid indicators of morale level. So are product defect rates and similar information, especially where it can be tracked over time.

Collectively, the above-described information enables the researcher to design a survey instrument that will elicit information necessary to plan the communication program. Data as to employee informational needs is especially important. So are employee preferences as to available communication channels. Employee perceptions of the organization, its products or services, and its management, also are helpful.

ADDITIONAL READING

D'Aprix, Roger. "Communications in Contemporary Organizations," in Carol Reuss and Donn Silvis, *Inside Organizational Communication.* New York: Longman, 1985.

Foltz, Roy G. "Communication in Contemporary Organizations," in Carol Reuss and Donn Silvis, *Inside Organizational Communication.* New York: Longman, 1985.

Goldhaber, Gerald M., and Donald P. Rogers. *Auditing Organizational Communications Systems: The ICA Communication Audit.* Dubuque, IA: Kendall-Hunt, 1979.

Louv, Richard. *America II.* Los Angeles: Tarcher, 1983.

Mitchell, Arnold. *The Nine American Lifestyles: Who We Are & Where We Are Going.* New York: Macmillan, 1983.

Oxford Analytica. *America in Perspective.* Boston: Houghton Mifflin, 1986.

Wilcox, Dennis L., Phillip H. Ault, and Warren K. Agee. *Public Relations: Strategies and Tactics.* New York: Harper & Row, 1986.

9
THE HUMAN FACTOR

Management has made a commitment to fairness and equity. Appropriate policies are in place. Managers, supervisors, and rank and file are operating under performance-based appraisal and reward systems. Now, one might assume, the communication program can begin. With the prerequisites fulfilled, the organization can proceed to reap the benefits.

Reality, unfortunately, is another matter. Management's commitment must be ongoing. A few weeks or months under new appraisal and compensation systems is merely a beginning. Communication, in fact, has been in progress for some time. Survival requires that these efforts be institutionalized; that they become woven into the cultural fabric of the organization. The process involved requires knowledge of organizational communication systems.

Organizational Communication

Organizational communication involves creating and exchanging messages within a network of interdependent relationships. The process occurs in a complex, open system, influenced by and influencing internal and external environments (see Figure 9.1). It involves the flow, purpose, direction, and media involved in message transmission, as well as people and their attitudes, feelings, relationships, and skills. The process requires time as well as communication. Most of all, it requires an understanding of communication in several contexts.

Successful communicators first must understand communication and individuals' roles in the process. The communication process is controlled by the receiver. Reactions and responses to communication are highly individualized. The factors that govern those responses must be considered if the process is to produce desired results.

Second, communicators must comprehend the nature of communication in organizations. Too many view organizational communication systems as consisting of mediated delivery channels; newsletters, bulletin boards, videotape presentations, and the like. The bulk of intraorganizational infor-

Figure 9.1.   Paradigm of Organizational Communication.

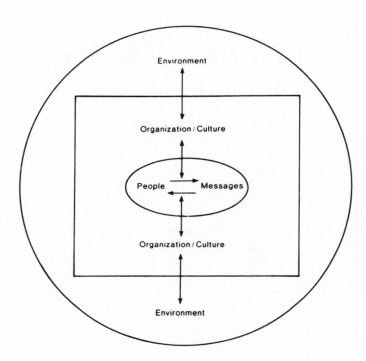

Source: From the International Communication Council newsletter, December 1981. Re-
    printed with permission.

mation, in fact, is transmitted informally. A substantial portion is delivered
orally, and a significant amount is conveyed by deeds rather than words.

Third, communicators must deal with the critical role of organizational
leadership in communication, since their behaviors are an essential part of
the process. Decision making and issuance of orders by senior executives
is inadequate. "Where the decision is painful," George deMare pointed out,
"it is quite possible to issue an order and have it drop into the bottomless
abyss of a company's hierarchy with no more effect than a whisper in the
Grand Canyon."

In the overall, these steps make productive a process that in most organizations has been far from adequate in design, content, and implementation.
The communication process is most productive where two sets of elements

are addressed: First, a climate conducive to communication must be created; second, all barriers to communication must be removed.

Communication Climate

Favorable communication climates exist in organizations only after several prerequisites have been met. First, communication must be perceived as helpful or supportive. Employees and supervisors must enter into the process without reservation and for mutual benefit. Upward communication must be seen as helpful. Organizations must be perceived as responsive, and the communication processes should be viewed as a form of participative decision making.

Several conditions must be met to fulfill these requirements. Message sources must be believable, which in turn requires mutual trust, confidence, and credibility on the part of all involved. Where intraorganizational relationships are perceived as open and candid, messages can be exchanged non-judgmentally, producing trust and confidence.

Finally, favorable communication climates require that goals, strategies, and individual assignments be mutually understood. Individuals want to understand their roles as well as those of their colleagues. They tend to understand them, and respond accordingly, where management takes steps to ensure that common barriers to communication are eliminated.

Barriers to Communication

Communication is a complex process. In simplified form, it involves a sender, a message, a channel of communication, and a receiver. "Failure" on the part of any of these components prevent communication from taking place. Communication in organizations is more complicated, primarily because more individuals are involved. Potential for failure compounds accordingly.

Inadequate information. Most common in organizational settings is failure on the part of the communication system to deliver adequate information relating to jobs and the organization. Relatively few employees are aware of the roles they play in moving the organization toward its objectives. Fewer still are aware of those objectives.

Most organizations are compartmentalized to a greater or lesser extent, usually along functional lines. Compartmentalization tends to compound as organizations grow and functions become more specialized. Information usually is distributed on a "need to know" basis, and employees and organization alike suffer as a result.

Most communication in organizations is perceived as an end in itself rather than a means thereto. Publishing personnel policy and procedure manuals

148   Communicating for Survival

and employee newsletters are worthwhile exercises only where they trigger desired responses among employees.

Lack of policy. The absence of a communication policy often is a significant barrier to organizational information flows. Many employers appear to assume that communication is a natural occurrence, although this is not the case. Policies establishing how messages are to be sent and how information is to be distributed are essential to organizational success. Every error explained by the phrase "but I didn't know" is a monument to lack of adequate communication.

Authoritarian management. "Need to know" policies and perceived management disinterest are major obstacles to communication in organizations. The former block downward flows and the latter prevent information from moving upward. Two sets of problems arise as a result. Ideas potentially valuable to management fail to reach those in a position to act on them and employee problems compound.

Absence of measurement. Seldom do organizations measure the results of their communication programs. Informal feedback often occurs, but no systematic effort is made to establish objectives and periodically determine the extent to which they have been achieved. If personnel manuals are intended to acquaint employees with policy and procedure, for example, the extent of their knowledge should be periodically measured.

Lack of follow-up. Problems are further complicated by lack of adequate response. Lethargy—or what many managers perceive to be lethargy—seems to compound with organizational size. The problem probably is more a function of tortuous communication channels, but nevertheless exists.

Upward communication slows radically. Downward communication suffers even more. Managers beleaguered by torrents of information requests from upper echelons find less and less time to respond to subordinates' inquiries, with predictable results.

Message timing. Senior managers tend to react to informational arteriosclerosis in a manner that further compounds the problem. They go "outside channels" with critical messages or transmit them earlier than would be appropriate. Thus, some messages continue to be late, while others may arrive so early as to have been forgotten by the critical moment.

Channel problems. Growing organizational complexity also results in an increasing substitution of impersonal channels of communication for face-to-face contact. Impersonality is a pervasive problem, especially for senior employees who once enjoyed person-to-person contact with organizational leadership. The problem is especially damaging where those involved feel they are consequently being deprived of opportunities to participate in decisions that affect their day-to-day activities.

Communicator ineptitude. Lack of communication skills is one of the most pervasive organizational problems. Managers and supervisors, especially at lower echelons, often are less than adequately skilled in conducting meetings and interviews. The best-designed communication system is dysfunctional in such circumstances.

Grapevine growth. Where these conditions prevail, communication between employees and management is supplanted by the ubiquitous "grapevine." Rumor replaces fact, and the organization suffers as a result.

Each of these problems must be overcome if communication is to succeed and organizations are to survive. This objective will be accomplished, however, only with considerable difficulty.

THE COMMUNICATION PROCESS

As has been noted, the communication process is complex. It involves a number of steps, some controlled by communicators, some by message recipients. And it usually fails. Peter Drucker described contemporary circumstances in admirable fashion:

> We have more attempts at communication today...yet communications *[sic]* has proven as elusive as the unicorn. The noise level has gone up so fast that no one can really listen anymore to all that babble about communications. But there is clearly less and less communicating. The communications gap within institutions and between groups in society has been widening steadily—to the point where it threatens to become an unbridgeable gulf of total misunderstanding.

Failure occurs in large part through the functioning of several principles of communication first described by Finland's Osmo Wiio. Communication efficiency is low, perhaps as low as 5 percent. Potential for successful communication declines as volume increases. Messages that can be understood in several ways will be understood in the most damaging manner. At least one recipient will understand the meaning of the message better than the originator. Most organizational communicators readily identify with four corollaries of Wiio's first law:

1. If communication can fail, it will. Carelessness, indifference, laziness, and lack of skill are the primary causes.
2. Communication fails even where it cannot fail, as communicators are defeated by nature's hidden flaws and misunderstandings.
3. Where communication succeeds, it must be in a way that was not intended. "Message receivers may misunderstand what they believed they understood. They also may merely be humoring senders, or avoiding admitting understanding."
4. Communication is bound to fail when communicators are satisfied it will succeed. Contentment with process design means it was developed to meet sender rather than receiver needs.

Breakdowns in communication most often occur where senders lack insight into human behavior or proceed on the basis of erroneous assumptions. They may be created by message transmission problems, receiver defensiveness, differences in perceptions, or variation in word definitions.

Barriers can be eliminated over time through honest communication and by reinforcing words with action. Repetition is helpful, but appeals based on community of interest and understanding of the human organism are more effective.

COMMUNICATION AND THE INDIVIDUAL

Contrary to popular political belief, individuals are not receptacles into which information can be poured for immediate assimilation and action. They are as likely, in fact, to reject as to accept information. The process is ongoing, for humans are constantly interpreting their worlds. They process all messages, rejecting many, accepting few, and modifying interpretations accordingly.

Individuals' worlds consist of constructed realities or beliefs modified from time to time in keeping with messages received from their environments. Their personal interpretive constructs serve as frameworks used to order and understand events. They create understandings of events and individuals and act on their interpretations of those persons, events, and situations.

Individual Beliefs

Beliefs can be viewed in a manner similar to that in which Abraham Maslow perceived human needs. They are essentially hierarchical in nature and strength. Basic beliefs and basic needs are primary behavioral governors. However, while Maslow's needs are often envisioned in pyramidal form, beliefs might better be depicted as a layered sphere.

Primitive beliefs are central to humans. These are beliefs shared with others, dealing with the nature of reality and enjoying social support. Superimposed over these beliefs are individuals' self-beliefs, including their sensitive concepts of self-worth.

The next layer consists of authority beliefs adopted through the influence of others considered trustworthy or otherwise. The latter group tends to implant negative beliefs.

Nearest the surface are derived and inconsequential beliefs. The former originate with trusted individuals, while the latter deal with such matters as product quality and similar minor matters.

Most significant from the perspective of organizational communicators is the fact that the levels of belief set out above are presented in descending order of strength. Primitive beliefs are more difficult to change than derived and inconsequential beliefs. Self-belief or self-concept is most significant in that it is central to individual perceptions.

Perceptions are organized, according to Swanson and Delia, in terms of the individual's (1) personal system of constructs or perceptual categories, (2) self-concept, and (3) goals, needs, and situational requirement.

Each person, within an individual system of perceptual categories, makes sense of the world. The sense that is made of the world is, hence, ultimately individual and persona:. . . . Each person lives only his own life; he knows the world only through his own personal system of interpretive schemes. Subjective experience, thus, in a very genuine way is private. It is the possession of only the single individual.

Compounding Factors

The situation is compounded, from communicators' perspectives, by factors that affect individuals' perceptions of messages. These include demographic elements, reference groups, personality variables, and the salience or importance of the message. Selectivity in exposure, perception, and retention also influence the process.

Demographic elements. Demographic variables are characteristics by which groups and subgroups are categorized, such as age, race, sex, education, and occupation. These elements help shape individuals' perceptions of messages to which they are exposed. Legislative action raising legal drinking ages in recent years, for example, was largely endorsed by older members of the population and opposed by younger members. Congressional elimination of the mandatory retirement age was welcomed by older workers. Others approved at the time, but may feel otherwise when those older employees linger overlong in senior organizational positions.

Reference groups. Humans belong to multiple groups. They are members of churches, social and fraternal organizations, work groups, and others. As such, they identify with and embrace group norms. Some contend that adopting these norms is the price of group membership.

Reference groups may be highly organized, as in the case of professional or trade associations. They also may be quite informal, as with veterans, antique fanciers, or coin collectors. Shared group beliefs in either case can complicate or facilitate communication.

Personality variables. Intelligence, authoritarianism, susceptibility to persuasion, and other personality variables influence individual responses to messages. Complex messages are better understood by more intelligent recipients. Authoritarian personalities tend to reject new ideas. Those with high levels of self-esteem are slow to modify their positions. Extroverts tend to be more receptive to new ideas than introverts. These are only a few of the factors that influence individual perception of messages, but they are among the strongest governors of the process.

Saliency. Most individuals screen messages in the light of their relative importance. Perceived usefulness of information, in other words, determines the extent to which messages are heeded. Those planning to buy new cars, for example, pay considerable attention to new-car advertising, consumer reports concerning automobiles, and comments by friends who recently have purchased models in which they are interested. Interest in such information immediately declines after purchases have been made.

Selective exposure. Individuals seek out or are receptive to information in which they are interested or that confirms their beliefs. Conversely, they tend to avoid or reject that in which they are disinterested or that which goes contrary to those beliefs. These factors influence selection of television programming, magazines, books, and even friends. At the extreme, selective exposure is readily seen in those who have made up their minds and prefer not be be bothered by facts.

Selective perception. Psychologists suggest that humans organize perceptions on the basis of need, experience, mood, and memory. Using these factors as filters of a sort, they tend to hear only that which is of interest to them. This results in striking variation, for example, in the recollections of individuals who hear political speeches. Older listeners may afterward recall comments on Social Security, while the younger among them may best remember statements about student loans.

Selective retention. Selective retention refers to the variation in individuals' retention of the content of messages to which they are exposed. Salience or information utility tends to play a role in retention. So do individual interests or beliefs. The latter factor may be positive or negative in impact. Ideas or concepts that individuals find especially repulsive are often among those best remembered.

Multiple problems. Problems facing organizational communicators are thus considerably more complex than they appear. Attempting to pour information into the heads of employees is an exercise in futility. Information alone seldom modifies individual beliefs interwoven with experience. Performance and communication, continued over an extended time span, is essential if attitudes and opinions are to be changed.

Continuing performance demonstrating organizational commitment to developing and maintaining a nurturing atmosphere based on truth, fairness, and equity is vital. This element, more than any other, influences employee perceptions of the organizational environment.

MANAGERS, CLIMATES, AND PATHWAYS

Success and failure in organizational communication are produced by several interrelated factors. Managers play a critical role. They can frustrate the best-designed system or achieve some semblance of success in the face of systemic weakness. The organizational climates they create are equally important. Managers may approach communication defensively, supportively, or from a perspective between the extremes. Employees respond accordingly, and results are predestined in the information exchange process. Finally, managers may use or abuse the several communication paths open to them. Most perform well in upward communication. Downward and horizontal communication often are less well handled.

Managers as Barriers

Organizational susceptibility to communication breakdown has several causes, size and complexity being the most obvious. Larger and more complex organizations often experience difficulty in maintaining timely communication. Managerial predispositions are less obvious, but probably more destructive of communication systems.

Beset by what they perceive to be more pressing matters, managers and supervisors are predisposed to use communication for remedial rather than preventive purposes. They permit minor difficulties to become major problems before responding. Their late responses then tend to be perceived as manipulative.

Time pressures also encourage attention to symptoms rather than to causes of problems, including those involving communication. Symptoms may subside as a result, but problems are prone to recur in more debilitating form.

Delayed and symptom-oriented responses are further weakened by managers' tendencies to "throw information" at employees and by managerial misperceptions concerning their status in the eyes of their subordinates. Transmission of information assures neither receipt nor understanding. Where managers have compromised their credibility, messages are prone to be rejected in any event.

Managerial weaknesses are often magnified by individual or organizational insensitivity to communication needs. Most view communication mechanistically rather than creatively. They may fail to transmit information due to laziness, procrastination, or "need to know" philosophies.

Climates as Barriers

The weaknesses that exist in many managers and organizations are magnified where managers tend to be defensive rather than supportive. Both defensive and supportive climates create predictable responses. Phillip Lewis identified six alternative characteristics of such climates.

Evaluation versus description. Managers may be judgmental or non judgmental. On the one hand, they can approach a situation to make moral judgments or question standards, values, and motives. On the other, they can present feelings or perceptions that neither ask nor imply need for behavioral change.

Control versus problem orientation. Control or collaboration are the options here. Managers can attempt to change attitude or behavior or seek collaborative solutions to mutual problems. They can proceed without preconceptions or on the assumption that others are inadequate. In the former case, workers are left free to solve their own problems with or without assistance.

Strategy versus spontaneity. A strategic approach is manipulative and attempts to create the appearance of involvement. The spontaneous approach is guileless and free of deception, conveying straight-forwardness and honesty in dealing with the problem at hand.

Neutrality versus empathy. Neutral approaches to individuals convey clinical detachment. Those involved are treated as objects, and readily perceive this to be the case. Empathy involves respect for individuals, interest in their problems, and acceptance of their feelings and values.

Superiority versus equality. Superior approaches arouse feelings of inadequacy and suggest unwillingness to enter into mutual problem solving. They denigrate the power, status, or worth of message receivers. Equality in approach, on the other hand, attaches no importance to differences in status or power. It implies willingness to help and inevitably induces a favorable response.

Certainty versus provisionalism. Certainty appears to message receivers as dogmatism, as "know-it-all-ism," as a desire to win an argument rather than solve a problem. Provisionalism is an investigative approach, implying intent to solve problems rather than debate them.

Managerial communication strengths and weaknesses are primary determinants of their individual successes and failures. They also influence the organization as a whole.

COMMUNICATION FLOWS

Communication in organizations flows in multiple directions: downward, upward, and laterally. Flows tend to be equal in direction. Variation in human communication ability and organizational structure, however, produce differences in directional volume and speed. Each flow also can be categorized by level of formality, as will be discussed later.

Downward Communication

Downward communication deals primarily with the principal functions of management: planning, organizing, controlling, and directing the activities of the organization. Downward flows consist largely of management directives concerning these functions.

Traditional organizations emphasize downward flows at the expense of the upward. Managers spend inordinate amounts of time and effort in preparing and sending messages to subordinates. They often appear little concerned over whether messages are received and understood, and pay a high price in waste and inefficiency. Gerald M. Goldhaber's study of 16 organizations led him to four conclusions concerning downward information flows.

1. Most employees do not receive a great deal of information in organizations.
2. Their information needs include (a) more job-related information from immediate supervisors, and (b) more information concerning organizational decision making from senior management.
3. Those closest to employees are the best information sources.
4. Information from top management is of lower quality than that received from other sources but lack of timeliness degrades information from all sources.

Upward Communication

Upward organizational information flows are impeded by workers' tendency toward reticence. Most workers believe that problems result when they express opinions to superiors. They also consider their thoughts unwanted by inaccessible and unresponsive managements.

These conditions erode the potential value of upward communication. The process should produce feedback in response to downward-flowing information and stimulate employees to participate in decision making.

Four perceived impediments to upward communication on the part of employees, which apparently would eliminate most of the potential benefit in the process, were identified by Goldhaber.

1. Inadequate opportunity for employees to send significant amounts of information upward
2. Inadequate opportunity to voice complaints and evaluate supervisors
3. Greater perceived need to receive rather than send information
4. Lack of response to information sent, especially to top management, which appears to increase as senders move up the organizational hierarchy.

Horizontal Communication

Horizontal communication tends to be even more neglected than the vertical variety. This phenomenon appears to stem from senior management perceptions that vertical communication is sufficient; that subordinate units need be aware only of what superiors elect to tell them.

The problem appears more a matter of habit than logic. Organizations once were more simply structured and moved more slowly than now. Time required by senior managers to coordinate communication between subordinate units created no undue difficulty.

In today's more complex organizations, workers are more isolated. Isolation limits mutual understanding and encourages rivalry and friction. Waste occurs while peer managers or supervisors attempt to cope with problems or conflict "through channels." Horizontal communication is essential, yet channels continue to be molded primarily by patterns of authority and work flow.

Enhanced lateral communication enables peer managers to coordinate their work better, solve problems more rapidly, share information, and resolve conflict. The process is discouraged, however, by interpersonal rivalries, departmental specialization, and lack of motivation. The latter may be generated by an absence of accountability. Organizations suffer when one unit's success is achieved at the expense of another's, but senior managers are often reluctant to extend the accountability concept to obviate such outcomes.

Communication Paths

Organizational structure is the primary shaper of communication channels. The organizational chart defines superior–subordinate relationships and in the process establishes how information will flow. In recent years larger corporations have acted to streamline organizational structures, although many continue to maintain as many as 12 management levels. Since multiple entities may need to be consulted at each level, a policy decision can require weeks or months to implement.

Work-flow patterns complicate the communication process. Individuals low in organizational hierarchies often initiate work processes for those of higher rank. While the manager may run the business, in other words, the secretary may run the office, and the interests of the two at any time may be in direct conflict. Consider, for example, the physician's office. The doctor presumably is in command, but subordinates schedule the work. Not a few physicians have thus found themselves working through lunch hours because their office staffs had an aversion to working beyond 5 P.M.

These formal and semiformal communication channels are complicated in every organization by the variation in levels of communication formality and several other factors.

COMMUNICATION LEVELS

Communication in organizations is complex, pervasive, largely uncontrolled, and only in part controllable. The complexity is created by multiple sources of messages. Virtually all the messages become pervasive, extending to the farthest reaches of an organization, often despite the senders' contrary preferences. Only a small part originate in formal communication systems.

Multiple Levels

Communication in organizations is usually considered to occur at three levels: the informal level, the formal level, and the executive level. DeMare defines the latter as the level at which "opinion or taste leaders are usually reached, where art and style are important."

In fact, communication in and by organizations is considerably more complex. It includes, for example, such factors as nonverbal communication, both animate and inanimate. It also includes organizational penetration by a flood of externally generated thoughts. Individuals and organizations are constantly exposed to thousands of messages from multiple sources.

Formal organizational communication systems encompass only a small percentage of the total volume, perhaps as little as 10 percent. DeMare suggested that the informal system alone accounts for "perhaps 70 percent of the communication in an organization." His estimate is perhaps accurate, but only if by "communication" he means intended communication—the transfer of thoughts through words. Organizations communicate with their personnel in many other ways, for better or worse.

Unspoken Messages

Consider, for example, such seemingly minor matters as the condition of employee restrooms or locker rooms; the cleanliness of cafeterias and work areas; the lighting in the parking lots. Each conveys a message. The messages may not be overly loud if conditions are good. They speak far more loudly than managerial platitudes when conditions are bad. Management proclamations of concern for personnel, no matter how loudly or frequently expressed, are futile when contradicted by deeds of omission or commission.

The same message-sending process is triggered by performance-appraisal systems, compensation mechanisms, promotions, disciplinary policies, and so forth. All of management's professed allegiance to equity and fairness go for naught in the face of consistent systemic malfunction.

Errors occur in the best of systems, of course. None is perfect. Occasional malfunction tends to be forgiven, especially when admitted and corrected. Consistent "error" patterns, however, destroy employee confidence.

The Resonator Effect

Whether or not deserving of support, organizational behavior is reported and magnified by the organization's informal communication network. The word "grapevine" is inadequate to describe its functions. The fruit at the extremes of a grapevine usually is no worse than that near the ground. If anything, it probably is better. Informal organizational communication systems tend to magnify and distort. At minimum they serve as resonators, amplifying perceived injustices and compounding credibility problems. Messages tend to become progressively more distorted at the extreme reaches of the network, and management pays heavy penalties

Gossip, hearsay, and rumor persist in organizations and will continue. A great deal of information—sound and unsound—is transmitted in the process. Casual commentary, unfounded portents of disaster, and rumors of all sorts abound, almost always to the consternation of management.

The grapevine. Managers, especially senior managers, often bemoan the efficacy of organizational grapevines and the impact of the messages they deliver. Their complaints are never heeded, of course, and their preoccupation with the grapevine's negative aspects precludes their recognizing its potential for good.

Informal information systems will exist in organizations until human beings are replaced by robots. They need not, however, be wholly destructive. Grapevines are easily bent, and managers are well positioned to do a bit of bending. Consider the impact, for example, of a chief executive's telephone call to congratulate a rank-and-file employee for some special accomplishment. What would the grapevine make of a senior manager's visit to the shop floor to personally thank an employee who on that very day had completed 20 years with the organization?

Feeding the vine. What about personal letters to employees whose children's or spouses' accomplishments are mentioned in the local newspaper? Luncheon invitations to those who make special contributions to the organization? Any number of gestures, sincerely made, will feed the grapevine, while adding immeasurably to the stature and productivity of those involved. Most important, they say once more to every employee that management really cares.

Compounding the Impact

Gestures of this sort can be readily encouraged where senior managers create appropriate inducements, but conscious effort is necessary to induce middle managers and supervisors to take a real interest in their personnel. Only rarely is such effort forthcoming in traditional organizations. Seemingly more pressing matters apparently consume every available moment, until organizational systems intervene.

Organizations that seek to engage the loyalty of personnel create systems conducive to development of such attributes. They reward managers and supervisors, for example, for controlling excessive absenteeism and tardiness. These problems are more a function of poor morale than of any other factor. Where employees know they are valued, where they are loyal to their peers and their units, absenteeism and tardiness quickly drop to irreducible minimums. Immediate superiors are best positioned to produce these conditions, but usually fail to make the necessary effort in the absence of appropriate incentives.

Successful use of informal communication channels is necessary but not sufficient for successful organizational communication programs. An atmosphere conducive to open communication is prerequisite to success in every form of communication. The process involved essentially is the same in all forms.

PROCESS COMPONENTS

The communication process consists of many components. Five—perhaps six—are of critical importance. The five are source or sender, message, channel, receiver, and feedback. The sixth, pertinent to but arguably not part of the process, is noise or interference that may impede or frustrate communication.

The relative efficiency of each of these factors is a function of several variables. Since all are present in every informational transaction, and each can facilitate or impede the process, each should be a matter of concern in every organization.

Message Source

Messages originate with people, each of whom is a complex organism, bringing to the communication process a set of personal attributes that inevitably become governors of success. Communication skills are most important, but other elements also play a role.

Attitude and knowledge. Communicator attitude and knowledge, often operating through individual assumptions, are critical. Attitude is the more important of the two elements in that it tends to precondition message sources and receivers. Where sources are open and caring, assuming the best rather than the worst in people, messages tend to be well received. Where they are insensitive or worse, the reverse is apt to be true.

Knowledge level is another matter. Most individuals tend to assume in others knowledge levels comparable to their own, but this is seldom the case. Receivers may be more or less knowledgeable than senders, usually less in organizations. Senders must compensate for differences in either direction. If senders are more knowledgeable than receivers, messages must be cast in terms understandable to prospective recipients. If not, senders must acquire sufficient knowledge to communicate at receiver knowledge levels.

Culture and credibility. Of lesser importance but nevertheless significant are the credibility of sources and their cultural backgrounds. Cultural factors may create difficulties when organizatinal cultures collide with those that have preconditioned senders. Not a few corporate executives in recent years have found such differences impossible to overcome.

The credibility of senders is only in part an attribute of the individuals involved. Their positions in organizational structures and their histories in the organization also have a bearing on success. Successful senders have a history of reliability among receivers. They also are appropriately positioned in their organizations. A new policy on health or safety, for example, would be more credible originating from human resources or safety departments than from a line manager.

Message Content

Variables in message content which are many and complex, should be of equal concern to managers and communicators. Facts and language are critical. So are message coding and audience characteristics.

Facts and language. "All the news that's fit to print" is an appropriate objective for the *New York Times,* but inappropriate in organizational communication. Senders must avoid information overload as well as the reverse. They must also assemble and sequence facts so that meanings are clear and potential for receiver uncertainty is kept to a minimum.

Words and coding. Messages must be well designed for receiver attitude, skill and knowledge levels, as well as sociocultural background. This requires careful selection of words to achieve precise meaning. The 500 most common English words, as Goldhaber pointed out, have more than 14,000 meanings. To assure clarity, senders may find it necessary to cast messages in nonverbal as well as verbal codes. Illustrations and diagrams, for example, may be desirable or necessary.

Channel Selection

Selecting channels today is arguably the most difficult decision involved in the communication process. There are more of them than ever before. They are producing audience fragmentation on an unprecedented scale, and they vary considerably in cost as well as efficiency.

Communicators caught up in proliferating technology often neglect basic concepts. All mediated communication substitutes for nonmediated communication. Group communication substitutes for individual communication. The best communication inevitably takes place with two individuals face to face with one another.

Channel variables. Variables that organizational communicators must consider include channel availability, cost efficiency, source and receiver preference, prospective message impact, and appropriateness of channel to message.

Source and receiver preferences—especially the latter—tend to be most important among the variables. Messages must be received to produce desired behavioral responses, and ease of access to channels thus is vital.

Prospective message impact may be equally important. Announcements of plant closings or layoffs, for example, probably are best handled in group meetings. They permit optimum opportunity for two-way communication and imply a greater level of caring on the part of managers. Less significant matters are more amenable to treatment through impersonal channels.

Other factors. Intervening variables may also require consideration. Does the organization function at one site or several? Are operations conducted 40 hours a week or on a seven-day, around-the-clock basis? How important is concurrent delivery of the message, as in the case of a plant closing?

Message Receivers

Receiver characteristics are, or should be, of greatest concern to communicators. Senders must be credible in the eyes of the receiver. Messages must be comprehensible. Channels must be convenient. The communication process fails where messages are not received and acted upon.

Receiver variables that communicators must evaluate are greater in number and prospective impact than those that apply elsewhere in the process. Literacy levels and/or attention spans must be accommodated. Ability to comprehend messages and their implications must be considered.

Recipient attitudes, circumstances, knowledge levels, expectations, and cultural backgrounds are all significant. All must be considered in message development and channel selection. Each can be a facilitator of or obstruction to the communication process.

Feedback

Feedback is essential in communication. With it, communicators can measure the results of their actions. Without it, assessment is impossible. Feedback should permit senders to determine the extent to which messages are received, understood, believed, and acted upon.

Monitoring communication results permits adjustment in communication processes and programs to improve subsequent performance. It also enables communicators to assess the impact of external interference on the process and attempt to avoid the problems involved.

Interference

Interference or noise, as it is sometimes called, can impinge upon almost any component of communication. Source, message, channel, and receiver are all vulnerable.

Messages sent may or may not be what the sources intended or perceived them to be. They may or may not have been what receivers received or thought they were receiving. They can be distorted by the sender or the receiver in the process of transmission.

Delivering information through impersonal channels produces mixed blessings. On the one hand, mediated information is less costly to deliver. On the other, it is less personal and more readily "tuned out." Most of all, mediated information inevitably is a substitute, usually a less productive substitute, for personal contact.

One of the primary advantages of impersonal or mediated communication is its relative efficiency. Messages can be brought within reach of significant numbers of individuals at low cost. The audiences involved, however, are beyond the direct control of message senders.

A concurrent disadvantage in using mediated information is the absence of immediate feedback. In face-to-face communication, the impact of information or its absence can be immediately calculated.

SUMMARY

Success in organizational communication requires mastery of a number of concepts and consequent action to assure systemic integrity. Primary among communicator concerns is the nature of the human organism and the manner in which it manages the communication process. Success is also influenced, however, by the organization's communication climate and its ability to overcome communication barriers.

Communication must be perceived by organization members as mutually beneficial. This requires a nonthreatening atmosphere, as well as a functional message delivery system. The latter entails adequate information delivered on a timely basis through functional channels and with adequate follow-up.

With potential technical problems controlled, the communicator can address the human organism with significant potential for success. Several factors are involved in this process as well. Most important among them are the nature and sources of human beliefs.

Beliefs are complex in nature, resembling a layered sphere. At the core are primitive beliefs, which deal with the individual's perception of reality. Superimposed on them are self-beliefs, including concepts of self-worth. Subsequent layers include authority beliefs, adopted from others the individual considers authoritative; derived beliefs, originating with those the individual trusts; and inconsequential beliefs concerning such things as the relative value of products.

Demographic elements, reference groups, personality variables, saliency, and selective exposure, perception, and retention influence the structure of beliefs. The structures constitute the individual's perceptions of reality. They can be modified, although not without difficulty, where barriers created by managers, occupational climates, and message pathways are cleared away.

The latter process requires creating conditions conducive to upward and horizontal as well as downward communication. The resulting formal communication system must convey messages in harmony rather than in conflict with others sent by the organization. The process requires adequate control of sender, message, channel, and receiver, as well as provision for adequate feedback.

ADDITIONAL READING

Andrews, Patricia H., and John E. Baird, Jr. *Communication for Business and the Professions,* 3rd ed. Dubuque, IA: Brown, 1986.

DeMare, George. *Communicating at the Top: What You Need to Know about Communicating to Run an Organization.* 2d ed. New York: Wiley, 1979.

Drucker, Peter. *Management: Tasks, Responsibilities, Practices.* New York: Harper & Row, 1974.

DuBrin, Andrew J. *Human Relations: A Job Oriented Approach.* Reston, VA: Reston, 1981.

Felsenthal, Norman. *Mass Communication,* 2d ed. Chicago: Science Research Associates, 1981.

Goldhaber, Gerald M. *Organizational Communication,* 4th ed. Dubuque, IA: Brown, 1986.

Lewis, Phillip V. *Organizational Communication: The Essence of Effective Management,* 2d ed. Columbus, OH: Grid, 1980.

Redding, W. C. *Communication within the Organization.* New York: Industrial Communication Council, 1973.

Swanson, David L., and Jesse G. Delia. *The Nature of Human Communication.* Chicago: Science Research Associates, 1976.

Wiio, Osmo. *Wiio's Laws—and Some Others.* Espoo, Finland: Welin-Göös, 1978.

10

DESIGNING THE PROGRAM

Successful employee communication programs are built on sound foundations. They include enlightened organizational philosophies, strong communication policies, and commitments by senior managements to support and participate in the effort. Weakness in any of these areas detracts significantly from programmatic outcomes. Strength compounds success.

ORGANIZATIONAL PHILOSOPHY

Organizations such as Weyerhauser and Hewlett-Packard have developed strong statements of philosophy or objectives, which provide guidance to organization members. Supported by management commitment, they go far toward establishing organizational cultures beneficial to all stakeholder groups. They bind organizations and stakeholders together for common good.

Clearly stated, openly communicated, and actively implemented, they also support organizational communication efforts. Hewlett-Packard's stated objectives have played a major role in keeping the company consistently on lists of best-managed organizations. They call on the company to

1. Achieve sufficient profit to finance company growth and provide the resources necessary to achieve other corporate objectives

2. Provide products and services of the greatest possible value to customers, thereby gaining and holding their respect and loyalty

3. Enter new fields only when the ideas and technical, manufacturing, and marketing skills assure that a needed and profitable contribution to that field can be made

4. Let growth be limited only by profits and ability to develop and produce technical products that satisfy real customer needs

5. Help Hewlett-Packard people share in the company's success, which they make possible; to provide job security based on their performance; to recognize their individual achievements; and to ensure the personal satisfaction that comes from a sense of accomplishment in their work

6. Foster initiative and creativity by allowing the individual great freedom of action in attaining well-defined objectives

7. Honor obligations to society by being an economic, intellectual, and social asset to each nation and each community in which H-P operates.

Communication Policy

Communication policy statements, based on organizational philosophy, can be logically developed. They should include, at minimum, the following objectives.

1. Avoiding misunderstandings, primarily through consistency in content of messages delivered to multiple stakeholder groups

2. Developing pride in the organization, with worthy performance a necessary prerequisite; transmission of information concerning organizational accomplishments to evoke the desired results

3. Establishing community of interest between employer and employees, primarily by educating employees in economics and in the interdependency of organizational stakeholders

4. Increasing understanding of political as well as economic systems to ensure that employees understand the manner in which external developments can impact the organization and themselves

5. Encouraging use of organizational products and services, where appropriate, to better equip employees to serve as organizational spokespersons in their communities

6. Eliciting cooperation for improved performance by informing employees as to organizational goals and objectives and the roles they play in achieving them

7. Promoting safety for the sake of employees and the organization, including educating employees in the cost of accidents

8. Selling the organization consistently to employees, as well as their families, through on-going information efforts

9. Making employees a part of public relations efforts through educational and informational programming supporting organizational citizenship

10. Obtaining support for those political and governmental entities whose activities influence the economic success of the organization and its personnel.

Research demonstrates that these results are reasonably achievable. Organizational climate and job satisfaction have been found to be related to organizational communication. Communication style as well as content have been shown to influence morale and employee relationships with their supervisors.

These are but a few of the research findings of recent date, attesting to the fact that effective communication programs produce tangible and profitable organizational results. Program productivity requires, however, that sound employee communication principles be applied.

Employee Communication Principles

Communication objectives can best be achieved where organizations adopt sound employee communication principles. No exhaustive lists of such principles exist. Those who have attempted to compile such lists, however, usually include the following.

Management commitment. Management must be committed to sharing with employees all information not of a proprietary or ultrasensitive nature in which they may be interested.

Two-way communication. Organizational communication systems should provide for upward as well as downward information flows.

Message delivery. Messages must be conveyed in words that employees will understand and through media selected to ensure timely delivery. Repetition in different terms should be used to assure understanding.

Clarity and accuracy. Messages should be factual, accurate and moderate. Content should be neither misleading nor distorted.

Community of interest. Messages should be based on the shared interests of employees and organizations.

Responsibility. Dissemination of information should be the responsibility of professional communicators skilled in message synthesis, media selection, and associated areas.

Context. Management should assume political and economic ignorance on the part of employees. Adequate context — the reasons why — must be provided with all messages and especially where policy and procedure changes are involved.

Strong Policies

The rationale for the guidelines set out above can best be understood in terms of contemporary organizational needs. They have increasingly been producing more enlightened communication policies among the nation's leading organizations. Eight guidelines set out in a very candid working paper for the Dow Chemical Company are exemplary of the trend. They were formulated by Corporate Communications Manager Richard K. Long and his colleagues to provide guidance for Dow's employee communication staff.

1. Employees should be told everything they can understand about their work environment and the company. We should trust the basic intelligence of our people to assimilate good *and* bad news.
2. Employees prefer hearing news about Dow from Dow rather than the local newspaper or the rumor mill. In the absence of forthrightness from Dow, the

"grapevine" becomes a major source of information — usually with unsatisfactory results.

3. All employees should hear the *same* story if we're to have common understanding, particularly in the case of policy shifts. Relying on "trickle-down" is risky because of varying supervisory attitudes. Some don't care if the troops understand a new policy. Others may actually misinform their people. In the case of "bad" news, many supervisors will simply blame "the system" or "management."

4. Telling only "good" news causes suspicion. Refusing to address "bad" news insults the intelligence and loyalty of employees.

5. In cases where policy changes are contemplated, employee communications can be used to condition the work force. Rather than have periodic blitzes, perhaps we should have more stage-setting.

6. Changing attitudes of the "new" employee dictate more openness and candor than ever before. At a time when we are faced with stiff challenges to retain bright young folks, we risk turning them off by not leveling with them.

7. Generally we over-do the confidentiality argument. Communicating about salaries and benefits, litigation, trade secrets and the like can build support and understanding. The alternative is a reputation for secretiveness, which is easily interpreted as contempt or disdain for our people.

8. Openness, candor, trust and freshness are consistent with the Employee portion of our new Core Values, as well as the "Towards Excellence" program. On the other hand, to be secretive or uncommunicative defeats the purpose of both programs.[1]

Economics and Politics

Potential for organizational success is especially strong where workers understand that their economic futures are inextricably linked with those of their employers. Understanding is difficult to achieve where employees lack adequate educational backgrounds; where they fail to comprehend the roles of ownership, management, and labor.

A lack of understanding was indigenous to the national work force during the rapid economic expansion of the post–World War II era. Managements in those years were more concerned over potential loss of market share than product cost. Consumers in the expanding economy could absorb higher prices. Thus, there occurred such ritual dances as the periodic "negotiations" between the Big Three automakers and the United Auto Workers. The ritual occasionally included a brief strike. The strikes universally resulted in agreements requiring higher wage rates and were followed within weeks by announcements of higher prices. As a result, workers were con-

[1] From a Dow memo circulated by Corporate Communications Manager Richard K. Long in 1986. Reprinted with permission.

vinced that organizational resources were inexhaustible; that every year should bring increased compensation, with or without enhanced productivity.

Improvement noted. Worker understanding of organizational economics improved during the mid-1980s amidst layoffs and multiple plant closings that signaled the nation's transition from an industrial to a postindustrial society. Employees caught up in these events were ultimately convinced that organizational resources were indeed limited. Disappearance of jobs in a climate of increasing competition changed their perceptions of employers and the economic system.

During that same period, many were educated concerning interrelationships between politics and economics. They saw Chrysler Corporation saved by governmental action, while other organizations were permitted to decline or die. They saw government in some cases grant and in others refuse tariff protection in selected industries.

These developments notwithstanding, employers cannot afford to assume adequate knowledge of economics or politics on the part of their employees. Ongoing educational efforts are essential components of employee communication programs.

Performance Improvement

The primary objective of employee communication is performance improvement. Knowledge of economic and political systems is a necessary first step in the process. It should be extended, however, to encompass some basic facts of organizational economic life. The economic implications of policies that employees often find unnecessarily burdensome are especially important.

Absenteeism and tardiness. Organizational need for employee attendance is seldom adequately understood. Policies that penalize those defined as "abusers" thus tend to produce undue antagonism. The antagonism often abates when employees are made aware of the costs involved and the fact that dollars expended to support high absenteeism rates are not available for other purposes.

Safety. Requirements that employees wear safety gear and follow established safety guidelines are often criticized as well. Knowledge of prospective Occupational Safety and Health Administration penalties, existing insurance costs, and prospective premium increases, which can result from high accident rates, tend to mollify protesters.

Organizational Commitment

The Dow document cited above captures the essence of an affirmative communication policy for an open organization committed to all stakeholder groups. Supported by committed senior managements, policies of this sort contribute to the health of communication systems and the organizations they serve. Commitment and support here imply more than lip service; more than written proclamations easily issued and as readily forgotten. The words mean active participation on the part of chief operating officers.

The extent of active participation necessarily varies from one organization to another. What might be considered the essentials are contained in a study by Professors Robert Rayfield and David Pincus, who set out the following guidelines for communication leadership (see Figure 10.1).

Successful organizational communication requires such extensive commitments. Business leaders must face the fact that effective communication takes place only where top management and organizational policy have established the proper atmosphere for communicating.

Unfortunately, this seldom is the case. Traditional organizations pay lip service to the value of communication and the benefits derived from maintaining open organizations. The extent of their real commitment is seen in the extent to which messages fail to reach recipients, reach them too late, or are distorted in the process.

Success requires three more or less innovative steps on the part of senior executives. First, they must get out of their remote offices and into every area of the plant or office complex. Second, they must become sufficiently familiar with operations to discuss them intelligently at every organizational level. Third, they must know local, national, and international affairs as they relate to the organization and its employees. DeMare described them in the form of managerial guidelines.

By getting out of the inner sanctum and into the office or plant, executives break the barriers that tend to seal them off from vital information inappropriate to or neglected by formal channels. In learning the languages of their subordinates, they become knowledgeable in worlds that otherwise often remain foreign to them. By keeping abreast of events in those worlds they better understand the trends and conditions with which their inhabitants must contend. They become far better leaders in the process.

INFORMATIONAL REQUIREMENTS

Designing employee information programs is a relatively simple process. It follows a pattern well established in public relations and other communication disciplines. The process is cyclical and repetitive. It begins with a definition of desired outcomes, comes full circle to an assessment of results, and begins again. Planners start with a series of simple steps that often require considerable effort. They must specify their objectives in behavioral terms; identify stakeholder groups directly and indirectly involved in creating desired outcomes; identify interests shared by the organization and

Figure 10.1.   Top Management Communication Table.

Objective	Approach	Channels
Top management trust and credibility	Communicate frequently, candidly and in a personal manner.	MBWA ("management by walking around"); regular business & social meetings with groups of employees; publish responses to employee questions/ complaints; share bad as well as good news; employee surveys & other feedback mechanisms.
Employee Security	Personal involvement in communicating significant organi- zation actions/ policies affecting employees' security concerns (e.g. wages, benefits, layoffs).	Live speeches/meetings with employees; public address system or telephone hotline; personal letters (e.g. mail-grams); video- taped remarks.
Employee Recognition	Personally & publicly involved in recog- nizing key employee contributions.	Personal presentation of awards; personal letters or notes; internal media coverage.
Employee Knowledge	Provide key organ- ization-wide infor- mation on a timely basis.	Organization public- ations or news vehicles; videotaped announcements; external media.
Employee Safety	During crisis, appropriate top managers serve as spokespersons in initiating distrib- ution of accurate, timely information for internal & external audiences.	Personal communication (e.g., telephone) with people most affected; personal (e.g., speech) or media delivery (e.g., memo, videotape) of key messages to employees, shareholders, customers, etc; news conferences, inter- views with media.

Source: From J. David Pincus and Robert E. Rayfield, "The Emerging Role of Top Management Communication: 'Turning On' Employee Commitment." Reprinted with permission from *Personnel Management: Communications*. Copyright 1985 by Prentice-Hall Information Services, 240 Frisch Court, Paramus, NJ 07652. All rights reserved.

the groups involved; determine what messages must be conveyed to engage those interests; and select those media or channels of communication most appropriate to reach the groups specified earlier.

In the process they must avoid several communication traps, including the temptation to conquer through volume, seduction, or secrecy. Lewis described them as "three popular theories of message transmission":

1. **Overpower 'em theory.** If you repeat something often enough, long enough, and yell loud enough, the message is bound to get through.

2. **Glamour theory.** If you take an idea and wrap it up in a very pretty package with a pretty bow, the receiver will be seduced into buying that idea.

3. **Don't tell 'em theory.** If you "don't tell 'em" anything, they don't have anything to gripe about, and they don't have anything to ask questions about. If you "don't tell 'em" anything, they don't have anything to form negative opinions about.

Types of Information

Information that should be conveyed falls into two basic categories, from which a number of subcategories can be derived. All of them have been developed over several decades through extensive research into what employees really want to know.

Studies of recent vintage have produced generally similar lists. Most employees want information concerning wage and salary policies, promotion opportunities, job security, and benefits. In recent years, company performance, management philosophy, and industry economic outlooks commanded mounting interest.

The basic categories thus become information that employees want and information that employers want them to have. Subcategories require a closer look. One recent survey by Foehenback and Rosenberg produced the following list of subjects in order of importance.

1. Organizations' plans for the future
2. Productivity improvement
3. Personnel policies and practices
4. Job-related information
5. Job advancement opportunities
6. Effect of external events on jobs
7. How jobs fit into the organization
8. Operations outside employees' departments or divisions
9. How the organization is doing competitively
10. Personnel changes and promotions
11. How the organization stands on current issues

12. How the organization uses its profits

13. Advertising and promotional plans

14. Financial results

15. Human interest stories about other employees

16. Personal news about other employees.

Much of the information that employers want employees to have relates directly to their jobs and to organizational economics. These topics in practice often are handled concurrently. Quality control, for example, has of late been high on the list of employee communication topics in manufacturing industries, for several reasons. High quality levels minimize waste in time and materials. They also attract and keep customers. Such information might also be categorized as that which management wants employees to have, but labels are relatively unimportant.

Management Information

Much of the information that management seeks to disseminate is designed to achieve organizational objectives. It falls in a lengthy list of categories. All are worthy of attention, but skilled communicators seek always to maintain an appropriate balance between "what they want" and "what we want them to have." Organizational information categories usually include

1. Organizational goals, purposes and directives, consistently identified in terms of common interests

2. Specific organizational tasks assigned to individuals or groups, which can frequently be "covered" in articles about promotions

3. Individual and group responsibilities, which can be conveyed while affording recognition to those involved

4. Use of communication channels, especially in a context encouraging their use

5. Encouraging compliance with policies, rules, and regulations, usually by explaining why they exist and why compliance is of benefit to all involved

6. Evaluating work performance and standards, often detailed in individual or departmental "success stories"

7. Coordinating organizational activities and maintaining high performance levels, also often cast in terms of recognition.

All of these needs must be satisfied through a comprehensive communication system that disseminates and gathers relevant information to facilitate achieving organizational goals.

Other Subjects

Both employers and employees benefit through mutual understanding of a multitude of other subjects. They vary in significance with circumstances, but almost always include the following.

New developments. What is new is necessarily news. Employees want any and all information indicating change in organizations. New products, new services, new divisions, and new markets are all of considerable interest.

Economic future. Employees are as interested in the economic health of the organization as shareholders and members of the financial community. Changing market conditions, sales projections, and the like should be regularly disseminated to them.

Employment prospects. Market data should be extrapolated to indicate any changes in the size or scope of the organization, especially as they may imply potential for promotions. Any anticipated organizational shrinkage with potential for layoffs should be communicated as well. Only where information is provided fully and on a timely basis will "rumor mills" be stilled.

Organizational information. Employees are interested in the background, history, and structure of employer organizations. Information that induces better understanding tends to create better attitudes.

Policy and procedure. Lack of understanding often creates more infractions of policy and procedure than any other factor. Employees are entitled to know organizational policies and procedures and the reasons why they exist. The latter element is especially important. Well-founded and well-understood policies tend to be far better observed than those that are not.

Employee accomplishments. Individually and in groups, employees want to know how they're doing. They take real pride in accomplishment. Recognition rewards accomplishment. From an organizational standpoint, it also serves to inform others as to what constitutes exceptional performance. Public praise and private censure should be organizational policy. Praise for performance tends to produce far better results than criticism of nonperformance.

Opportunity for advancement. Organizations should capitalize on every opportunity to encourage renewed employee effort by focusing on individual successes. Information concerning promotions, especially of long-time employees, should be freely disseminated. Characteristics that typify those selected for promotion should be emphasized. Successful employees can thus become role models for those who follow.

Job importance. Information about promotions can also serve to underscore the importance of the jobs involved. Employees want to know where their jobs fit into their organizations and how important their jobs are. They seek identity and accomplishment.

Income and profits. Other than in close-held organizations, income and profit figures almost always become public knowledge. They can be destructive or constructive where workers are concerned. They must be presented in contexts meaningful to employees, if the latter objective is to be achieved. What appears on newspapers' financial pages seldom produces that result.

Developmental plans. Announcements appearing in the mass media of organizational plans for the future are also usually deficient from an employee-relations standpoint. Information as to their meaning to current employees is often missing. Capital expenditure figures, which tend to prompt questions from workers, inevitably are included. The internal communication program should provide information from an employee perspective.

Communicators often sort information for employees into four basic categories, which might be used to expand the foregoing list in terms of specific organizations:

1. News and information about employees, management, the work, or the organization that keep employees abreast of contemporary conditions
2. Feature material showing all aspects of the organization and the ways in which its products and services benefit consumers; this category may also include information about employee skills, talents, extramural activities, and so forth
3. Policy, progress, technology, and other aspects of the organization of general interest, which should be oriented to illustrate the organization's goals and accomplishments
4. The current thinking in the organization as to its future, trends in its industry, and so on.

The lists are by no means all inclusive. They are exemplary of the types of information that interest employees and that employers should provide. When well disseminated, they can assist organizations in avoiding fundamental employee communication problems. Most often encountered among them are

1. Too much downward communication, often interpreted as "dictating to employees," and too little listening to their opinions
2. Misunderstanding of message content and, more often, message meaning, which most frequently occurs where managers and/or communicators fail to provide information in understandable context
3. Too much information about "what we want" and too little about "what they need"
4. Excessive propagandizing at the expense of candor
5. Too little specific information as to how the parties can work together for their mutual benefit.

Further insight into development of messages for employee groups can be gained by examining some of the message typologies that have been developed in recent years.

TYPES OF MESSAGES

Messages are created and exchanged by individuals seeking to advance their objectives or those of the organizations by which they are employed. Many message typologies have been developed over the years, seeking to categorize messages in one manner or another. Two most applicable to organizational communication were advanced by Katz and Kahn and by Goldhaber.

Katz and Kahn Typology

Five types of messages were identified by Katz and Kahn: job instructions, job rationale, procedures and practices, feedback, and indoctrination.

They defined job instructions as directives on how to perform specific tasks. Job rationale messages relate individual tasks to organizational tasks. Procedure and practice messages relate to organizational policies, rules, and regulations, and employee benefits. Feedback messages let employees know how they're doing in their jobs. Indoctrination messages are intended to motivate them by reinforcing overall organizational missions.

Goldhaber Typology

Goldhaber sorted messages into four categories: task, maintenance, human, and innovative.

Task messages, he said, give employees all information necessary to the performance of their jobs. They deal with products, services, and activities of interest to the organization. They relate to organizational outputs and include such subject matter as training, orientation, and goal setting.

Maintenance messages he defined as pertaining to organizational policy and regulation. They direct organizational progress toward generating products or services. They deal with achieving organizational output, while task messages deal with output content.

Human messages involve feelings, interpersonal relationships, self-concept, and morale. They are directed toward people and occur in praise for achievement, conflict solving, performance appraisal, and informal activities. Where human messages are neglected, morale problems tend to arise.

Innovative messages contain information concerning new plans, activities, programs, directions, projects, and products. They enable organizations to adapt to environmental change.

Message Management

Productive organizational communication programs, as indicated earlier, are designed to achieve specific purposes. These purposes are not arbitrarily

Figure 10.2. Organizational Goals and Communication Objectives.

If the organization's goal is to ...	Then the communication goals/objectives could include ...
Bring a new facility on line by March of next year.	Support development efforts by recognizing milestones and people who achieve them.
Add 100 nurses and medical technicians to the hospital staff within 60 days.	Help attract good people by publicizing opportunities and presenting the hospital as a good place to work.
Close the 200-employee regional headquarters in East Snowshoe by the first quarter of next year.	Mount a comprehensive internal and external communication program to generate understanding and support among employees and others in the East Snowshoe community.
Achieve 10% market penetration for a new product during the first year.	Support marketing communication efforts by rallying the sales force, other employees, shareowners and others with a stake in corporate success.
Reduce the year-to-year fleet accident rate by 50%.	Make safe driving a dominant theme in future issues of the organizational publication and other organizational media.

Source: From Thomas A. Ruddell, "Chartering the Communication Function." From *Inside Organizational Communication* 2E, edited by Carol Reuss and Donn Silvis. Copyright © 1985 by Longman. All rights reserved.

determined in the communication department. They are functional outgrowths of the organization's short-term goals and objectives. Communication programs must support management's efforts to move the organization from Point A to Point B.

Organizational priorities thus produce logical guidelines for message management, essentially a planning task through which communication priorities are established. Thomas A. Ruddell provided several appropriate examples (see Figure 10.2).

MANAGING COMMUNICATION

While the manager's role is increasingly a communication role, the organizational communicator's role too infrequently is a management role. These and other circumstances can create barriers to informational flows. They often occur because communicators lack adequate access to information and information sources. Less frequently, senior managers knowingly block communicator access to information.

Barriers become evident when employee use of communication channels is closely examined, as the results of a 1982 International Association of Business Communicators study show in the accompanying chart.

Employee Sources of Organizational Information

Current Rank		Preferred Rank
1	Immediate supervisors	1
2	Grapevine	15
3	Employee handbook and other booklets	4
4	Bulletin boards	9
5	Small group meetings	2
6	Regular employee publication	6
7	Annual report to employees	7
8	Regular local employee meetings	8
9	Mass meetings	11
10	Union	13
11	Orientation program	5
12	Top executives	3
13	Audio-visual programs	13
14	Mass media	14
15	Upward communication programs	10

The IABC data suggest that workers are no more enamored than managers of the grapevine as a communication channel. They also indicate strongly, however, that the grapevine can be best supplanted by top executives and improved orientation programs.

Access to Information

Information amenable to inclusion in employee communication programs exists in almost every component of contemporary organizations, from board rooms to supervisors' offices. Senior management's commitment to free information flows, however, may not be reflected at lower levels. "Need to know" approaches to organizational information handling, ingrained over time, do not readily yield to new systems.

These approaches have created the same sort of problems in organizations that security systems have triggered in government. The federal government, especially, has become notorious for overuse of security classification systems. Only in recent years, through the Freedom of Information Act, have the media been able to gain access to information of public interest that for no good or apparent reason had been classified.

Information Sources

Much of the information needed by those responsible for implementing communication programs may be denied them in like manner by middle managers. The problem can be minimized to some extent by positioning communication managers at organizational levels that afford access to necessary information. Constant reminders from senior management will, nevertheless, be necessary.

Organizational "freedom of information legislation" in the alternative may be necessary to facilitate "declassifying" nonsensitive materials. Senior managers, otherwise, will find it beneficial to assign high staff rank to senior communication executives, giving them access to meetings and memoranda from which such information may be obtained.

Communicator Skills

Responsibility for the communication function is best assigned to professionals. Most are skilled in human relationships, as well as communication, and are equipped to build intraorganizational relationships that enable them to develop necessary access to information. They also are sufficiently knowledgeable to determine what information should be communicated and how it can best be communicated to the benefit of the organization.

Organizational communication requires skills and knowledge of a sort that seldom exists, and they are not readily developed in senior management. They include technical as well as creative capabilities. Communication specialists are expert in message synthesis, and are also sufficiently familiar with alternative channels of communication to select those that will be most productive in any given set of circumstances. They will follow five rules enunciated by Robert M. Fulmer for successful communication necessary to communicator and manager alike:

Clarity. Words should be selected with care and used sparingly. Communicators should be sensitive to different meanings which can attach to words and be governed accordingly.

Completeness. All important facts must be provided. The journalist's formula provides a valid guideline when doubt arises: who, what, when, why, where and how.

Conciseness. Use as few words as possible and avoid technical or other difficult language, especially with newcomers to the organization or industry.

Concreteness. Be specific. Flowery memoranda have no merit in organizational communication. Avoid the vernacular and regional colloquialisms.

Correctness. Be accurate and truthful at all times. False and misleading information inevitably returns to haunt the communicator.

SUMMARY

Successful organizational communication programming begins with a strong philosophical commitment by senior management, which those involved are prepared to support with individual efforts. Philosophical statements ideally express the organization's commitment to all stakeholder groups. They also serve to support communication policies dedicated to the mutual interests of organizations and their employees.

The economic welfare of organizations and their employees today are inextricably intertwined. Commitment to fair dealing enables management to engage employees in this context, enhancing their understanding of political and economic problems with which organizations must deal, and enlisting their support.

Design of informational programs then becomes a relatively simple task. Types of information in which employees are interested have been well established through research. Communications managers need only adapt existing lists to meet the needs of their own organizations.

Organizational goals provide sound bases for the development of communication goals and objectives that provide ongoing guidance for communicators. If the communicators are to fulfill their objectives successfully, however, they must have access to information within their organizations. Access can best be assured by granting the communication unit adequate authority to obtain necessary data.

Communication tasks should be assigned to communication professionals if programs are to have optimum potential to achieve desired results.

ADDITIONAL READING

Aiello, Robert J. "They Hear You...But They're Not Listening," *Public Relations Journal,* March 1983.
Baird, John E., and Patricia H. Bradley. "Communication Correlates of Employee Morale," *Journal of Business Communication* 15:3
DeMare, George. *Communicating at the Top: What You Need to Know about Communicating to Run an Organization,* 2d ed. New York: Wiley, 1979.
Foehenback, Julie, and Kam Rosenberg. "How Are We Doing," *Journal of Communication Management* 12, 1984.
Fulmer, Robert M. *Practical Human Relations.* Homewood, IL: Irwin, 1983.
Goldhaber, Gerald M. *Organizational Communication,* 4th ed. Dubuque, IA: Brown, 1986.

Kreps, Gray L. *Organizational Communication: Theory and Practice.* New York: Longman, 1986.

Lewis, Phillip V. *Organizational Communication: The Essence of Effective Management,* 2d ed. Columbus, OH: Grid, 1980.

Moore, H. Frazier, and Frank B. Kalupa. *Public Relations: Principles, Cases and Problems,* 9th ed. Homewood, IL: Irwin, 1985.

Muchinsky, Paul M. "Organizational Communication: Relationships to Organizational Climate and Job Satisfaction," *Academy of Management Journal,* December 1977.

Nolte, Lawrence W. *Fundamentals of Public Relations: Professional Guidelines, Concepts & Integrations.* New York: Pergamon, 1979.

Reuss, Carol, and Donn Silvis, eds. *Inside Organizational Communication,* 2d ed. New York: Longman, 1985.

Ruddell, Thomas A. "Chartering the Communication Function," in Carol Reuss and Donn Silvis, eds., *Inside Organizational Communication,* 2d ed. New York: Longman, 1985.

11
SELECTING
COMMUNICATION CHANNELS

Channel selection in organizational communication involves a series of compromises. There are many substitutes for face-to-face discussion, but none are perfect. All involve sacrifices. Their use, nevertheless, increases with organizational size and complexity. Managers must select from among them in keeping with changing circumstances.

Five criteria are usually involved in selection processes in four channel categories: personal, print, electronic, and display. The criteria are speed, selectivity, acceptance, feedback, and cost.

Personal communication channels include social functions, interviews, meetings, letters, memoranda, directives, reports, and agreements. Print channels consist of organizational publications, booklets, manuals, paycheck stuffers, books, reprints, and the like. Motion pictures, videotapes, slide/tape presentations, filmstrips, audiocassettes, audiodiscs, telephones, television, radio, teletype, facsimiles, and so on comprise electronic channels. Display channels include billboards, bulletin boards, and exhibits.

SELECTION CRITERIA

The five selection criteria in making channel selections are outlined below.

The speed with which messages will be delivered. Variation in speed of delivery is probably the greatest differentiator of communication channels. Messages can be transmitted and received in moments by telephone. Memoranda may require an hour or more. Newsletters or magazines can take weeks or months.

The selectivity of the channel. Here, selectivity means the extent to which messages will be confined to particular audiences. Personal letters and telephone calls provide the greatest selectivity. Information delivered through group meetings or circulated memoranda is addressed to larger groups. Bulletin-board or organizational-publication messages are nonselective within the organization.

The credibility of the channel from the perspective of message recipients. Information reduced to printed or other durable form is generally perceived as more credible than that delivered verbally or electronically. Variation also exists within the print area. Books are usually deemed more credible than leaflets. Informal word of mouth is generally considered least credible.

The extent to which feedback is necessary and to which it is generated by various channels. The greatest amount of feedback is obtained in face-to-face communication. Small meetings usually come next, in order of volume. When the value of feedback does not deteriorate with time, surveys can measure the effectiveness of other channels of communication.

The cost involved. Cost must be considered in terms of time as well as dollars. A few hours of senior managers' time in meetings can be considerably more expensive than circulating a memorandum or newsletter.

All of these factors must be taken into account in selecting any communication channel. They can be successfully considered, however, only in the light of specific circumstances. Relative urgency in message delivery tends to be the most significant among them, but others can become paramount in certain situations.

A major organizational announcement, for example, may be of such significance to personnel that concurrent notification is considered necessary. Audio or video teleconferences may then prove to be the best channels. Information as to a pending change in employee benefits, however, might be adequately disseminated through the next issue of the organization's employee publication.

PERSONAL CHANNELS

Personal communication involves more than face-to-face meetings. Individually addressed letters, memoranda, or postcards fall in this category. So do telephone calls and interviews.

Somewhat less personal, since they usually involve several individuals, are conversations during social events, reports, proposals, and directives. Small group meetings also retain a somewhat personal flavor.

Each of these devices should be used to the greatest possible extent in organizational communication. Relative cost can be high in larger organizations, but benefits are correspondingly great. Employee perceptions of impersonality tend to mount with organizational growth. Individuals come to perceive themselves as being treated like cogs in a machine, whether or not this is the case.

Several remedial devices are available to management. One of them, a relatively informal approach, has come to be called "management by walking around." Another requires periodic meetings between managers and their immediate subordinates. These latter are expensive in manager and worker time, but benefits will increasingly outweigh cost, as competitive labor markets develop. A third involves planned use of personal communication techniques on the part of all organizational managers and supervisors.

Management by Walking Around

The concept is what the name implies: senior managers getting out of their offices and spending time on the shop floor or in other operational departments. In practice, somewhat more is required. The process should not involve a series of inspection tours of a militaristic sort. Visits should be unscheduled, informal, and undertaken on a leisurely basis.

Those involved should conscientiously pause in every department or operating unit and engage workers selected at random in conversations concerning their jobs. Their ideas for improvement should be actively solicited. Their suggestions should be requested as to products or services as well as policies and procedures.

Most important, there should be follow-up. Managers should note the names and ideas of those with whom they speak. Thank-you notes may be in order. Responses in writing are appropriate in any event.

Not a few senior managers have found such activities highly productive of ideas and suggestions. More important, they gain a far better insight into the workings of their organizations and the thinking of their personnel.

Small Group Meetings

Quality circles have of late become increasingly popular in business and industry. They also have been highly productive for organizations in several ways. Money-saving ideas have been generated in quantity by quality circles. Often more important, they have created greater understanding on the part of individuals involved as to their roles in organizations.

Regularly scheduled, small group meetings in operational units can institutionalize the employee-input process on a less formal basis. Unlike quality circles, which most frequently meet on members' own time, such meetings would have to be scheduled during working hours. Productivity might suffer a bit as a result, but mid- to long-term benefits more than offset costs.

Formal agendas, covering employee as well as managerial or supervisory concerns, should be followed. Time should be allowed to discuss individuals' work-related problems or suggestions for improvement. Most important, reports to middle or senior managers, covering the concerns of all involved, should be required.

The latter process provides a basis for still further personal communication. Middle or senior managers should acknowledge worthwhile ideas and suggestions. A brief note on the reverse side of a business card is sufficient. It tells the employees involved that they are important; that management is listening and responding to their concerns.

Personal Communication

Listening, responding, and caring are what personal communication is all about. It is a dying feature of contemporary civilization in many ways. Thank-you notes to hosts and hostesses are seldom seen today. Their counterparts in organizations are even more rare.

The problem in organizational settings arises out of timeworn and now inapplicable concepts of employee–employer relationships. They were founded on the premise that wages should buy productivity and loyalty, and that managers' primary responsibility is to see that these "commodities" are diligently delivered. As a result, communication tends to fall into largely negative patterns. Directives and reprimands flow freely. Employee contributions are taken for granted.

Relatively little effort, however, is required to modify this pattern. In the process, managers earn and receive greater loyalty and productivity than otherwise would be forthcoming. Senior management need only require that middle managers and supervisors seek out and acknowledge meritorious conduct on the part of individual employees. The acknowledgment may be nothing more than a thank-you, although preferably delivered in writing with copies to senior management and the employee's personnel file.

The process deals with the "little things," which are often disproportionately significant in differentiating one organization from another in the eyes of employees and prospective employees. They generate unusually high returns on small investments. This is inevitably the case, for example, where supervisors' thank-you's are expressed in public, and where interoffice mail brings the executives' thank-you notes. Recipients are more flattered and others work harder as a result.

PRINT CHANNELS

Organizational communication for the most part is intended to inform or educate. Impersonal channels of communication—print and electronic—for the most part can be categorized as primarily informational or primarily educational. The former category includes organizational newsletters and magazines. Manuals, handbooks, paycheck stuffers, brochures, and booklets are usually in the latter group. The five criteria listed above—speed, selectivity, acceptance, feedback, and cost—are all involved in the selection and use of these channels of communication.

Informational Channels

Employee publications are probably the most frequently used of the organizational communication channels. They range in form from relatively sophisticated magazines to tabloid newspapers and often are circulated as newsletters. Although many in the graphic arts would argue strongly to the contrary, publication content is of greater importance than packaging in determining effectiveness.

Editorial response to the question, What's in it for me? is the key to success. Articles about new products or services are as interesting as those about benefit programs, provided management is prepared to handle them in appropriate fashion. Employees want to know what new products or services mean in terms of anticipated revenues and profits. They are concerned with what percentage of revenues is allocated to wages and benefits. They are interested in the market for the new product and the competition it may face.

Publication content. Employees expected to be concerned about the organization and its efforts must be informed about them. Unnecessary secrecy must be avoided. If the organization is preparing a new advertising campaign, ads should appear first in the employee publications. When a plant is expanding—or closing—employees should be informed before the events are reported in newspapers.

Virtually any topic can be addressed in terms of employee self-interest. Accidents cost dollars, which otherwise can be used for other purposes—including employee compensation. Absenteeism produces similar results and places unnecessary burdens on coworkers. Legislative proposals can make organizational operations more costly and/or less profitable.

Other publications. The publication concept can be applied in several other ways. Many organizations supplement monthly or quarterly magazines or newspapers with single-sheet bulletins distributed on a weekly or even a daily basis. Some are designed for general distribution, others for smaller audiences.

Management newsletters or bulletins are often published in large organizations. Most are issued daily or weekly. Many deal primarily in policy and production matters, but senior managers are increasingly using newsletters to convey information concerning organizational problems and opportunities.

Daily bulletins for general internal consumption also appear to be increasing in number in larger organizations. These often are circulated in employee lunchrooms and include industry-related information as well as timely internal announcements.

EDUCATIONAL CHANNELS

Education has long been an ongoing process in most organizations. It begins with employee orientation through personnel policy and procedure handbooks, employee-benefits manuals, and similar documents. Orientation processes also serve to introduce organizations' performance-evaluation and compensation systems and documents associated with them.

These and related subjects are usually dealt with in books, booklets, brochures, or similar mechanical formats. As is the case with informational publications, content is more important than format. It must be designed to meet the needs of the groups to which it is directed. This may be no small task. Organizations such as hospitals employ individuals with diverse educational backgrounds. Physicians and maintenance personnel may be members of the same audience.

Mixed Uses

The groups of communication channels described above function primarily in specified categories. None can be wholly excluded, however, from "doing double duty" as need and circumstances occasionally dictate. Safety regulations propounded in policy/procedure manuals, for example, can readily be and often are reinforced through newsletters and other publications.

It is appropriate here to underscore a point made earlier. Channels of communication must be applied in keeping with overall communication plans. Plan objectives and audience characteristics dictate the nature of messages and the channels through which they should be delivered. They are discussed here in groups as a matter of logical organization, rather than implying any rigidity in their application. Electronic channels must be considered in like manner.

ELECTRONIC CHANNELS

Electronic channels are equally useful in delivering educational and informational messages and are more effective than the print variety in some circumstances. Audiovisual media are especially helpful where detailed instructions are necessary, where a more personal vehicle is preferred, or where senders seek to evoke emotional responses. Some offer distinct advantages where message-transmission-time factors become critical. They are most amenable to examination in terms of user time factors. Some produce almost instantaneous communication. Others can be activated in a relatively short time. Still others require considerable preparation.

Instantaneous Communication

No form of communication, science tells us, is instantaneous. Nevertheless, several channels available to contemporary communicators are tantamount to being instantaneous.

The telephone probably best approaches the concept of instantaneous, especially where communication is taken to mean verbal exchanges or two-way communication. Communication of this sort can be accomplished through wired and portable systems, including air-to-ground links being introduced by some airlines.

The teletype permits communication at an only slightly slower speed and is advantageous where verbatim written records are necessary. The same result can be achieved in computer-to-computer communication, where at least one machine is equipped with components and software necessary to preserve verbatim transcripts.

Facsimile transmission is another high-speed vehicle through which messages can be transmitted almost instantaneously. It is most appropriately used where relatively close copies of original documents are necessary. Federal Express Corporation's now defunct ZAP Mail service was essentially a facsimile system. Similar equipment is available from commercial vendors to transmit typed or printed information within or between organizations.

Short-Term Channels

More time, although not a great deal more, is necessary where some of the devices listed above are used to link more than two individuals. Telephone conference calls, for example, require little more time to complete when all of the parties are available. The same is true in the case of computer conferences.

Time requirements tend to increase with group size. Prearrangement is usually necessary when telephone or computer conferences involve more than three persons. This is especially true where computers are used. Those equipped with modems (modulator–demodulators) necessary to link them to telephone lines are not always readily available.

Where one-way communication is adequate, other devices can be used in relatively short time frames. They include unedited audiotapes and videotapes. The former are often used to disseminate quickly, to those unable to attend, the content of professional meetings. Videotape is less often used in unedited form.

Audiotapes or videotapes of a meeting can be transported, with contemporary package delivery service, to remote sites around the world in little more than a day. Their content can be transmitted by satellite, where time pressures override the costs involved.

Telephone "hot lines" are also used by many organizations to facilitate response to employee questions and concerns. They are usually linked to tape recorders, from which messages are periodically extracted for review and response.

Long-Term Channels

Long and short are relative terms. Their meanings may vary with message sophistication as well as technology. Audiotape and videotape, for example, technically can be played back immediately after recording. Users, however, may insist that "raw" tapes be edited for any of several reasons, delaying their availability for playback. User criteria as to message quality thus becomes the limiting factor.

Videoconferencing, on the other hand, can immediately create instantaneous contact among groups of individuals at several distant sites. Considerable preparation is required, however, in bringing groups involved to sites equipped with the necessary equipment. Even where this problem does not exist, satellite transponders may not be readily available. Technology may thus impose significant time requirements.

Longer-Term Channels

There is considerable variation among communication channels that impose lengthy production-time requirements. Technology again is the primary determinant. The channels involved include edited videotape, slide-tape, film strips, and audiodiscs. In each instance, temporal requirements can be minimized where budgets permit.

Time required in producing slide/tape presentations, for example, usually is governed by slide-developing processes. Audiotape production can be completed quickly, once there is a script. High-speed duplicating equipment is available in most major cities.

Processing time. Preparing slides is another matter. Multiple subjects at several sites are often involved. When photography has been completed, film must be processed before duplicates can be made—a relatively time-consuming process. Laboratories can be persuaded to work overtime, but costs escalate at a disproportionate rate.

Film strips can be prepared from slides and audiodiscs from audiotapes, but these processes also are time consuming. Videotape editing and duplicating can usually be accomplished more rapidly than slide/tape and film-strip production. Only motion picture production takes more time. The motion picture process, however, is more often eliminated from consideration by cost than time or utilitarian factors.

Film versus tape. Commercial motion picture production costs can involve thousands of dollars per minute of finished film. Equipment is more delicate and bulky than that used in videotape production, and lighting requirements are considerably more rigorous. Time required in exposing, processing, and editing film in normal circumstances consumes months. Videotape requires none of the processing necessary with film, and fidelity is only marginally inferior. The finished, edited product in its most sophisticated form can be ready in days or weeks, rather than months.

On the reverse side of the coin, finished motion picture film is often easier to use than videotape. Many organizations lack the necessary equipment for tape. Where equipment is available, tape widths can vary, potentially rendering any given tape valueless.

Another variable. One other variable influences decisions concerning videotape and motion pictures: alternative dissemination channels. Some organizations, most notably hospitals, maintain extensive internal electronic communication systems. Where cable video systems exist, film or videotape content can be quickly disseminated, so that either vehicle can be valuable.

"Captive" radio outlets also are occasionally available to some organizations—for example, campus radio stations—and can sometimes be useful communication channels. And organizations often purchase radio time to notify employees of changes in work schedules during periods of bad weather.

Thus, use of electronic channels is a matter of time in several senses. One is the amount of time necessary to prepare materials. The other is the amount of time needed for planning. Where adequate planning time is available and no substantive cost constraints exist, communicators are free to select channels that will best suit audience characteristics.

DISPLAY CHANNELS

The best way to communicate in terms of a given issue at any time usually involves several channels. Usually time is a limiting factor, but many if not most subjects on which management should communicate can be anticipated. Many are strongly calendar oriented. Fiscal years, holiday periods, and health insurance contract renewal dates are well known. Others are less definite, but highly predictable. Organizational managers are aware months or years in advance of impending changes in policy, of construction or closing of production facilities, and of the introduction of new products. Other than in crises, organizations seldom are pressed to select less than the best channels to meet any need, which makes display channels highly productive.

Channel Characteristics

Display channels, like others, vary in applicability. Developmental time is a major variable. Bulletin boards can be used in minutes within individual buildings. With some coordination, messages can be posted at near-identical times in multiple locations.

Bulletin boards are considerably more complex channels than they appear. Materials must be displayed to attract the eye. They also must be changed at appropriate intervals. Nothing is quite so ineffective as a bulletin board at which no one stops. Messages removed too soon also fall short of producing optimum benefit.

Perhaps the best solution to the two problems developed to date involves a color-coding scheme. Items to be posted are mounted on craft paper. A different color is used for each day. Every item remains on the board for exactly one week. Employees who know the code can readily find items posted since last they checked the board.

Another successful approach involves a divided, two-purpose board. One segment is reserved for management use; the other for employee use. The latter postings attract personnel who inevitably read the former as well. Like the employer segment of the board, the employee segment requires maintenance. It is most palatably managed by requiring messages be dated and left for predetermined times. They are removed by those who maintain the management component of the board.

Bulletin boards are also appropriate for externally supplied materials, ranging from United Fund posters to those available through the National Safety Council and the many health and welfare-related agencies, private and public. Some of these can also be used on internal billboards.

Billboard Applications

Billboards, either large outdoor models or smaller indoor versions, require something more. Materials must be prepared by printing or photography, which may take days or weeks.

Time requirements, as in the case of other channels, should not discourage billboard use. In many organizations they are quite common and serve many purposes. Manufacturing plants often use billboards as safety reminders. A plant's consumer products can also be featured from time to time at locations visible from the premises and surrounding areas. Product billboards in most cases are designed to instill pride in employees as well as sales in the community. They have proven successful in both respects.

Displays

Conceivably, displays may require still more time in preparation than bill-boards. In many organizations, however, displays already exist, but remain in storage for much of each year. These are the displays that virtually every manufacturer takes to trade shows; those that some use in recruiting activities, that others use at sales meetings; and that still others use as airport display units. They can be major components of organizational education programs.

Using these displays in areas frequented by employees is a simple matter in single-site organizations. It is little more difficult where multiple locations are involved. Those involved in employee communication need only contact other departments involved and schedule in-house displays just before or after other uses. This process minimizes handling and maximizes return on the organization's investment. Ideal display locations are in or adjacent to cafeterias, lobby areas, and other points at which employees congregate.

SUGGESTION SYSTEMS

One communication channel, the suggestion system, cannot logically be considered a part of any of the groups specified above. Suggestion systems are used in several designs, varying primarily in formality. They range from full-featured systems with major reward potential in large organizations to informal systems often incorporated in employee publications.

Large organizations' systems usually offer rewards in either lump sums or as a percentage of savings realized through implementation of the idea proposed. Some also offer lump-sum awards for suggestions pertaining to organizational safety.

These systems are complex and expensive, due to the need for user anonymity in the evaluation process and potential legal pitfalls. Meeting these requirements entails considerable paper work as well as reviewer time and effort. Active systems may require as many as one staff member for each 2,500 to 3,000 employees.

Informal systems, sometimes referred to as Good Idea programs, may entail nothing more than a suggestion coupon published in an employee newsletter. A small reward, usually $25 to $50, is given each month to those submitting either usable ideas or the best idea.

Suggestion system benefits often extend beyond the obvious. The systems are conducive to employee anonymity and often encourage messages concerning real or perceived problems. Senior managers are well advised to monitor these closely and provide for adequate follow-up. Not a few major organizational problems have been identified from time to time, as a result of what appeared to be a "crank note."

COMPOUNDING BENEFITS

Most organizations spend large sums over the course of a year in producing and distributing messages of various kinds in a multitude of formats. Ongoing communication efforts may be directed toward shareholders and the financial community; governmental agencies at municipal, county, state, and federal levels; dealers, distributors, and customers; community groups; and the mass media. As in the case of trade-show displays, almost all programs involved generate materials that can be used in enhancing employee communications.

Such efforts are beneficial for several reasons. First, they compound the organization's return on communication investments. Second, they minimize the potential for delivery of conflicting messages to diverse stakeholder groups. Third, they promote cooperation among the several communication disciplines within the organization.

Return on Investment

Extended use of materials produces incremental additional costs, ranging from negligible to near nonexistent. As any who have dealt with printing understand, additional copies of a brochure or newsletter add little to basic production costs. Additional audio or videotapes may be a bit more expensive on a unit basis than is the case with printing. The bulk of the production cost is incurred in producing the first tape, however, and any productive expansion in audience is economically accomplished.

The same principle applies in other areas. Advertising, marketing, and sales-promotion materials can add to the impact of employee communication programs, especially where they are exposed to personnel before being used in their primary applications. This is readily accomplished in almost every case, since these materials must be completed by the departments and/or agencies involved far in advance of ultimate publication or distribution dates.

The benefits are twofold. First, prior internal exposure tends to enhance morale. Employees perceive themselves as being made party to "inside" information, as being "in the know." Second, their conversation with outsiders about impending promotional efforts serves to attract greater attention to those efforts. Where consumer goods are involved, this can be a significant sales advantage as well.

Eliminating Conflicts

Apparent conflict in messages prepared for diverse audiences occurs too easily in many organizations. Those synthesizing and transmitting information are well intentioned, but resultant perceptions can be damaging.

Consider, for example, the content of annual or quarterly reports, as well as executives' speeches reported by the media. They tend to be strongly affirmative in nature, using the best-foot-forward approach almost without exception. Where economic results are less than anticipated, management tends to counter them with a brightly painted picture of the future. The organization may be concurrently caught up in an internal austerity program involving a wage freeze, a hiring freeze, or worse. If the future is so bright, employees wonder, why is the organization taking such harsh measures?

Conflict compounding. Further conflict often occurs where senior managers' rewards become public knowledge during austerity campaigns. Bonuses granted to top executives in such conditions can seldom be kept secret, even in nonpublic organizations, and they tend to generate considerable rank-and-file dissatisfaction, no matter how well deserved.

Such unnecessary conflict can be eliminated or minimized through cross-application of communication devices or modification in management practices. Chrysler Corporation's handling of Lee Iacocca's compensation during the organization's economic crisis of the early 1980s is exemplary of the latter approach. Iacocca announced that he was working for a dollar a year although his stock options later permitted him to reap disproportionately high rewards. Any salary commensurate with his position would have been an irritant to employees, who were being asked to take wage cuts at the time. When the company's fortunes had improved and rank-and-file wages were being increased, his huge stock-option profits produced no significant negative response.

Eliminating negatives. A potential for negative employee response is readily eliminated in normal circumstances by providing employees with copies of annual reports, together with explanatory material. Some organizations go so far as to publish annual reports for personnel as separate documents or in supplemental pages bound into limited numbers of copies of the shareholder report.

Considerable care must be taken in developing the messages involved, especially where employee economic education traditionally has been neglected. The value of cash or stock dividends, for example, must be explained with exquisite care. Millions of dollars in dividends to shareholders can appear disproportionately generous in the eyes of individuals whose wage increments are measured in pennies per hour. Where dividends are expressed in percentile terms as return on investment, and where the percentages involved are compared with contemporary bank interest rates, amounts involved become more reasonable.

Enhanced acceptance. Dividends are especially acceptable where management discharges its commitment to equity in dealing with stakeholder groups. Comparison of amounts allocated to wage/benefit programs with those earmarked for dividends then tend to be viewed favorably by employees. Such comparisons produce the most favorable responses where performance-based compensation systems are in place and management can compare percentages of increased revenues or profits allocated to employees and shareholders.

Virtually every document and speech used in shareholder and financial communication programs should be made a part of the employee communication effort. The process enhances the economic education of employees while creating greater message consistency.

Interdepartmental Conflict

The same process of avoiding negative responses should be applied in every communication program both to enhance message consistency and for another significant reason. Communicators aware that their messages will be broadly disseminated to multiple stakeholder groups will be more prone to avoid potential conflict.

This occurs because messages involved are examined from the outset in the light of their impact on the audiences involved. Communicators should be required, for example, to weigh potential affirmative impact on shareholders and the financial community against prospective negative responses on the part of employees.

Alternative controls. Multiple applications of communication materials is one of several organizational procedures that tend to minimize potential message conflict. A more beneficial long-term approach involves reorganizing traditionally independent communication functions in a single cohesive unit responsible for all communication functions, internal and external.

Historical development of the communication functions in the United States has produced traditional fragmentation in most organizations. Advertising, public relations, marketing, and employee communications are often housed in free-standing units. They compete in most cases for organizational resources and turf, the latter created primarily by delineating the constituencies they serve.

Unified organizations. Most organizations would be better served by unified communication staffs. Substantive benefits would accrue economically and in the consistency of messages. Multiple communication units produce duplication in resources. Expenses are unnecessarily high, even when this does not occur, since little effort is made to coordinate programs or minimize overlaps.

Larger organizations, as indicated earlier, frequently produce many newsletters. Content at times is duplicative. Even greater duplication is often advisable to give stakeholders as much information as possible in a consistent fashion.

This objective is most economically achieved in a unitary communication organization. Such an organization, with all information at hand for all stakeholder groups, can design publications whose content would be of interest to all the groups involved. Two four-page newsletters, for example, might consist of six original pages. Two of the pages would be different in the two newsletters and the remaining two would be the same. Net result: two fewer pages produced and audiences better served.

Other economies occur as well, especially where state-of-the-art technology is in use. Where text material is compiled with compatible microcomputers, and both typesetting and composition are handled from original computer files, production costs are substantially lowered. Another benefit, in the form of reduced operating expenses, is thus created.

MESSAGE EFFECTIVENESS

While message consistency is vital to the effectiveness and productivity of communication programs, repetitiveness is equally important. Communicators often neglect this aspect of their efforts, falling victim to what has been termed the "if-it's-raining-here-it's-raining-everywhere syndrome." They assume, naturally if erroneously, that messages they send are universally received, understood, and acted upon.

They tend to neglect some of the well-know but seldom-pondered features of contemporary communication reality. First among them is information overload. Virtually no individual today can receive, assimilate, and store all information to which he or she is exposed. Second is media audience fragmentation. In a day when the strongest daily newspapers reach less than 70 percent of households in their market areas, the term "mass media" is virtually an oxymoron. Third is individual selectivity among media as well as messages. Organizational communication channels are far from universally used among employees.

Lessons from Advertising

The circumstances described above require that messages be repeated within and across channels. Organizational communicators dealing with employee audiences need to adopt some of the tactics of their colleagues in advertising and marketing, with repetitiveness foremost among them. The tactic need not be "done to death" in the manner of some broadcast commercials, but must be adopted if adequate audience penetration is to be achieved.

Other advertising and marketing techniques are also worthy of emulation. Messages must be cast in terms of self-interest rather than organizational interest. Consumers may sell products or services, but individuals buy real or perceived benefits, often the latter. As the president of a major corporation once said during a television interview, "We manufacture cosmetics, but we sell hope." A plant safety campaign will be more prone to succeed with the theme, "Don't Make A Widow of Your Wife" than with "Reduce Our Insurance Costs."

Lessons from Marketing

Marketing has successfully embraced a military concept worth incorporating in other communication disciplines: Know your enemy. Marketing has succeeded through results obtained by understanding motivators and audiences, especially the latter. These understandings have led to enhanced message synthesis and media selection.

While advertising deals traditionally with the mass media—newspaper, radio, television, and outdoor—marketing has gone beyond to reach the prospective consumer where he or she lives. Innovation has been the watchword. In recent years it has produced a host of new media, ranging from coupons to miniature billboards attached to grocery store shopping carts.

The latter device was prompted by a decline in mass-media audiences, coupled with research that demonstrated that 60 percent of grocery-store purchasing decisions were made in the store.

Success in employee communication requires similar insights based on research. Where audiences are highly literate, newsletters may be most productive. Where literacy is marginal, they should be supplanted by audiovisual devices. Motivators, messages, and media all must be audience oriented.

SUMMARY

Selection of communication channels is a complex process, with many variables requiring careful consideration. In many cases several channels must be used to assure message delivery. Criteria for channel selection include speed of transmission, selectivity of audience members, credibility of the channel, necessity for feedback, and cost factors involved.

Channels of communication can be categorized as personal, print, electronic, and display. Personal channels involve direct communication in person or otherwise. Display channels include bulletin boards, posters, and displays.

Personal channels arguably are the most neglected and potentially the most productive in organizational communication. They require the individual effort of managers using multiple techniques. "Management by walking around," small group meetings, and a variety of personal communication techniques are among them.

Print channels include publications, manuals, handbooks, paycheck stuffers, brochures, booklets, and the like. These can be grouped by primary purpose. Most are oriented either toward informing or educating, although all can be used for both purposes. Publications, in any of a number of forms, are probably the most popular. They range in sophistication from mimeographed newsletters to sophisticated magazines. Content, however, is of far greater importance than production technique.

Electronic channels are more amenable to categorizing by time required for their use. They range from the telephone to motion pictures. The former produces communication in seconds, while the latter may require months in production.

Displays are the most neglected of devices in the display channel category. Many that are presumably available for use with employee groups are created for trade- and professional-show use and may sit idle for most of any given year.

Benefits attaching to any group of communication channels can be compounded where materials created for one stakeholder group are made available for others. Extensive use of materials produces greater economy, by limiting potential for conflicting messages and inducing greater cooperation within communication disciplines.

ADDITIONAL READING

Alten, Stanley R. *Audio in Media,* 2d ed. Belmont, CA: Wadsworth, 1986.

Breach, Mark, Steven Shepro, and Ken Russon. *Getting it Printed: How to Work with Printers and Graphic Arts Services to Assure Quality, Stay on Schedule and Control Costs.* Portland, OR: Coast to Coast, 1986.

Degen, Clara, ed. *Understanding and Using Video.* New York: Longman, 1985.

Kindem, Gorham. *The Moving Image: Production Principles and Practices.* Glenview, IL: Scott, Foresman, 1987.

Lazer, Ellen A., et al. *The Teleconferencing Handbook: A Guide to Cost-Effective Communication.* White Plains, NY: Knowledge Industry Publications, 1983.

Pickens, Judy E. *The Copy To Press Handbook: Preparing Words and Art for Print.* New York: Wiley, 1985.

White, Jan V. *Mastering Graphics: Design and Production Made Easy.* New York: Bowker, 1983.

12
GETTING THE JOB DONE

One further ingredient is necessary to produce new organizational settings and new managers to meet the needs of new workers. Organizations require multiple bodies of knowledge, communication skills, and the will and ability to apply them entrepreneurially. These elements may be embodied in a single individual or a group. Given the requirements, the latter is more often the case.

Successful organizational communication units require more diverse capabilities than once was the case. Professional communicators must be adept in handling personal, print, and audiovisual communication. They must be expert writers in all areas and knowledgeable in associated production techniques. They must be armed with insight into human behavior generally and in organizations. Most important, they must be prepared to serve as the organization's early warning system. Successful communicators must identify social, political, and economic trends that may impact the organization and define alternative courses of action for management.

Put another way, success in communication requires knowledge of organizational suprasystems and subsystems and the skills necessary to communicate with all their components. Professionals must know their organizations, the industries of which they are part, and the social, political, and governmental milieus in which the industries operate. They must be equally at home with the organization's divisions, departments, and workers and with other stakeholders, understanding their formal and informal interrelationships.

EDUCATIONAL BACKGROUND

Communicators' educational backgrounds may or may not be individually critical to their organizations. Collectively, however, they should contain certain essentials. These include, at minimum:

1. Communication, including course work in writing for the print and electronic media; production for the print and electronic media; and communication strategies

2. Specialized communication disciplines including public relations, advertising, marketing, and organizational communication
3. Business, including economics, management, and strategic planning
4. Social sciences, including psychology, sociology, and anthropology.

Communicator knowledge in all areas should include both the theoretical and the practical. Undergraduate liberal arts course work necessarily includes English, history, physical sciences, mathematics, and philosophy. Graduate degrees most favored for communicators are in business and communication.

Media Backgrounds

Least appropriate, in the absence of extensive practical experience, are communicators educated for careers with the news media. Changes in communication techniques have rendered traditional journalism education programs inappropriate in organizational communication, public relations, and other disciplines.

This is due to the relatively narrow scope of curricula involved. Print and electronic journalists are ill equipped to cope with each others' specialties. Broadcast personalities, in addition, may have little or no training in communication beyond that necessary to read a script and project well on camera.

Journalists are often employed in organizational settings at lower and middle echelons. Equipped with print backgrounds, they may be qualified to serve apprenticeships writing for employee publications or other media. Those with electronic backgrounds may be similarly employed where organizations make extensive use of audiovisual technologies. Several years of organizational experience may ultimately equip them for broader responsibility.

Business Backgrounds

With one exception, business graduates are seldom adequately equipped educationally for organizational communication. The exception involves those whose academic backgrounds are in human resources management. They may or may not, however, be appropriately skilled in communication.

Graduates of traditional business curricula tend to be more oriented toward dollars or widgets than the people who produce them. Organizations require the services of accountants, production managers, and others oriented toward business management. They are apt to be inept in organizational communication, however, in an era in which exceptional skills are essential.

EXPERIENTIAL BACKGROUND

Skilled communicators, with diverse experiential backgrounds, are found in many organizations. Some are adequately equipped for organizational situations. Others are not.

Organizational communication units require personnel with experiential backgrounds in similarly structured organizations. Experience in manufacturing, distribution, or institutions, for example, is a major asset to those who would succeed in such settings.

The critical factor is not in the nature of the organizations but in their generally similar structures, functions, and personnel complements. Exposure to each of these, and especially to structural idiosyncrasies and personnel, is invaluable to the communicator.

Organizational Structures

No two organizations are identically structured. Within specific industries, however, they are generally quite similar. Hospital organizational structures, for example, are unduplicated in other settings. Many have adopted corporate nomenclatures in recent years, but hospitals remain unlike any other organization. Each consists of a multitude of small departments artificially grouped into administrative units. The former are usually directed by technically rather than managerially oriented individuals, who are products of educational curricula essentially similar to those of business schools.

Manufacturing, distribution, and institutions have similar sets of differences. Nonprofit and service organizations have theirs as well. Communicators can and do successfully move from one sector to another, but no organization can afford to be wholly without communication personnel conversant with its basic operations.

The communication function is best served where one or more of those involved are experientially equipped in the organization's specific areas of endeavor. Here again, there are varying degrees of suitability. Experience in a community college or technical school might be acceptable in a university setting, but not nearly so helpful as university experience. Similarly, a background in mortgage banking or the savings and loan sector might be helpful in a large commercial bank, but not nearly so beneficial as banking experience.

Personnel Complements

The nature of personnel complements is of greater importance to communicators than organizational structure. Organizational function dictates their composition. Distribution firms, for example, employ large numbers of freight handlers and truck drivers, but have relatively small professional and managerial complements. Manufacturing organizations are more diverse. Production personnel may predominate, but the numbers of professionals and managers are greater.

Such differences produce variation in the demographic and psychographic profiles of personnel involved. These imply a potential need for different communication strategies and consequent differences in messages and channels.

Skilled, knowledgeable communicators can and do adapt over time to differing circumstances they encounter in moving from one organization to another. Their learning periods, nevertheless, can create potential difficulties for employers. Successful transitions are not unknown, especially where larger communication departments are involved.

Junior communicators often make such changes without difficulty, especially in moving to established organizations with experienced senior personnel. Senior communicators may succeed as well, particularly where experienced staffs await them. Considerable risk exists, however, where organizations employ only one professional. Newcomers to those positions should be as experienced as possible in their employers' fields of endeavor.

MAINTAINING PROFICIENCY

The half-life of contemporary knowledge has been estimated at five years. That with which fledgling communicators leave the educational system rapidly becomes obsolete without continued learning. Three primary tools are available in maintaining state-of-the-art communicator knowledge and skill. All are educational in nature.

Continuing Education

Continuing education and/or professional development programs are accessible to virtually every communicator. They are offered on national, regional, and local bases by professional groups, such as the Public Relations Society of America (PRSA) and the International Association of Business Communicators (IABC).

Both of these groups sponsor professional accreditation programs and journals that assist members in maintaining a contemporary knowledge of their fields. PRSA is organized in sections by areas of operational interest. The sections also support educational programs and publish member newsletters.

Many larger business and institutional groups also provide professional development opportunities. The American Hospital Association, for example, sponsors the American Society for Hospital Marketing and Public Relations. Similar organizations exist for communicators in the nation's colleges and universities and in other organizational groups.

Organizational communicators should be encouraged to participate in these organizations and their activities, and communication budgets should provide for attendance at regional and national meetings. Where organizations provide educational benefits, these should be used as well.

Formal Education

Educational benefit programs should be applied to further communicators' knowledge and skills. The nation's educational system has evolved to a point at which one need not live near a college or university to achieve this objective. A broad range of external degree and extension programs are available through accredited postsecondary institutions, and more are being introduced each year.

Most major universities offer executive programs leading to the master's degree in business administration (MBA). These can usually be completed in two years and require only weekly or semiweekly visits to the campus. For those relatively distant from its compuses, the California State University system offers master's degrees in many disciplines wholly by mail. In 1986 Purdue University started offering an executive MBA primarily by computer, but with some required on-campus sessions. Trinity University in San Antonio offers an external master's in hospital administration, which includes some on-campus sessions supplemented by telephone conferences.

Communication and public relations courses are also being developed for off-campus delivery. Telelearning Systems, Inc. of California is marketing a set of computer-mediated courses, including one in public relations developed at Memphis State University in Tennessee. Memphis State is working to develop further computer-mediated programming in public relations at both graduate as well as undergraduate levels.

Supplemental Activities

Individual communicators' personal commitment to maintaining an adequate knowledge base is of equal importance in organizational communication. Knowledge of business or industrial sectors in which individuals practice, of the national economy as a whole, and of organizational communication should all be involved.

An appropriate professional reading program would consist of academic and professional journals in communication, trade and/or professional journals serving the field in which the communicator practices, and general business publications. For those in the health-care sector, for example, required reading would include:

Professional journals: Public Relations Journal, Communication World (published by the International Association of Business Communicators), *International Public Relations Review* (published by the International Public Relations Association), *Public Relations Review*, and the publications of the American Society for Hospital Marketing and Public Relations.

Health care publications: Hospitals, Modern Healthcare, the Journal of Healthcare Administration, and state hospital association publications in the region served by the communicator's employer.

Business publications: Wall Street Journal, Business Week, Forbes, Fortune, American Demographics, and *Across the Board* (published by the Conference Board).

The above constitute only part of what is available. Newsletters today serve virtually every industry. Several are in the health care and communication areas. These, with the addition of the communicator's local newspapers and, perhaps, the *New York Times,* should be required reading.

New Technology

Other major information sources today include a burgeoning number of electronic data bases and special interest groups, accessible at low cost by personal computer. CompuServe, The Source, and other computer utilities offer general and special information of considerable interest to communicators.

Special interest groups. CompuServe's Public Relations and Marketing Forum (PRSIG) is exemplary of the special interest groups. PRSIG maintains multiple data bases containing information of contemporary interest to communicators. Leading authorities in the field come on line regularly for conferences as well.

Perhaps most important, members of PRSIG and similar groups can be of inestimable value to communicators in need of information on special topics. The system seems to breed a form of camaraderie that induces multiple detailed responses, via an electronic bulletin board, to any question a participant poses.

Data bases. Electronic data bases accessible by computer are available in many forms. The majority are standing files updated on a regular basis, and their content ranges from magazine articles to newsletters. Others are especially valuable where communicators or their employers want to monitor developing news stories.

CompuServe's Executive Service, for example, enables users to establish electronic file folders, identified by key words or terms. The CompuServe computer monitors wire-service reports and, on detecting the key words or terms, automatically places copies of items involved in the electronic file folders. Subscribers can review file-folder content at any time, discarding items in which they are not interested and retaining or downloading the remainder. Information obtained in this manner can be especially important where communicators are functioning as entrepreneurs within their organizations.

EARLY WARNING SYSTEMS

Information flows that communicators monitor position them to serve their organizations in the early stages of strategic planning processes. Organizations must be viewed in a systems context. They are part of a set of suprasystems and composed of subsystems, influenced for better or worse by events and trends in both areas.

Successful managers constantly monitor these events and trends and their prospective impact on the organization. Contemporary demographic trends, with which this book is concerned, are among many that require attention.

Environmental Assessment

The knowledge base required by communicators and the extent of information acquisition processes in which they are involved make them ideally suited to play a part in monitoring processes. Technically labeled "environmental assessment," they consist of two parts: scanning and monitoring.

Scanning requires consistent observation of organizational horizons for events that may signal trends or might prove troublesome to the organization. The first Tylenol poisoning incident, for example, should have been a signal of potential difficulties to come to every manufacturer of over-the-counter drugs. In like manner, published reports of shortages of unskilled labor during the summer of 1986 were clear evidence of impending nationwide manpower problems.

Handling of the environmental assessment process varies with organizations. Some commit significant resources to internal efforts. Others subscribe to commercial services, such as those offered by the Naisbitt Organization. More than a few take an ad hoc approach. Most, however, maintain a strategic planning function in one form or another.

Communicators should be part of the strategic planning group in the light of the information they assimilate and for another significant reason: They ultimately will be concerned with virtually every trend or event that impacts the organization.

If the nuclear family continues to decline, child-care services will become more and more important to employees. If governmental pressure to shift responsibility for social programs to the private sector persists, a perceptible impact on shareholders is almost inevitable. Drug testing, worker retraining, and other issues have similar organizational problem potential. These and similar concerns will be especially significant to communicators who function in entrepreneurial fashion within their organizations.

ENTREPRENEURIAL APPLICATION

Organizational communication units function for the most part in one of two basic postures or patterns. In the traditional, communicators handle assignments from senior managers or other organizational units on request. In the entrepreneurial pattern, they actively seek out assignments. They assume responsibility for identifying as well as meeting organizational communication need. The latter approach is by far the better of the two. It requires, however, that senior management organize the function and position the communication unit to ensure the best results.

Unit Positioning

Several prerequisites must be met if communicators are to be productive. In addition to adequate resources, they must be granted sufficient rank and/ or stature in the hierarchy to command the attention of managers and supervisors.

For optimum productivity, the organizational communication unit should be part of a larger complex dealing with all communication functions. Marketing, advertising, sales promotion, and public relations ideally should be components of the unit. Organizing in this fashion enhances coordination, assures optimal use of resources, and minimizes the potential for message conflict.

The communication complex should be in a staff rather than a line situation, reporting directly to senior management. Senior communicators should report to chief executive officers. The critical nature of the communication function and communicator need for appropriate organizational stature militate in this direction.

Unit Function

There must also exist a system that encourages the use of communication services within organizations' operational components. This is readily accomplished where managers and supervisors are accountable for the performance of units operating under their direction.

Where managerial and supervisory rewards are governed by productivity, those involved will be predisposed to use communication services in resolving organizational problems. Should attendance become a problem, for example, managers involved will be prone to accept any assistance the communication unit can offer.

The unit thus provides both staff support and services. It offers professional counsel to line managers, assisting them in identifying and fulfilling their communication roles. Concurrently, it may provide appropriate communication programs.

Information sources. The communication unit system is based on a simple concept. Line managers rather than communicators are preferred sources of information in any organizational unit. Their personnel look to them for information and guidance. From the employee perspective, most communication problems are a matter of not knowing what is expected of them or of not having adequate information on which to act.

In these circumstances communicators are placed under obligation to managers and supervisors, as well as their personnel. At minimum they should: educate and support managers in communicating with their personnel; provide communication programs to support managerial efforts by giving personnel the information they need; and identify and eliminate obstacles to communication.

Information needs. People's need for information is almost insatiable, due in part to their basic need to reduce uncertainty. It also reflects their desire to understand how the organization is doing, which in turn bears on the security of their positions. The vigor of organizational grapevines is a direct function of the extent to which management fails to meet these needs.

Economic System

Accountability on the part of managers and supervisors for operational results enables senior management to install systems designed to create optimum performance by the communication unit. It renders the unit entrepreneurial, in fact as well as concept, by establishing it as a consultancy within the organization.

This objective is accomplished by basing unit budgets on minimal essential duties prescribed by senior management. Other funds that might be expended for organizational communication are allocated to the operational unit rather than the communication unit budget.

Unit functions. Thus, the communication unit is required to identify operational unit problems, design appropriate communication programs, and sell them to operational unit managers at mutually acceptable prices. In this manner it "earns" revenues necessary to a communication organization of a size in keeping with organizational need.

This consultant approach to organizational communication, as it is called, creates a self-policing system on which managers at all levels can depend. Senior managers need not be concerned over excessive communication budgets. They are governed by the willingness of junior managers to use communication services to meet the needs of operational units. Accountability on the part of junior managers for operational results encourages them to use communication services to the extent to which they produce positive net results.

Operational constraints. Constraints of the same sort limit any tendency on the part of communication managers to oversell, overpromise, or overprice their services. Their continued success is dependent on satisfied clienteles. Clients (other managers) are satisfied only when communication services are productive, when they engender results in keeping with costs involved.

COMPREHENSIVE PROGRAMMING

The consultant system is especially beneficial from an organizational stand-point when other conditions cited above have been met. Most significant among them is the structure of the total communication unit. Where communication services are colocated, managers can achieve optimum operational economy by the best use of the resources available to them. The unit should be prepared to offer personal as well as print and electronic services. It should also be alert to fast-changing technologies and their potential for enhancing communication systems.

Personal Communication

Developing personal communication skills among managers and supervisors is often the most neglected component of organizational programs. The problem is most prevalent in the absence of effective accountability systems.

Without accountability for results, managers and supervisors are content to let print or electronic communication devices substitute for the personal attention that employees need, want, and deserve. The problem grows where organizational communicators are oriented primarily to print or electronic channels. Their predispositions lead them to neglect organizational need for personal communication skills.

The consultant approach encourages them to innovate rather than cling to the familiar. It predisposes them to develop services in which clients and prospective clients may be interested. Services may include seminars and/or training programs designed to better equip managers and supervisors in such communication techniques as meeting management, interviewing, counseling, and small-group communication. Public speaking programs might be added for senior managers or executives.

Print and Electronic Channels

The same sort of outcomes can be expected in communicator handling of print and electronic channels of communication. Accountability inevitably defeats inertia. Economic accountability provides the best results.

Evidence of change in the use of these channels can be found in two areas. The first is the interest in emerging technologies and the manner in which they can be used to enhance communication systems. The second is a constant questioning of contemporary techniques. The latter is the more important of the two.

The status quo. There are always two reasons to continue existing practices: "We've never done it the other way," and "We've always done it this way." To a certain extent, this philosophy is perpetuated in the remonstrance, "If it ain't broke, don't fix it."

The issue is not whether the system is working, but whether it can be made more productive. In the absence of incentives for improvement, lethargy and inertia discourage any tendency to question long-standing methods or systems.

Emerging technologies. New technology is placing more and more tools at the disposal of communicators. Relatively few communicators display any marked tendency to replace the new with the old. The computer, for example, has become well accepted as a substitute for the typewriter and calculator. It is far from realizing its potential as a communication device, however.

Few organizations have emulated the 3M Company in establishing a sophisticated bulletin-board communication system for internal and external communication. The system consists of sets of data bases established on the company's mainframe headquarters computer for personnel at different organizational levels as well as the news media.

Using access codes issued in keeping with informational needs, supervisors, managers, and executives of 3M around the world can obtain at any hour of the day and night information and messages left for them. They also can leave messages for others. News media representatives can access files containing all recent company news releases on a host of subjects, as well as basic information about the company.

Computer communication. A system of the same sort would be an invaluable employee communication device in larger companies, in organizations operating around the clock, and in those operating in multiple time zones. Typical questions and answers concerning employee benefit programs, for example, could be programmed into the computer for immediate access at any time by any employee. The system could also permit employees to leave questions for human resources personnel on an individual basis. It could even maintain employee records of accrued benefits, such as leave time. As in the 3M Company case, these would be accessible only through the use of assigned identification codes.

Other prospective applications include maintaining electronic copies of personnel policy and procedure manuals, indexed by subject for instant access. These documents tend to be bulky and difficult to use and maintain in printed form. Easy access to electronic versions would make content more readily available and assure recipients that they have the latest versions of policies in which they are interested.

Other technologies. Continuing communicator attention is also necessary in such areas as satellite-based communication systems, new audiovisual technologies, and the like. New videotape equipment, for example, is rapidly expanding the applicability of these systems in such areas as employee training.

A self-contained video and sound system approximately the size of a 35 mm camera already has been demonstrated at a major electronics exposi-

tion. Readily transportable equipment of this sort radically enhances organizations' ability to train and retrain personnel, especially in manufacturing
environments inhospitable to older and bulkier videotape units.

SUMMARY

Productivity in organizational communication is created by several factors.
Primary among them are the characteristics of individuals involved and the
manner in which organizations are structured.

Organizations require diverse communication skills, which can best be
acquired in graduate-program accredited curricula in public relations or
mass communication. The curricula require breadth as well as depth of
background. They require proficiency in personal as well as print and electronic communication. They also require background in the social sciences
which is essential to communicators' understanding of the world in which
they function.

Successful organizational communicators are seldom found among those
trained in journalism—print or broadcast. Neither discipline includes appropriate education in personal communication. Curricula in both areas are
overly narrow. The organizational communicator must be equally at home
with interpersonal, print, and electronic message delivery.

The knowledge and skill required at the beginning of an organizational
communication career must be maintained in one or more of several ways—
among them, continuing education programs, advanced formal education
curricula, and supplemental activities. Supplemental activities, which are
necessary in any event, require extensive reading in professional journals,
business publications, and those specialized media serving the industry in
which the organizational communicator practices. They may also include
use of electronic data bases as information sources.

The extent of successful communicators' reading makes them ideal candidates for inclusion in organizations' strategic planning teams. These groups
employ environmental assessment processes to identify events and trends
that suggest potential organizational response.

Communicator knowledge and skill are best applied entrepreneurially
within organizations. Communicators in this organization pattern serve as
consultants to line managers who require communication services to enhance the performance of their operating units.

The ideal system provides a minimal budget for the communication function and places most necessary funding in the hands of line units. Communicators, then, are compelled to perform entrepreneurially. They must
identify client needs, develop services to meet those needs, and market
them to the operational units involved.

This system requires that communication professionals develop and offer
a broad range of innovative communication services to meet client need.

Personal as well as mediated communication efforts may be indicated. Where the former are necessary, communication units may find it appropriate to train managers in becoming better communicators. Employees prefer them as information sources to any controlled channel.

The system is especially helpful where the organization employs a coordinated approach to communication by housing marketing, advertising, public relations, and organizational communication in a single operating entity. The manager should report to the organization's chief operating officer.

ADDITIONAL READING

Brody, E. W. *The Business of Public Relations.* New York: Praeger, 1987.
D'Aprix, Roger. *The Believable Corporation.* New York: AMACOM, 1977.
Kreps, Gary. *Organizational Communication.* New York: Longman, 1986.
Reuss, Carol, and Donn Silvis. *Inside Organizational Communication.* New York: Longman, 1985.

13

A MODEL FOR SUCCESS: FEDERAL EXPRESS CORPORATION

Few of the many how-to-succeed business books published in recent years fail to mention Federal Express Corporation. The tale of Frederick W. Smith's success in turning a less-than-applauded term paper into a multi-million-dollar business is well known. Less well known are the philosophy, policies, and operating methods through which Smith and his colleagues achieved success. All but unknown is the fact that they continue to aggressively follow this pattern to maintain leadership in an increasingly competitive industry.

The Federal Express philosophy developed in part through Smith's experience during two tours with the Marine Corps in Vietnam. Where leaders treated people with respect, fairness, and genuine concern, he found, they performed under any and all conditions. Otherwise, they met minimum standards and little more. Thus, Federal Express was founded on a commitment to people in order to produce a level of service necessary to reap a profit.

This commitment from the outset was evidenced in a no-layoff policy, coupled with compensation and benefit programs among the industry's best. The compensation system was oriented to employee growth and development through a strong promote-from-within policy. It was also performance based and supported by an effective performance-evaluation system. Supervisors and managers at every level were held accountable for results, and employees were guaranteed fair treatment.

Federal Express supported these efforts with a communication organization arguably second to none in the United States. Employee communication became increasingly difficult as the organization grew. In response, says Thomas R. Martin, the company's managing director for employee communications, Federal Express built an organizational communication staff of 60 with an annual budget of some $3 million.

In fiscal 1986 (May-June) the company had assets of $2.8 billion, annual sales of $2.6 billion, and a net income for that year of $132 million. It was the dominant entity in the air-express industry and had earned a reputation for excellence, reliability, and customer satisfaction. Enlightened communication policies alone could not and did not produce this result, Martin said, but they contributed to high morale, which in turn helped produced the unprecedented service levels necessary to industry dominance.

COMPONENTS OF SUCCESS

There is no simple formula for success in organizational communication. All of the elements mentioned above are necessary, but not sufficient. Organizational commitment to employees is a beginning point. Expression of that commitment through compensation, benefits, and performance-appraisal programs is important. Ensuring functional outcomes through supervisory and managerial accountability is vital. These are prerequisites to communication, but they in no way ensure that communication will succeed. Success in communication can be achieved through the active support of managerial and supervisory personnel and the efforts of a professional employee communication unit.

Managerial Requirements

Federal Express establishes its expectations of all managers unequivocally in a *Manager's Guide* section under the heading, "A Leader Must Communicate and Cooperate."

A Federal Express Manager Must Be a Good Listener
The foundation of Q = P (quality equals performance) management is involvement of the people actually doing a job in order to simplify and improve operations. This vital feedback can take place only in an atmosphere of mutual trust and confidence under the encouragement of the first-line manager. Where there is no fear of retribution or embarrassment, when workers believe job improvement will benefit them personally, the employee ranks form an incredible resource for a huge reservoir of knowledge. *Not only are employees motivated by the obvious respect afforded to their ideas, but they naturally support decisions based on their input.*

Removing Barriers to Listening

The biggest obstacles to improving productivity in this way are (1) *managerial hang-ups* and (2) the *inability of many in authority to listen.* The traditional boss did not consult his or her subordinates. Such a practice would be "beneath" a manager's place in the scheme of things and, as a result, threatening to his or her authority. The increasing democratization of society and the understanding that such management practices are counterproductive have melted away many of these psychological barriers to greater worker involvement. Even so, there are still far too many in the management ranks that either can't or won't tap this incredible font of knowledge.

In addition to cultural inhibitions to employee involvement, the human mind's natural difficulty in listening is a significant problem. For years psychologists have studied the phenomenon of people's inability to hear—really hear—what's being said to them. One reason for this is the *natural egocentricity of most human beings.*

When others are speaking, many of us are simply tuned into our own concerns to the exclusion of others.

We all realize that speaking is a far less effective communications medium than seeing and, especially, doing. Despite this, limits of time and other job pressures make verbal communications the primary method for transmitting thoughts.

The manager must make a great effort to overcome these deficiencies. And it is hard, hard work to listen. It takes maximum concentration to do so. Self-discipline is essential as is genuine interest in the other human being. Without both *attentiveness and empathy,* most talk is not retained for any time at all.

A good exercise is to commit the important ideas of others to brief, written highlights. Not only does this practice facilitate *remembering* what was said, but it forces the listener to *organize* the points being made. If you don't invest a significant effort, there is a high risk that the value of others' thoughts will be lost to you almost immediately.

Effective listening builds tools for success in many managerial skills. It aids in both the subjective areas and in the *quantitative* areas, by succinctly identifying problems and opportunities. Careful listening always reveals subtleties that indicate important things about the speaker. Having a window on subordinates' attitudes and convictions is an important factor in successful leadership. Listening as carefully and respectfully as possible reiterates as no other management action can that the employee is a *valued member* of our team.[1]

The foregoing is the content of one of five full pages of general instructions to managers concerning communication. Managers are called on to groom successors from among their subordinates, use education and training as communication, and recognize employee performance. Among the tools available to them in the latter context is a "Bravo Zulu" sticker program, which uses a replica of a U.S. Navy flag signal meaning "well done." Federal Express has rendered the two flags in the form of a sticker that managers use to immediately recognize "above and beyond" performance on the part of subordinates.

Organizational Support

Successful communication requires constant attention in any enterprise, whether the process is undertaken by a single professional or the 60 in the Federal Express department. It involves a clearly defined mission and a set of precisely expressed goals. Communicators must be organized to meet those goals, and their progress must be measured. Further, their success requires management support, expressed through unequivocal organizational policy.

[1]From Federal Express Corporation's *Manager's Guide.* Courtesy of Federal Express Corporation.

Communicating for Survival

EMPLOYEE COMMUNICATION POLICY

A clearly stated policy applicable to all employees and supported by guidelines that defy misunderstanding delineates the Federal Express employee-communication program: "It is the policy of Federal Express to maintain a positive communication climate where the flow of timely, accurate and candid information supports achievement of company goals and strengthening of corporate values."

Much of the Federal Express policy is not unusual. It is exceptional, however, in two respects. First, it requires information be timely, accurate, and candid. Second, it produces that result. When the company abandoned its ill-fated Zap Mail project in mid-1986, for example, employees were made aware of the decision, the reasons for that decision, and its anticipated impact on the organization. The information was conveyed to them before it appeared in the next morning's newspapers—rather than after.

Management Responsibilities

The seriousness with which Federal Express views employee communication is expressed in guidelines set out in support of the policy.

Each member of management serves as the primary communicator to the workgroup he manages. In this role, as shown on the model below [see Figure 13.1], the manager must identify and satisfy information needs of the workgroup, including but not limited to the following areas: individual job responsibility; individual performance feedback; individual needs and concerns; work unit goals, role and progress; company goals and progress.

The word "individual" is most important. Its presence mandates intrapersonal communication. Managerial compliance defeats any tendency toward dependence on mediated communication.

The Federal Express policy continues in detail seldom encountered in similar documents. The language involved, in addition, establishes managerial accountability beyond question.

The manager must encourage upward communication and employee involvement through regular and well-planned face-to-face and group meetings. Every manager is expected to have a planned, organized meeting with his direct reports a minimum of thirty (30) minutes at least every two weeks. Senior managers should meet with the staff of their direct reports [those who report to them] preferably each quarter and, in no case, less than twice a year. Concise records should be kept of these sessions and the issues addressed.

Managers also have the responsibility to communicate upward any questions, concerns or suggestions that emanate from the workgroups and provide employees feedback on the status of such upward communications.

Figure 13.1.   Federal Express Corporation's Manager's Communication Model.

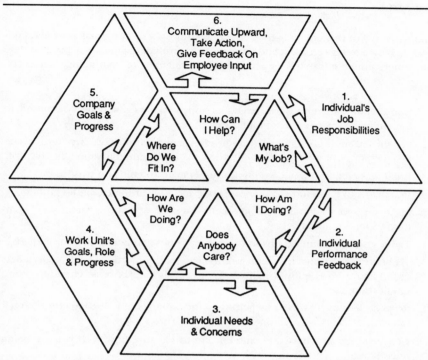

Source: From "Employee Communication Policy," *Federal Express Personnel Policy & Procedure Manual*. Courtesy of Federal Express Corporation.

Managers should ensure that all employees in their workgroups receive general corporate information through such media as Employee Pak, video programs, posters, and newsletters in a timely, effective manner.

Managers must communicate laterally with their peers in other workgroups in an effort to correct operational problems and improve coordination and teamwork.   Failure to comply with the intent of this policy may result in disciplinary action.[2]

While the latter admonition at first appears most striking, other provisions of the policy are equally significant. Managers are enjoined to provide opportunities for small-group communication. They are required to see that subordinates' concerns and ideas are conveyed to senior managers, and that

[2]From Federal Express Corporation's "Employee Communication Policy." Courtesy of Federal Express Corporation.

responses are delivered as well. An appendix to the employee communication policy is even more explicit as to organizational expectations of
managers.

The objective of this policy is to establish an atmosphere of mutual trust and confidence between management and employees by providing guidelines for complete
and timely communications. Federal Express principles of communication excellence are as follows:

1. Know your communication strengths and weaknesses and be committed to
   becoming an excellent communicator.
2. Set the example for communication excellence within your workgroup and
   take responsibility for your workgroup's overall communication effectiveness.
3. Build an open, two-way communication climate to cultivate trust.
4. Practice active listening to increase your accuracy at understanding others.
5. Make sure your actions are consistent with your words to protect your communication credibility.
6. Tailor your communications to the needs, values and beliefs of your audience.
7. Maintain regular and frequent face-to-face communications with your workgroup and each employee individually to satisfy the six basic employee communication needs.
8. Respect the time of others by getting to the point and eliminating non-essential
   information.
9. Get feedback on what you communicate to measure how well you are being
   understood.
10. Take the risk of disclosing your true thoughts to others to gain the rewards of
    mutual understanding.[3]

   Item 7 is especially significant in that it requires one-on-one as well as
small-group communication. Item 10 also is noteworthy in that it urges
individual openness and candor. This admonition tends to produce skepticism among those not familiar with the Federal Express organization. Few
individuals exhibit such traits beyond early childhood. Most learn early to
conceal their thoughts. In the Federal Express organization, however, complete candor is accepted and expected. It is an integral part of the corporate
culture, reduced to writing more as a reminder to veterans and for the
benefit of newcomers than for any other reason.
   Openness and candor are similarly encouraged among nonmanagers. "All
Federal Express employees," the communications policy declares, "have the

---

[3]From Federal Express Corporation's "Employee Communication Policy." Courtesy of Federal Express Corporation.

responsibility to communicate upward to management, and laterally to each other pertinent information such as: suggestions for ways to improve the operation; concerns and complaints; questions about the company or department; information that is helpful to others."

The policy establishes several areas of responsibility for the Employee Communications Department—research and analysis, organizational communications, communications development, graphic communications, and video production. Other than graphic communications and video production, which are combined in a media design and development unit, each area of responsibility is handled by a separate operational group within the department (see Figure 13.2).

EMPLOYEE COMMUNICATION

The Federal Express Employee Communications Department is guided by a mission statement and goals congruent with the organization's overall philosophy. The mission: "to support Federal Express in accomplishing its goals and objectives by facilitating effective, two-way communication throughout the company." The goals: to help management become more effective as the primary communicators in the company; to facilitate two-way communication that is timely, credible, relevant, receiver oriented, and results oriented; to measure the effectiveness of all communication programs; and to accomplish departmental goals and objectives in a cost-effective manner.

Other than as to cost effectiveness, the department's goals encompass considerably more than the same words imply in other organizations. Assistance to management, for example, involves training managers in interpersonal communication techniques as well as providing impersonal communication vehicles. Credibility, relevance, and receiver/results orientation are evident in every communication department component and product. Effectiveness is measured both objectively and subjectively. The latter includes random telephone calls to employees by members of the communication staff.

RESEARCH AND ANALYSIS

To a greater extent than most organizations conceive, much less achieve, the research and analysis unit is central to Federal Express employee communication programming. The unit is significantly involved in delivery services as well as data gathering and analysis. Its primary functions include developing effective communication practices, periodic communication audits, ongoing surveys, and a new program called EmpComm.

Figure 13.2.   Organization of Federal Express Corporation's Employee Communications Department.

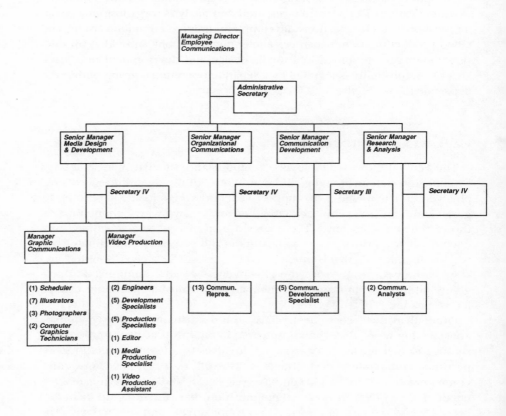

Source: Courtesy of Federal Express Corporation.

Effective Communication Practices

The effective communication practices effort involves two components: assessing and developing communication skills in managers. As always, program objectives are purely functional. "The key is to bring our managers to understand that if they involve employees in finding solutions to problems, they are most likely to find the solutions," Martin says. "Otherwise, the solutions are less likely to be found."

To enhance communication practices, employee communications personnel monitor the effectiveness of managerial communication efforts and provide guidance and programming to induce improvement. The latter includes skill development to meet specific managerial needs in a program called Effective Communication Practices (ECP).

The ECP program enables managers to assess their skills and abilities as communicators. They also have at their disposal survey data indicating how their employees perceive them. Developmental activities, including self-instruction materials and classroom instruction, are made available to enable them to enhance their communication skills.

These activities reflect Federal Express's recognition that first-line managers are the most important link in the communication chain. This concept has been reinforced by surveys undertaken within Federal Express and by other organizations.

"They support the notion," Martin says, "that employees want to receive most information about the company from their immediate supervisor. If they don't have a good communication relationship with their direct management, they don't place much faith in the newsletters or video programs produced by the corporate communications function."

Ongoing Surveys

Communication effectiveness in the Federal Express organization, therefore, is monitored constantly at every level. After managing directors' meetings, for example, participants are asked to evaluate the meeting and the presentations involved. Results are used to plan ensuing meetings. Similar evaluative techniques are applied in the wake of every major event or communication effort.

The process amounts to constant self-questioning. How are we doing? Can we make it better? How can we make it better? Any tendency toward self-satisfaction, any inclination toward acceptance of the status quo, any assumption that the communication system necessarily is achieving desired results is thus immediately rejected.

Communication Audit

The organization's periodic communication audits, supported by other programs are designed to produce similar results. Audits are designed to assess the efficacy of the employee communication program and all of its components. They involve formal surveys dealing in depth with interpersonal as well as mediated communication.

The organization's annual Survey Feedback Action (SFA) questionnaire, for example, asks personnel to evaluate Federal Express by marking response scales for 27 statements.

1. Management tells us about company goals.
2. Management listens to ideas from my level.
3. I am confident of fair management.
4. I can tell my supervisor what I think.
5. My supervisor tells me what is expected.
6. Favoritism is not a problem in my area.
7. Our supervisor helps us do our job better.
8. My supervisor listens to my concerns.
9. My supervisor asks for my ideas about my work.
10. My supervisor tells me when I do a good job.
11. My supervisor treats me with respect.
12. My supervisor keeps me informed.
13. My supervisor does not interfere with the job.
14. I am sure of having a job if I do good work.
15. I am proud to work for the company.
16. My work is leading to the kind of future I want.
17. The company does a good job for our customers.
18. Working for the company is a good deal.
19. I am paid fairly for this kind of work.
20. Benefit programs meet most of my needs.
21. People cooperate between workgroups.
22. There is cooperation between workgroups.
23. Rules and procedures do not interfere.
24. We are able to get supplies and resources.
25. We have enough freedom to do the job well.
26. My supervisor doesn't expect me to sacrifice quality.
27. Management doesn't expect us to sacrifice quality.[4]

Employee responses to items 4 through 13 are used to create an SFA leadership index—a set of point scores by which the organization measures and monitors the effectiveness of managers' communication efforts. Percentages of favorable responses are calculated for these items and compared with the same set of percentages for the prior year. The result is a set of data that reflect improvement or deterioration in managerial performance as well as raw scores.

[4]From the Federal Express Corporation Survey Feedback Action Comparison Worksheet. Reprinted with permission.

EmpComm

The annual communication audit is supplemented by a program called EmpComm. It involves 300 interviews a month, conducted by telephone or in writing, with employees selected at random from throughout the organization.

EmpComm deals with specific communication products, such as publications or videotapes, as well as organizational issues. The program is designed to keep communicators abreast of "how we're doing," and enable them to fine-tune their efforts to achieve desired results.

COMMUNICATIONS DEVELOPMENT

Data produced by the research and analysis unit have many uses. They are provided to managers for their guidance and to senior managers for use in evaluating subordinates. Some also are occasionally helpful to the communications-development unit in fine-tuning message content to improve understanding.

The communications-development group deals primarily with four communication vehicles: *UpDate,* a monthly employee newspaper; *Manager's Pak,* a monthly magazine for managers; *This Week,* a weekly newsletter for managers; and the "Family Briefing," an annual mass meeting of Federal Express personnel and their families, conducted by satellite at multiple locations around the world. In each case the content reflects the organization's underlying philosophy, its personnel policies, and its communication strategy.

Update

Federal Express's primary employee publication is a monthly tabloid newspaper that addresses organizational and employee concerns, "warts and all." Consider some of the subjects covered in one 16–page issue (December 1986):

—Testimony before Congress regarding a package route to Japan

—A new jumpseat reservation system for employees

—A complaint from an employee whose personal package was delayed

—Letters—favorable and unfavorable—from customers

—Customer satisfaction data, emphasizing Federal units that were recording exceptional service levels.

—Problems with "Wrong-Day" deliveries

—A summary of mass media news items about Federal Express, its competitors, and its industry

—A report on the "final shakedown period" for a new package-tracking system

—A summary of information conveyed to the financial community during an annual
—analysts' and lenders' meeting.

—A new employee health program.

—Reports from various departments covering subject matter ranging from forthcoming benefit plan changes (personnel) to protection of employees' personally
owned computer systems (information systems).

Publication content, like messages delivered through other employee-
communication vehicles, thus meet organizational and departmental criteria: timeliness, credibility, relevance, and receiver/results orientation.

Manager's Pak

The same criteria can be seen at work in Federal Express's managers' magazine, known as *Manager's Pak*. A list of contents from the December 1986
issue illustrates this point:

—A Federal Express Christmas Carol: Teamwork Is Our Christmas Present to Our-
selves.

—Communicating with Employees: Maintaining an Open Channel.

—Managing MBOs: Seven Steps for Setting Objectives.

—Strange New World: Managing in a Losing Situation.

—MP Magazine Topics: June through December 1986.

—MP Reprint: With Problems More Visible, Firms Crack Down on Sexual Harass-
ment.

—GFTP: Defining the Company Document.

—Summary of Timely Information.

—Back-Page Editiorial: Leadership.

The contents of several articles were especially significant in terms of
organizational communication objectives. "Communicating with Employees" reminded managers of the company's SFA leadership index and the
survey questions on which it is based. "Strange New World" took Houston,
Texas, sales problems as a model and told how managers can deal with
declining business volumes. "MP Magazine Topics" is a semiannual index
provided to enable managers to keep copies of the magazine and use them
productively as a reference resource.

"GFTP" dealt with the termination of an employee who falsified a doctor's
note, which was defined as a "company-related document." The article
spelled out the terminology involved, explained how organizational policy
was applied, and urged managers to inform their employees that

The broad scope of the term "company-related document" includes any document which has a meaning or relationship to an individual's employment at Federal Express.

The highest degree of intergrity and honesty is expected of an employee when submitting paperwork in any form. Anything less than complete honesty can result in termination.

Since careless mistakes might be viewed as falsification, extreme caution should be stressed to employees when completing any company-related document. The distinction between a mistake and deliberate falsification is not always obvious.

Any documentation submitted by an employee to the company, such as a physician's statement, which is used as documentation for a medical absence, is considered a company document. Any alteration to that document is looked upon as falsification, and is a terminable offense.

As is the case with *UpDate, Managers' Pak* includes a summary, from media reports, of timely information for managers and a reminder of another service to managers: "Ask Senior Management," defined as "a confidential information-sharing forum" through which managers can obtain answers to questions about the company and its policies. An internal mailing address was provided with the reminder.

The "Back Page Editorial" also was illustrative of organizational philosophy. It defined training as "an opportunity for operations and district support staffs to work together to provide new employees the opportunity to do their jobs correctly and professionally"; and as "a team effort that requires total cooperation and communication between managers and instructors to educate and reinforce corporate expectations of employees."

This Week

In contrast with *Manager's Pak, This Week* is a no-nonsense summary of information managers need, published on both sides of an $8\frac{1}{2} \times 14$—inch sheet. A typical issue dealt with collect billing at international agent locations, problems regarding unauthorized use of customer account numbers, and regulations on firearms shipments.

Employee informational needs, however, are never forgotten. The same issue described discounts extended to Federal personnel by commercial airlines and ceilings on credit-union auto loans.

Family Briefing

Of the many communication channels Federal Express uses to convey information to employees, "Family Briefing" is perhaps the most complex and sophisticated. It is an annual 90—minute telecast for employees and spouses that reviews the past year and explains plans for the year ahead.

Family Briefing started in 1975, when Federal had but a few hundred employees. It then consisted of personal visits by executive managers to a relatively few operating locations. By 1986 Federal had grown to a global audience of more than 40,000 employees at 350 sites. Broadcasts originated in London, Hong Kong, Chicago, and Federal Express headquarters in Memphis, and were beamed live via satellite around the world.

The elaborately produced program, featuring Gladys Knight and The Pips, explained company policies and plans for the coming year. Between 35 and 50 percent of Federal Express employees attended Family Briefing on their own time, in spite of competition from the National Football League in the United States and late hours in Europe and the Far East.

Like *UpDate, Manager's Pak,* and *This Week,* Family Briefing is a broad-spectrum communication channel designed for all Federal Express personnel. By the summer of 1987 the company expected to be broadcasting on a regular basis, perhaps as frequently as daily, to more than 500 operating locations around the world.

Together with assorted audiovisual productions for training and educational purposes, Family Briefing broadcasts require a significant portion of employee-communication resources. These corporate programs are supplemented, however, with more targeted efforts involving a variety of communication channels at divisional levels.

ORGANIZATIONAL COMMUNICATIONS

The organizational communications unit in Federal Express's Employee Communications Department is uniquely designed to serve two purposes. It supports the company's operating divisions in meeting employee-communication needs, while serving as the department's coordinating arm.

These objectives are achieved through a 13–person communications-representative network. The 13 are members of the organizational communication unit assigned to Federal Express divisions. They also have a matrix or "dotted-line" relationship to the managers of those divisions. Their tasks fall into three basic divisional areas: communication plans, communication vehicles, and divisional meetings.

Pragmatically, the Employee Communications Department is thus organized in large part in the "consultant model" defined by Brody in *The Business of Public Relations* (New York: Praeger, 1987). Communication representatives serve as consultants to divisional executives. They assist in developing communication plans, vehicles, and meetings. They provide divisional managers with guidance, counsel, and expertise on messages and media. And they assist in disseminating divisional information to the rest of the company. Communication representatives also help divisional managers adhere to Federal Express employee communication policy as to newsletters, video programs, and other forms of communication.

Newsletters

Guidelines for newsletter production incorporated into the organization's employee communications policy prescribe the manner in which divisional and departmental newsletters should be developed.

Newsletters should address intra-divisional issues, programs and news. Corporate-wide information intended for inter-divisional audiences should be reserved for the publications produced by the Employee Communications Department.

Newsletters produced at the division head or officer level must receive authorization by the Editorial Review Board [see below] prior to the initial publication.

Newsletters produced at the manager, senior manager or managing director level must be approved initially by the responsible officer prior to publication.

Each issue of approved newsletters must be reviewed by at least two levels of management prior to publication.

Every effort should be made to control production costs by avoiding expensive processes such as two and four-color printing, elaborate typesetting, heavy covers, etc.

Good editorial judgment should be used to avoid using off-color material, offensive humor, profanity, or any material which could prove embarrassing to any individual or the company.

Overly aggressive or derogatory references to our competitors should be avoided.

Potentially libelous statements about individuals or companies should be avoided. When in doubt, consult with the Legal Department or the Employee Communications Department.

Previously copyrighted material should be used only after permission is obtained.

Release of newsletters to vendors, suppliers or customers should be avoided, unless prior approval from Legal is obtained.[5]

The Editorial Review Board is more and less than its name implies. It consists of Federal's chairman and president and the heads of the firm's Marketing, Legal, and Employee Communications Departments. They meet monthly in informal sessions chaired by Martin. Their agendas typically deal with projects in progress rather than issues requiring resolution. The primary purpose is to "better define elements of policy and occasionally resolve disputes rather than to serve as an approving body," according to Martin.

Similar guidelines are prescribed in the Federal Express Employee Communications Policy for video programs. "If a division head or officer should choose to issue a divisional or departmental video, approval of the Editorial Review Board must be obtained prior to implementation.

All approved video programs will be produced in conjunction with Employee Communications.

---

[5]Federal Express Corporation Newsletter Guidelines. From Federal Express Employee Communications Policy. Reprinted with permission.

All video programs will include a brief corporate news update produced by Employee Communications.

All video programs must be reviewed and approved by Employee Communications and appropriate division head prior to release.

To avoid duplication of effort and messages, Employee Communications should be informed prior to production of any video programs on special topics, training programs or other single-use applications for employee audiences.

Bulletin-board and poster guidelines prescribed for all Federal Express managers are similarly complete:

The senior member of management in any department or location is responsible for all bulletin boards and postings in that department or location. Day-to-day implementation of this policy may be delegated to any member of management.

Because of limited space in Federal Express locations, all poster requests and personal advertisement of items for sale, rent, give away, or personal services for employee audiences should be channeled through the Corporate Communications Support Center.

With approval from their management, announcements of special interest to employees (including messages of condolence or thanks) may be posted on the bulletin board. The Career Opportunity Posting will be displayed on all Company bulletin boards consistent with the Promotion from Within Policy.

Notices which cannot be displayed on bulletin boards or other space provided by the company include: controversial or political notices and any notice, writing, poster, sign or object which does not have prior approval from management.

The bulletin-board policy is more noteworthy for what it requires than for what it prohibits. Bulletin-board controls are prevalent in most organizations. Few of them specifically require managers to use their boards to promote career opportunity postings in keeping with a promotion-from-within policy.

MEDIA DESIGN AND DEVELOPMENT

Development of posters, other formal materials for bulletin boards, graphic communication devices, and video production are the responsibility of the Employee Communication Department's media design and development unit. This is the largest component of the department in number of personnel, with 14 assigned to graphic communications and 16 to video production.

Extensive production facilities are attached to each unit. They include computer graphics, photography and typography equipment in the graphics area, and complete production and duplicating facilities in the video sector.

The graphic communications group produces art work, graphic design, and photo support for posters, publications, slide shows, and other media. It also maintains a library of corporate slides and negatives for prints.

The video group produces corporate programs for management and general employee audiences. Some also are produced on a regular basis for one or more departments. One serves telecommunications and information systems. Another is designed for personnel, legal, finance, and marketing. A single program in five regional versions is produced for ground operations, and several are produced for sales and customer service.

Responsibilities of the video group also include special live broadcasts over the Federal Express satellite network for Family Briefing and other programs, including the daily broadcasts described earlier. A training/interactive support program is in the early stages of development. It will incorporate audio visual and computer technologies to produce interactive training programs.

Video production personnel also provide ad hoc duplicating and consultation services. The latter range from such routine matters as conference room design and audiovisual equipment selection to more critical decisions such as selection of outside video producers.

PERFORMANCE FIRST

Federal Express communication policies are universally based on prior performance. Employees are afforded every protection. Performance thus precedes communication in a system designed to produce equity and credibility.

Policies require that managers and supervisors communicate. They require that personnel be directly and indirectly exposed to the content of organizational communications. They hold managers and supervisors accountable for results. Most important, they guarantee that personnel will be equitably treated in every respect.

Guaranteed Fair Treatment

The company's "Guaranteed Fair Treatment Policy" is a five-step process. The third and fourth steps afford employees an unusual if not an unprecedented level of protection. The fourth involves a Board of Review consisting of five members. Three are selected from a list of six nominees named by the employee involved. Two are from a list maintained by management.

The board may uphold or overturn the management decision involved or recommend other "relief action," although the company is not bound to follow any relief action recommendation. Employees who are dissatisfied with the Board of Review action may apply to an appeals board consisting of Federal's chief executive officer, chief operating officer, and senior vice-president of personnel. Their decision is final.

The guaranteed fair-treatment policy was designed to insure fairness and equity for both parties. "Perhaps the cornerstone of Federal Express's operating philosophy in general and the PEOPLE philosophy in particular," says the firm's *Personnel Policy & Procedure Manual,* "is the Guaranteed Fair Treatment Procedure.

In any company with an "employee first" philosophy, it is paramount that employees have a viable means of venting complaints to management without fear of retaliation. As many companies have found out too late, employees will find a method for venting their complaints. In the absence of a viable procedure, employees sometimes vent their complaints to those people or agencies who do not have the company's best interest at heart. It is to assure that Federal Express maintains the right and the flexibility to control its own destiny that this policy is addressed.

Other Policies

The guaranteed fair-treatment policy is supported by several others. Federal's "Acceptable Conduct Policy"—what in other organizations might appropriately be called a disciplinary policy—specifies conditions that may lead to termination, but includes ample safeguards to prevent misuse. Discharges of personnel at or below the level of managing director, the highest nonofficer rank, must be approved at two management levels and by a member of the organization's Personnel Services staff.

More impressive is Federal's "Performance Improvement Policy," which deals with employee proficiency rather than rules of conduct. Where performance deficiencies exist, managers are required to employ counseling procedures in efforts to correct problems.

The policy prescribes three counseling sessions. The first is informal. No written record is required. The second produces a written record signed by employee and supervisor, which includes "the facts supporting the deficiency, the action plan jointly developed to correct the problem, and an established follow-up date."

Should the deficiencies continue, the manager must schedule a third meeting with the employee to review the seriousness of the situation. This meeting may result in the employee's being granted a "decision day" (with pay) to determine whether or not he desires to remain in the employment of Federal Express. In those situations where the deficiency is job specific (i.e., driving), the employee (in concert with his manager) may at this point wish to consider an alternative position to which the particular skill deficiency is unrelated.

If the employee decides to remain with the Company, he must, upon return from the "decision day," present a written personal performance agreement acceptable to the manager. This performance agreement must detail specific actions and timetables to overcome the deficiencies and state a personal commitment by the employee to abide by that agreement. Failure to agree on a mutually acceptable action plan and commit to the desired level improvement will be considered voluntary resignation.[6]

Outcomes

The product of these and related policies is only in part measurable in the abstract. Least measurable and most important in an era of declining labor pools will be the cumulative impressions of Federal Express they create in communities where the firm maintains operations. Employee perceptions of an organization, as reflected and amplified by friends and neighbors, arguably are most influential in community perception.

Community perception, in turn, governs the relative willingness or reluctance of employees to depart for "greener pastures." It also is a governor of the percentage of qualified workers in a given community ready to accept employment when vacancies occur. Federal is an unchallenged leader in this respect in Memphis, Tennessee, its headquarters city.

Time will demonstrate the value of Federal's philosophy as well as the firm's human resources and communication policies. The organization almost inevitably will benefit, however, in one respect. Organizations are not static entities. All of them at any given time are either improving or deteriorating. Federal inevitably will be part of the former group.

SUMMARY

The Federal Express success story is well known. Considerably less well known is the commitment to employees on which that success was based. The company maintains no-layoff, promote-from-within, and performance-based compensation policies, together with a guaranteed fair-treatment policy and an accountability mechanism that demands managerial and supervisory support.

The Federal Express formula is complex. Managers are expected to be good listeners and are given five full pages of general instructions in communication behavior. They are supported by an employee communication policy that casts managers as the company's primary communicators. Mediated communication support is provided by a sophisticated Employee Communications Department, but managers are held accountable for use of departmental products. They are enjoined to build strong interpersonal communication systems within their operating units.

The Employee Communication Department's functional components include a research and analysis unit charged with monitoring organizational

---

[6]From the *Federal Express Personnel Policy & Procedure Manual.* Reprinted with permission.

communication needs, a communication development unit that produces multiple publications and videotapes as well as international satellite broadcasts, an organizational communication unit that serves operating divisions of the company, and a media-design-and-development unit that meets Federal's production needs.

Their combined efforts are supported by a "performance first" philosophy centered on Federal's guaranteed fair-treatment and performance improvement policies. They are designed to assure equitable treatment of personnel and encourage their productivity.

ADDITIONAL READING

Brody, E. W. *The Business of Public Relations,* New York: Praeger, 1987.

Federal Express Corporation. "Employee Communications Policy," in *Personnel Policy & Procedure Manual,* 1986.

———. "Open Door Policy," in *Personnel Policy & Procedure Manual,* 1985.

———. "Promotion from Within," in *Personnel Policy & Procedure Manual,* 1986.

———. "Acceptable Conduct Policy," in *Personnel Policy& Procedure Manual,* 1986.

———. "A Leader Must Communicate and Cooperate," in *Manager's Guide,* 1986.

———. "Performance Improvement Policy," in *Personnel Policy & Procedure Manual,* 1986.

———. "Guaranteed Fair Treatment Policy," in *Personnel Policy & Procedure Manual,* 1984.

———. "Appendix: Background Discussion, Fair Treatment Procedure," in *Personnel Policy & Procedure Manual,* 1984.

14
ALTERNATIVE FUTURES

Mortality rates among labor-concentrated organizations in the United States through the first decades of the next century will be governed by two factors: their human resources policies and their communication systems. Federal Express Corporation long ago made its commitment to the future. Some others are following suit. Many organizational destinies remain to be determined, however, as the turn of the century approaches.

Two distinct trends are developing among domestic organizations. Some are committing themselves to policies patterned after those of Federal Express, Weyerhauser, and Hewlett-Packard. Others appear equally committed to a contrary view. The two patterns appear in organizations of all sizes and in a broad range of endeavors. Management philosophy rather than size or nature of business appears to be the primary policy determinant.

Which of the two groups ultimately encompasses the greatest number of survivors remains to be seen. Equitable dealings with all organizational stakeholder groups will be necessary to success. In some cases, however, it may not be sufficient. A global economy is supplanting national economies. National, organizational, and individual values, life-styles, and priorities appear to be in the process of redefinition around the globe. Economic survival will require mutual accomodation to change.

THE SCOPE OF CHANGE

The extent to which the nation and the world will change in ensuing decades is difficult to forecast with accuracy. Some developments are quite predictable; others defy prediction. In the former category are demographic changes, which will produce multiple difficulties in organizations. Younger workers will decline in numbers. As baby boomers achieve seniority, however, other predictable problems will occur. The boomers will compete for fewer senior positions in organizations. Many may retire in frustration, but the upper reaches of the career ladder will remain congested. Busters will be prone to frustration as well. Shortages of personnel in lower age groups thus will be complicated by surpluses in higher age groups.

Haves and Have Nots

These conditions will be one factor in a growing disparity between the nation's "haves" and "have nots." The onset of this trend was already in evidence in the mid-1980s. Commerce Department data suggested significant decline in the so-called middle class. Layoffs among managers were increasing in number. New jobs were being created, but most were in a growing service sector with significantly lower wage rates. The change from industrial to postindustrial society was primarily responsible, but this made the changes no more conducive to worker satisfaction.

Dissatisfaction can be expected to increase if the low economic growth rates of the mid-1980s continue. Low growth implies a low rate of technological innovation, with accompanying social and political problems. The first half of the decade was atypical of the past but could be typical of the future. If the historic trend has finally been reversed, the nation will be denied the incremental resource growth that facilitated the American Dream. Potential for economic and social mobility will decline and personal frustration will grow.

These developments have been avoided in recent years only through growth in multiple wage earner households and in the so-called underground economy. The former trend apparently is close to having run its course. The latter probably will be inadequate to sustain popular perceptions of a better future. Workplace difficulties can only compound as a result.

Moderate growth rates would not necessarily prevent these problems from developing. They would be apt to create a spotty economy in which some sectors grow while others stagnate, again compounding dissatisfaction among the have nots. This might be the case in a high-growth situation as well. High economic growth rates at this writing appear to be the least likely scenario. In addition, they are not problem free. The origins of the nation's psychological "malaise," to use a former president's term, can be traced to the high-growth 1950s and 1960s. Material wealth then was not creating psychological well-being. This frustrating dichotomy could reappear in high-growth circumstances.

Limits of Technology

Perhaps second only to demographic dislocations as a source of potential concern are prospects for technological progress. The United States, over time, has apparently come to the conclusion that any problem can be solved, in large part technologically. Advancing technology over the years has solved problems and produced "progress." As a facilitator of enhanced productivity, it also has played a role in individual economic and social mobility. Whether this will remain the case is another matter.

More and more of the conflicts with which the nation seeks to deal seemingly defy technological solution. Reliance on nuclear energy can be reduced only through greater use of fossil fuels and resultant increases in air pollution. Use of agricultural chemicals can be curtailed to protect the nation's water supplies, but only at a price. Crop yields inevitably would decline and food prices would escalate. The nation's health care problems can be resolved by embracing the concept of universal entitlement, but who will pay?

The United States came to rely economically on technological advances in the form of labor-saving devices, which enhanced productivity and fueled the American Dream. New technologies have not been uniformly beneficial, and those of the future appear unlikely to be so, yet faith in technology appears to persist. These circumstances enhance the potential for continued economic and social dislocation, which inevitably would impact worker and workplace. Thus, organizations can be seen at a fork in the road. They can prepare to cope with a new set of realities or ignore them. One fork offers potential for survival. In the other direction is disaster.

THE FORK IN THE ROAD

Consensus apparently has been reached in the United States as to the need for change. Still to be resolved are the questions of what to change and how. Can traditional organizations and traditional management systems meet tomorrow's needs, or must traditional techniques be abandoned to enhance the potential for organizational survival? Radical steps have been taken by many organizations in efforts to prepare for the future, but outcomes often have been less than anticipated. General Motors Corporation's acquisition of Electronic Data Systems, Inc. (EDS) is a case in point.

The acquisition occurred amidst considerable fanfare early in the decade. General Motors (GM) acquired EDS with two stated objectives. The automotive giant primarily was seeking EDS expertise in computers and automation. Concurrently, however, GM Chairman Roger Smith hoped to bring Electronic Data System's entrepreneurial style and organizational culture into the tradition-ridden GM organization. For reasons not immediately apparent, the "culture transplant" failed to take. GM ultimately purchased the stock of board member and former EDS chairman H. Ross Perot, who had been publicly criticizing the company's policies in an era in which its market share steadily dwindled. Perot left the board and agreed not to further criticize the company in public.

Uncertain Outcomes

The long-term impact of the EDS acquisition on GM remains to be seen. The automotive giant conceivably could lose much of what it paid for the company as well as the millions paid to Perot. EDS is a labor-concentrated organization. Personnel are its primary assets, and while Perot and two key EDS executives accepted a three-year non-competitive agreement, others were not similarly bound.

GM also was likely to encounter considerable internal difficulty over the buy-out, which Perot himself considered inadvisable. The company was losing money, closing plants, and laying off workers at the time. Its much-heralded Saturn project in Tennessee had been reduced to almost a third the size earlier announced, and GM's unions had yet to be heard from.

Future Shock

The continuing layoffs and plant closings, coupled with GM's apparent fail-ure to successfully assimilate the technological expertise and organizational culture of EDS did not bode well for the nation's largest corporation. Perhaps more significant in the long run, these elements almost certainly made GM less attractive as an employer. Diminished attractiveness inevitably will exact a price in terms of existing and prospective employees. The former doubtless will be more prone to quickly seize any opportunity to escape to greener pastures. The latter will tend to view GM with a jaundiced eye.

The extent to which these circumstances will impact GM's efforts to retain its market share by offering better products at more competitive prices remains to be seen. Few would argue that the task will be more difficult than otherwise would have been the case.

Alternative Approaches

An alternative approach to organizational health was advanced by busi-nessman/columnist K. C. Mosier II in the August 1986 issue of *Nation's Business*. It is best told in his own words in a column entitled "Assuring the Future: Corporate Survival Through Labor Management."

Again and again I have read about the demise of American manufacturing. Yet it still has plenty of life in it: The manufacturing sector employs almost 22 million Americans and comprises over 20 percent of our gross national product. I have every reason to wish it good health. My well-being as a manufacturer of custom components for the capital goods industries depends on its survival.

My company, which has 110 employees, makes pneumatic cylinders and valves. Our customers range from the largest corporations, such as International Business Machines and General Electric, to the smallest job shops and custom machinery builders. In spite of heavy competition from more than 40 companies, including strong competitors in Germany and Japan, we are highly profitable, and our market share is increasing.

Few of my customers make effective use of an essential resource—their employees.

But a sound labor management program can have a dramatic effect on a company's productivity and profitability.

One such program certainly has done so at my company. Here are its keys points:

1. Treat employees as individuals within the framework of the organization. Use common sense and have empathy.

   One of our employees asked that his anniversary date be changed so he could get his vacation paycheck early to pay overdue bills. Rules were rewritten to help him and others.

2. Never defend the company image when management is wrong; that undermines mutual trust.

   At an employee meeting, a factory hand asked if he could wear shorts at work. Our plant manager said no. As voice levels rose, I realized this unimportant matter was becoming a real issue. I stepped in and announced that employees could wear shorts, unless it was determined on an individual basis to be hazardous.

   The manager told me he had vetoed wearing shorts because "I just don't think it looks right." Managers should not attach their value systems to the labor force.

3. Top managers should spend time working in each factory department so that employees know they take personal interest in what is happening on the shop floor.

   Our large-cylinder assembly department's production was way below both projection and demand. Supervisors blamed workers' attitudes. I decided to spend a week in the department and see from the inside what was happening.

   In two hours, I knew the problem. The department was woefully short of assembly bench space and tools. Things soon changed for the better.

4. Give employees as much information as possible about the company's financial welfare—including an annual review of the income statement, highlighting key statistics. Such openness by the company will build a "we're in this together" spirit.

5. Create a cash incentive system, based on overall labor costs, for both salaried and hourly employees.

   We started an efficiency bonus program in 1979 and have paid out $202,548. Size of individual bonuses depends on seniority, job classification and attendance—both for regular working hours and overtime.

   Shipments per employee as well as company profitability have increased markedly. Our employees know there is something in it for them, too, when they do their best.

6. Establish minimum work qualifications to be met by all employees.

   We test manual dexterity by requiring applicants to disassemble and reassemble a variety of nuts and bolts in a certain period. We also use a 50–question intelligence test to determine ability to take instruction.

7. Establish a clear-cut rulebook for all employees. Make sure each has a copy. People want to know they will be treated equally, even though each considers himself or herself a special case.

   We require that employees, including managers, work the day before and the day after any scheduled holiday period that falls between regular work days. Several middle managers had to be called on a Monday following the long Thanksgiving weekend (we do give Friday off) and informed they would forfeit holiday pay if they did not come to work.

8. See that the work environment is clean and well lit, with good air circulation. Employees will reason that if management doesn't care enough to keep the place clean, employees shouldn't care about what they produce.

9. Establish a fund to make emergency loans that employees can repay through payroll deductions. Interest should be modest. Employees troubled by finances will not be at their best.

10. Promote from within, so that skilled workers—you may want to develop a training program—will come from the ranks of employees. This will show employees there is a future for them if they work for it.

And that is what a labor management program is all about.

There may be no future for manufacturers that don't work for it by doing a better job with their employees.[1]

Underlying Principles

Mosier's words are worth rereading for what they do not say as well as for the thoughts they express. The system he describes encompasses a majority of the principles espoused in earlier chapters:

1. Treat employees as people.
2. Make policies people-friendly.
3. Hold managers accountable for results.
4. Get senior managers out of their offices and into areas where the work is done.
5. Develop an effective communication system.
6. Offer economic incentives to workers and managers.
7. Define minimum acceptable performance.
8. Establish clear policies and procedures and enforce them equitably at all organizational levels.
9. Create physical environments that reflect management's commitments to workers as well as products or services.
10. Assist and encourage employee development.

"DISPOSABLE" LABOR

While many organizations have embraced these concepts, a significant number have taken the opposite fork in the road. They are using alternative

---

[1]Reprinted by permission from *Nation's Business*, August 1986. Copyright 1986, U.S. Chamber of Commerce.

forms of employment to limit labor costs and thereby enhance competitive position. They do so, unfortunately, at considerable cost to their workers.

The concept they use involves what have been generously described as "contingent workers." They include part-time and "leased" personnel, who might better be identified with a term used by *Business Week* as "disposable employees." These are workers who voluntarily or involuntarily work part time. At mid-decade they were estimated to account for some 25 percent of the total work force or some 25 million individuals.

As many as 70 percent of them may have been involuntarily placed in these circumstances, where they are considered "dispensable" employees. As City University of New York Professor Kathleen E. Christensen told *Business Week,* "We're creating a second-class tier in the labor force."

Bureau of Labor Statistics (BLS) data show that there are 3.8 million of these part-time workers who would prefer to have full-time work. Several million others are consultants or other professionals who prefer to work part time, but BLS data are imprecise.

The disposable employee receives lower wages and no fringe benefits. Government data show that part-time workers earn an average of $4.17 per hour, as opposed to $7.15 for their full-time colleagues. Some 70 percent have no retirement plans and more than 40 percent lack health insurance coverage.

They are not unlike a large group of Japanese part-time workers who also are subject to frequent layoffs. In the Japanese organizations, relatively small groups of "core" workers hold well-paid jobs guaranteed for life. Some 75 percent have less comfortable situations, and 8 percent are in the part-time category.

In the United States more than a third of retail workers are part-timers, and about 40 percent of the past decade's growth in retail workers consisted of part-timers. The greatest growth in the part-time sector, however, has been among individuals who work at home. Between 1980 and 1986 they increased fourfold to almost nine million. Compensation and benefits for some are identical to those in their employers' offices. Others are less fortunate.

The latter category consists of so-called leased workers. They once were employed by companies that technically terminated them. They then were hired by outside companies whose only function was to pay them and administer their benefits—all paid for with money from their prior employers.

People leasing began as a service to smaller organizations. Leasing companies obtain employee benefits at lower rates because of the numbers of personnel they "employ." Employees often receive better benefits through leasing than could have been the case if they were full-time employees of their original employers.

The practice now is spreading to larger organizations, however, with questionable results. One of the nation's larger for-profit hospital chains has announced plans to staff a psychiatric hospital in California largely with leased personnel.

A similar growth trend is evident in manufacturing, where International Business Machines Corporation and others increasingly are using part-time personnel and subcontractors. The process enables them to avoid laying off permanent staff, but adds to the ranks of contingent or disposable workers.

Motorola, Inc. has been using three categories of employees since the 1970s. About 30 percent of the firm's 90,000 personnel have guaranteed jobs. Another 40 percent are regular employees without such assurances. The remainder can be terminated on 24 hours' notice.

"Outsourcing" in the automotive industry and elsewhere produces similar results. Work once done internally is subcontracted to organizations that provide inferior wages or benefits and free employers of the stigma of potential layoffs. The layoffs may occur, of course, but former employers don't handle them directly. They merely terminate the subcontracts, which results in layoffs.

Organizations thus create short-term benefits and long-term problems. The benefits accrue in the form of profits achieved through lower costs. The problems are less evident but more pervasive. Reduced investment in personnel over time will tend to create the same sort of circumstances that resulted from the steel industry's failure to renew production facilities after World War II.

Work may be done less expensively but, as *Business Week* pointed out, contingent workers are seldom trained for more highly skilled jobs. Companies thus become less competitive in what is increasingly a global marketplace.

Equally significant, workers involved are less able to purchase the products and services offered by their employers. They ultimately may become a permanent economic underclass in a society once relatively free of such volatile components. This prospect also raises a substantive question as to social as well as economic responsibility, an issue that *Business Week* raised in part in an editorial.

What are the employers really buying? Business complains increasingly that workers have less and less loyalty to their companies and that it doesn't pay to spend large sums to train them and upgrade their skills when they are not likely to stay in their jobs long. Executives bewail the short-term mentality of the financial markets and corporate raiders. But if companies themselves are weakening their workers' long-term attachment to their jobs in the interest of short-term savings, their reasoning is circular. Corporate leaders may be reducing rather than strengthening their ability and that of the U.S. to compete internationally. Business must take care not to carry cost-cutting to the point of false economy.

Other contingent problems are of equal moment. What are the attitudes and opinions of former employees of the companies involved? What do those who remain on their pay rolls think of them? Expect of them? Will they not be prone to depart for greener pastures as the labor crunch sets in? And what of the organization's responsibilities to other stakeholder groups? Stockholders arguably are relatively well served, for the short term at least. But what of customers? Will products really be of lower price or better quality? And what of the communities in which these firms are located? Will they not be forced to cope with higher social costs growing out of employee disposability?

THE CENTRAL ISSUE

The central issue is quite pragmatic. Are organizations experiencing a people problem or are people—and society—experiencing an organizational problem? Organizations' manipulative tendencies are not new. Now they appear to be impacting communities as well as individuals, with results that over time can be only destructive.

Organizations, industrial psychologists, management consultants, and communicators have traditionally directed their effort toward two goals: increasing productivity and reducing intraorganizational frictions. Workers have been manipulated with every technique applicable to alienated individuals. Organizations have embraced worker contentment and human values as manipulative tools, rather than worthwhile objectives in and of themselves. They have been adopted in the interests of productivity or efficiency, rather than for their own sake. They have been applied as manipulative tools to render workers a part of the organization's productive machinery.

These activities are all predicated on a single tenuous assumption: that productivity and associated problems are people problems. Their use has persisted in the face of fast accumulating evidence that the problems are, instead, organizational in nature; that managements would be far better advised to mold organizations to the needs of people rather than the reverse.

Systemic Problems

"The system" has been designed to compartmentalize workers' lives in the interest of productivity. It has, instead, resulted in a near total alienation of people from their work, which has, in turn, produced crises in credibility and communication. The two can not be viewed separately. They are interdependent. Communication is impossible without credibility. "Formalized communication," as D'Aprix put it, "won't motivate anyone. It won't make anyone more productive. It won't increase their loyalty. And it won't make them one damn bit happier."

Successful organizational communication requires real commitment to people expressed in behavior rather than words. Successful communication programs are tailored to individual organizations. They address organizational problems and serve educational as well as informational purposes.

They deal in truth—nothing more and nothing less. They are consistent in behavior. They address employee concerns as well as those of other stakeholders, and they do so specifically rather than in glowing generalities. Most important, they can only reinforce and induce understanding of what the organization really is.

Weakness in Words

Words are the least effective of communication devices. Organizational policy and procedure, managers' styles and personalities, and the decisions that these produce each day define the organization and its leadership. Words may enhance understanding. They can not change reality.

Organizational commitment, behaviorally expressed, earns employee loyalty day by day. It is neither earned nor granted on a one-time basis. It is slow to be given and quick to be withdrawn. The stakes are high. They are much higher, in fact, than most are aware. D'Aprix may have best expressed organizations' prinicipal contemporary problem.

What is at stake is the whole question of trust. A public—including an employee public—that even occasionally has been led down the garden path, lied to, and in some cases even hoodwinked by powerful business interests is not going to begin to believe those interests until it sees tangible evidence that it should—indeed, that it **can**....

And this is the responsibility of both management and the professional communications people who assist them: to see that the actions are correct and then to see that the words are right for communicating those actions.

While the issue requires policy decisions, communicators' subsequent actions are equally critical. Like managers, many tend toward narrow viewpoints. Both become caught up in the process of communication to such an extent that it distracts them from the purpose: behavioral change.

COMMUNICATION PROBLEMS

Senior managers, more than communicators, tend to become entrapped in what arguably are the trivia of the communication process. The vehicles or channels of communication, because many are tangible in nature and require sophisticated production techniques, too often become the primary concerns of both groups. They become more concerned with the process, in other words, than with the objectives it has been created to accomplish.

Such difficulties are understandable, although unacceptable. Today's communicator must be more a social scientist than a designer and sender of messages. The latter remain significant components of the communication process, but the objective is growing in importance. The objective is behavioral change. The results of communication can be measured in no other context.

What Has Been Accomplished

Are the organization's stakeholders aware of the issues that involve their futures and the organization's? Are they well informed on these topics? Are they adequately educated in the subject matter to apply their knowledge? Are their attitudes and behaviors supportive of the organization adequately reinforced by the communication program? Have the attitudes of those who disagree with organizational positions been changed? Have their resultant behaviors been changed?

Communicators' objectives, in other words, may include (a) awareness, (b) information, (c) knowledge or education, (d) reinforced attitudes/behaviors, (e) changed attitudes, and (f) changed behaviors. Messages must be created, transmitted, and received, if any of them are to be realised. Creation, transmission, and induced reception are valueless, however, unless the objective is gained.

Some years ago, for example, the chief executive officer of an industrial insurance company, which sold weekly-premium burial insurance to lower socioeconomic groups, asked the author for an opinion of advertising prepared for insertion in a sophisticated city magazine. The response: "If you're interested in something that will produce salutary comments from your friends at the country club on Saturday, this will do a great job. But it won't sell a nickel's worth of burial insurance."

The message might have been more bluntly expressed in this manner: "If you're interested in massaging your ego, do it. If your objective is sales, forget it." Neither messages nor channels of communication are inherently good or bad. They can be successfully evaluated only in terms of desired results and potential for inducing them.

Barriers to Communication

The principle also applies in organizational communication. A company with a large population of Spanish-speaking personnel may need to use an interpreter in producing an annual report to employees. If a professor of classical Castilian Spanish is employed, the message is unlikely to be received or acted upon. The report, no matter how attractive or how close to technical perfection, will be valueless. The time, effort, and money involved will have been wasted.

The electronic media are no different. Users are less apt to communicate effectively because of inexperience or histrionics, even if message content is candid and appropriate. Viewers are able to "read" style and sincerity as well as hear words. The organizational executive may be seen as a Jimmy Carter as easily as a vintage Ronald Reagan.

The outcomes of communication, as public relations counselor Patrick Jackson wrote in *International Public Relations Review,* can be unexpected. "Every communication or course of action is probably going to be countered in our society," he said, using as an example an anecdote about a minister's attempt to use public relations techniques. The minister's first message appeared on the church's lighted outdoor sign: "If you're tired of sin, come in." Very shortly, written beneath in lipstick were the words, "and if you're not, phone 753–6267." Jackson's point is that communicators must be strategic thinkers to look successfully beyond the communication process to anticipated outcomes.

Variation in Results

Results of communication may be more or less than the communicator anticipates. Absence of response, in other words, is not the worst possible outcome. Unanticipated consequences can create or compound problems, rather than resolve them. This can occur in at least five areas.

First, messages or actions impact those to whom they are exposed with varying results. Change in an organizational policy to require all personnel to work rotating shifts, for example, might well create as much protest among those who prefer evening and night shifts as previously existed among those who objected to them.

Second, messages can produce favorable or unfavorable secondary results. A change in timing of work shifts to enable workers to sleep later in the morning could create objections among spouses who expect them home at an early hour for dinner. Announcing record dividends similarly may induce negative responses among workers.

Third, messages can produce varying results among stakeholder groups. Liberal wages and benefits welcomed by workers are not going to produce joy among other firms in the community competing for those workers.

Fourth, messages that conflict with preexisting organizational images can be especially destructive, as when the organization committed for years to a no-layoff policy is forced by economic exigencies to release personnel.

Fifth, messages can harbor potentially destructive negative symbolism, as in the case of an animal shelter selling unclaimed and unwanted animals for laboratory research.

Thus the focus of organizational and every other form of communication must be on the perceptions of stakeholder groups. More time and effort are required to analyze in advance the impact of proposed communication

efforts. Tendencies to become so involved in message development or channels of communication as to permit unforeseen consequences to develop
must be resisted at all costs.

All of these factors ultimately will command the attention of organizations'
senior managers as well as their communicators. Some will recognize the
trends that threaten them and respond in time to avoid disaster. Others
inevitably will not.

SUMMARY

Labor-concentrated organizations are beginning to establish strategies for
survival through the early decades of the new century. Some are opting for
policies paralleling those of the nation's most successful organizations. They
are based on equity in dealing with all stakeholder groups. Others are
electing to maintain and expand upon the concept of personnel as disposable
components of production.

Neither of the two policies alone will determine success or failure. To
the extent possible, many organizations will attempt to replace humans with
machines, especially computers and robots. Their potential for success is
limited by the nature of the organizations. Some, such as the fast-food and
accommodations industries, will never be able to supplant significant numbers of lower-echelon personnel in this manner. Computers and robots are
incapable of cleaning hotel rooms or serving as hamburger stand clerks.

Contemporary organizational strategies must also be cast in a manner to
accommodate continuing change. While some changes, such as those inherent in demographic data, are inevitable, others remain difficult to calculate. New technology is limited in its ability to enhance productivity.
While older technologies performed well in that respect, the newer tend
to be spotty in application and replete with unpleasant side effects. These
circumstances are compounded in that many contemporary societal problems are resistant to technological solution.

While the need for change in keeping with external and internal circumstances apparently has been accepted in the United States, accomplishing
change successfully is another matter. The troubled marriage of General
Motors Corporation and Electronic Data Systems, Inc., is exemplary of the
difficulties that can occur when managers seek to integrate two very different organizations.

Organizational problems, nevertheless, appear solvable other than where
exacerbated through use of disposable labor. Organizations using this concept are turning to part-time and leased personnel, as well as outsourcing,
to achieve optimum economy and/or avoid layoffs. Whether these devices
will be beneficial over time remains to be seen.

Layoff avoidance that destroys employee loyalty is unlikely to be productive over time. Neither is creation of a new underclass of workers paid at considerably lower wage rates and receiving no benefits.

These concerns raise a more basic question. Are organizations experiencing people problems or is society encountering organizational problems? Organizations have long been manipulative in their treatment of personnel. The extent of their manipulation now threatens to create social problems and long-term, comparable difficulties for organizations. These ultimately may destroy society's already tenuous confidence in organizations, with potentially devastating results.

Given organizational environments developing along these lines, managers and communicators must take a significantly different approach to communication than heretofore has been the case. Predispositions toward focusing on the communication process must be set aside in favor of concentrating on results. Messages must be based on organizational realities. More sophisticated workers are less susceptible to being misled and more suspicious of organizational motives. Message channels must be selected for delivery efficiency rather than superficial appeal, and care must be taken to avoid negative outcomes arising out of unforeseen audience reactions.

ADDITIONAL READING

D'Aprix, Roger M. *The Believable Corporation*. New York: AMACOM, 1977.
Jackson, Patrick. "Let's Lift Our Eyes above Process and Concentrate on Outcomes." *International Public Relations Review*, November 1986.
Pollock, Michael A. "The Disposable Employee Is Becoming a Fact of Corporate Life," *Business Week*, December 15, 1986.
"The Danger of Disposable Labor." *Business Week*, December 15, 1986.

BIBLIOGRAPHY

Albert, Kenneth J., ed. *The Strategic Management Handbook.* New York: McGraw-Hill, 1983.

Anthony, William P. *Participative Management.* Reading, MA: Addison-Wesley, 1978.

Arnold, L. Eugene. *Parents, Children and Change.* Lexington, MA: Lexington Books, 1985.

Bailey, Catherine T. *The Measurement of Job Performance.* London: Gower, 1983.

Belker, Loren B. *The First-Time Manager: A Practical Guide to the Management of People.* New York: AMACOM, 1978.

Bennis, Warren. *Leaders: The Strategies for Taking Charge.* New York: Harper & Row, 1985.

Bennis, Warren. *The Unconscious Conspiracy: Why Leaders Can't Lead.* New York: AMACOM, 1976.

Bennis, Warren, and Burt Nanus. *Leaders: The Strategies for Taking Charge.* New York: Harper & Row, 1985.

Bennison, Malcolm, and Jonathan Casson. *The Manpower Planning Handbook.* Maidenhead, England: McGraw-Hill (UK), 1984.

Berko, Roy M., Andrew D. Wolvin, and Ray Curtis. *This Business of Communicating.* 3rd ed. Dubuque, IA: Brown, 1986.

Botkin, James, Dan Dimanecescu, and Ray Stata. *The Innovators: Rediscovering America's Creative Energy.* New York: Harper & Row, 1984.

Bramson, Robert M. *Coping with Difficult People.* Garden City, NY: Anchor, 1981.

Briggs, Vernon M., Jr. *Immigration Policy and the American Labor Force.* Baltimore, MD: Johns Hopkins University Press, 1984.

Cascio, Wayne F. *Managing Human Resources: Productivity, Quality of Work Life, Profits.* New York: McGraw-Hill, 1986.

Chung, Kae H. *Motivational Theories and Practices.* Columbus, OH: Grid, 1977.

Cialdini, Robert B. *Influence: the New Psychology of Modern Persuasion.* New York: Quill, 1984.

Coffin, Royce A. *The Negotiator: A Manual for Winners.* New York: AMACOM, 1973.

Crosby, Philip B. *Quality without Tears: The Art of Hassle-Free Management.* New York: McGraw-Hill, 1984.

Crystal, Graef S. *Financial Motivation for Executives.* New York: American Management Association, 1971.

Cummings, Paul W. *Open Management: Guides to Successful Practice.* New York: AMACOM, 1980.

Diebold, John. *Making the Future Work: Unleashing Our Powers of Innovation for the Decades Ahead.* New York: Simon & Schuster, 1984.

Dowling, William, ed. *Effective Management and the Behavioral Sciences: Conversations from Organizational Dynamics.* 8th ed. New York: AMACOM, 1978.

Dowling, William F., Jr., and Leonard R. Sayles. *How Managers Motivate: The Imperatives of Supervision.* New York: McGraw-Hill, 1971.

Duck, Steve. *Human Relationships: An Introduction to Social Psychology.* Beverly Hills, CA: Sage, 1986.

Fendrock, John J. *Managing in Times of Radical Change.* New York: AMACOM, 1971.

Ford, Robert N. *Why Jobs Die and What to Do about It: Job Redesign and Future Productivity.* New York: AMACOM, 1979.

Fulmer, Robert M. *Practical Human Relations.* 2nd ed. Homewood, IL: Irwin, 1983.

Gallup, George, Jr., and William Proctor. *Forecast 2000: George Gallup Jr. Predicts the Future of America.* New York: Morrow, 1984.

Gellerman, Saul W. *Motivation and Productivity.* New York: AMACOM, 1963.

Gellerman, Saul W. *Management by Motivation.* New York: AMACOM, 1968.

George, Claude S. *Supervision in Action: The Art of Managing Others.* Reston, VA: Reston, 1979.

Ginzberg, Eli. *The Development of Human Resources.* New York: McGraw-Hill, 1966.

Ginzberg, Eli. *The Manpower Connection.* Cambridge, MA: Harvard University Press, 1975.

Ginzberg, Eli. *Beyond Human Scale: The Large Corporation at Risk.* New York: Basic Books, 1985.

Glueck, William F. *Personnel: A Diagnostic Approach.* 3rd ed. Plano, TX: Business Publications, 1982.

Hall, Richard B. *Dimensions of Work.* Beverly Hills, CA: Sage, 1986.

Handy, Charles. *The Future of Work: A Guide to a Changing Society.* New York: Basil Blackwell, 1984.

Harrington, H. James. *The Improvement Process: How America's Leading Companies Improve Quality.* New York: McGraw-Hill, 1987.

Hersey, Paul, and Kenneth H. Blanchard. *Management of Organizational Behavior: Utilizing Human Resources.* 3rd ed. New York: Prentice-Hall, 1977.

Howrath, Christine. *The Way People Work.* New York: Oxford University Press, 1984.

Hunt, John. *Managing People at Work.* Maidenhead, England: McGraw-Hill (UK), 1979.

Imundo, Louis V. *The Effective Supervisor's Handbook.* New York: AMACOM, 1980.

Kaagan, Lawrence. "America's Changing Social Agenda: Measuring Its Impact on Business." *New Jersey Bell Journal,* Fall 1984.

Kakabadse, Andrew, and Christopher Parker. *Power, Politics and Organizations: A Behavioral Science View.* New York: Wiley, 1984.

Kellogg, Marion S. *What to Do about Performance Appraisal.* New York: AMACOM, 1975.

King, Patricia. *Performance Planning and Appraisal.* New York: McGraw-Hill, 1984.

Kirkpatrick, Donald L. *How to Improve Performance through Appraisal and Coaching.* New York: AMACOM, 1982.

Kochan, Thomas A., ed. *Challenges and Choices Facing American Labor.* Cambridge, MA: MIT Press, 1985.

Kopelman, Richard E. *Managing Productivity in Organizations: A Practical, People-Oriented Perspective.* New York: McGraw-Hill, 1986.

Landy, Frank J., and James L. Farr. *Measurement of Work Performance: Methods, Theory and Applications.* New York: Academic Press, 1983.

Latham, Gary P., and Kenneth N. Wexley. *Increasing Productivity Performance Appraisal.* Reading, MA: Addison-Wesley, 1981.

Lawler, Edward E., III. *Pay and Organization Development.* Reading, MA: Addison-Wesley, 1981.

Lesley, Philip. *The People Factor: Managing the Human Climate.* Homewood, IL: Dow Jones–Irwin, 1974.

Levering, Robert, Milton Moskowitz, and Michael Katz. *The 100 Best Companies to Work for in America.* New York: New American Library, 1985.

Londgren, Richard E. *Communication by Objectives: A Guide to Productive and Cost Effective Public Relations and Marketing.* Englewood Cliffs, NJ: Prentice-Hall, 1983.

Macarov, David. *Worker Productivity: Myths and Reality.* Beverly Hills, CA: Sage, 1982.

Marting, Elizabeth, Robert E. Finley, and Ann Ward, eds. *Effective Communication on the Job: A Guide for Supervisors and Executives.* 8th ed., New York: AMACOM, 1963.

Masnick, George and Mary Jo Bane. *The Nation's Families: 1960–1990.* Boston: Auburn House, 1980.

McCaffrey, Robert M. *Managing the Employee Benefits Program.* New York: American Management Association, 1972.

McCaffery, Robert M. *Managing the Employee Benefits Program.* New York: AMACOM, 1983.

McConkey, Dale D. *No-Nonsense Delegation.* New York: AMACOM, 1974.

McGregor, Georgette F., and Joseph A. Robinson. *The Communication Matrix: Ways of Winning with Words.* New York: AMACOM, 1981.

McLean, Adrian, et al. *Organization Development in Transition: Evidence of an Evolving Profession.* New York: Wiley, 1982.

McPhee, Robert D., and Phillip K. Tompkins, eds. *Organizational Communication: Traditional Themes and New Directions.* Beverly Hills, CA: Sage, 1985.

Merrett, A. J., and M. R. M. White. *Incentive Payment Systems for Managers.* London: Gower Press, 1968.

Meyer, John W., and W. Richard Scott. *Organizational Environments: Ritual and Rationality.* Beverly Hills, CA: Sage, 1983.

Michael, Donald N. *The New Competence: Management Skills for the Future.* San Francisco: Jossey-Bass, 1985.

Milkovich, George T., and Jerry M. Newman. *Compensation.* Plano, TX: Business Publications, 1984.

Miller, Lawrence M. *Behavior Management: The New Science of Managing People at Work.* New York: Wiley, 1978.

Morgan, Gareth. *Images of Organization.* Beverly Hills, CA: Sage, 1986.

Murphy, Robert D. *Mass Communication and Human Interaction*. Boston: Houghton Mifflin, 1977.

Nash, Allan N., and Stephen J. Carroll, Jr. *The Management of Compensation*. Belmont, CA: Wadsworth, 1975.

Organ, Dennis W., and W. Clay Hamner. *Organizational Behavior: An Applied Psychological Approach*. Plano, TX: Business Publications, 1982.

Paluszek, John L. *Will the Corporation Survive?* Reston, VA: Reston, 1977.

Perelman, Lewis J. *The Learning Enterprise: Adult Learning, Human Capital and Economic Development*. Washington, DC: State Council of Planning Agencies, 1984.

Pincus, J. David and Robert E. Rayfield. "The Emerging Role of Top Management Communication: "Turning On' Employee Commitment," in *Personnel Management: Communication Service*. Paramus, NJ: Prentice-Hall, 1985.

Putnam, Linda L., and Michael E. Pacanowsky, eds. *Communication and Organizations: An Interpretive Approach*. Beverly Hills, CA: Sage, 1983.

Reeves, Elton T. *How to Get Along with Almost Everybody*. New York: AMACOM, 1973.

Rothman, Jack. *Using Research in Organizations: A Guide to Successful Application*. Beverly Hills, CA: Sage, 1980.

Roxe, Linda A. *Personnel Management for the Smaller Company: A Hands-On Manual*. New York: AMACOM, 1979.

Ruben, Brent D., ed. *Information and Behavior*. New Brunswick, NJ: Transaction, 1985.

Sanzotta, Donald. *Motivational Theories and Applications for Managers*. New York: AMACOM, 1977.

Schaefer, Susan Davidson. *The Motivation Process*. Cambridge, MA: Winthrop, 1977.

Stanton, Edwin S. *Successful Personnel Recruiting and Selection within EEO/Affirmative Action Guidelines*. New York: AMACOM, 1977.

Stanton, Edwin S. *Reality-Centered People Management: Key to Improved Productivity*. New York: AMACOM, 1982.

Stone, G. Harry. *The Corporate Survivors*. New York: AMACOM, 1986.

Tracey, William R. *Designing Training and Development Systems*. New York: AMACOM, 1984.

Tuleja, Thaddeus F. *Beyond the Bottom Line: How Business Leaders are Turning Principles into Profits*. New York: Facts on File, 1985.

Viola, Richard H. *Organizations in a Changing Society: Administration and Human Values*. Philadelphia: Saunders, 1977.

Von Kass, H. K. *Making Wage Incentives Work*. New York: AMACOM, 1971.

Weeks, David A., ed. *Rethinking Employee Benefit Assumptions*. New York: The Conference Board, 1978.

Weger, John J. *Motivating Supervisors*. New York: AMACOM, 1971.

Weiss, Carol H., and Allen H. Barton, eds., *Making Bureaucracies Work*. 2d. ed., Beverly Hills, CA: Sage, 1980.

Zander, Alvin. *Making Groups Effective*. San Francisco: Jossey-Bass, 1982.

INDEX

Freedom of Information Act, 179
Fulmer, Robert M., 179

Galbraith, John Kenneth, 27
Gay rights, 2, 43
General Dynamics, 66
General Electric, 68, 238
General Motors Corporation, 33, 56, 74, 237–238, 247
General systems theory. *See* Systems theory
Goals: communication vs. corporate, 177; individual perception and, 151; information dissemination, 173; intraorganizational understanding of, 147; statements of, 217, 221
Goldhaber, Gerald M., 137–140, 155, 160, 176
Gooding, Judson, 30, 49, 123
Gossip, grapevine and, 158
Government: protectionist role of, 31; spending on elderly, 40
Grapevine: communication breakdown and,149; informal communication and,157–158; as information source, 178; organizational credibility and, 167
Gray-power revolt, 40
Groups, reference. *See* Reference groups

Harris International, Ltd., 102
Harris, Louis, 81
Harris, Philip R., 102–104
Harvard Business Review, 69
Harvard Business School, 69
Hayes, Robert H., 56
Herman Miller Company, 90
Hersey, Paul, 62
Herzberg, Frederick, 67–69
Hewlett Packard, 66, 165, 235
Hickman, Craig R., 34–35
Hierarchies: corporate culture, 95–96; lateral vs. vertical, 70; messages in, 146; systems theory and, 60; work flow and, 156
High technology, displacement by, 33

Hiring, deceptive practices and, 75
Honda of America, 68
Hospitals, 206
Hot-lines, 189
Human resource management: accountability of, 100; communicator training in, 202; computer applications in, 211; counter-productive, 6–11; ethical approach to, 93; Federal Express, 214–234; generational problems and, 49; guidelines for, 239–240; IBM, 13–14; jobs as products, 85; new age skills for, 35; organizational survival and, 235; peer review and, 68; survey research and, 130; theory of, 59; undereducation and, 102
Humanist organizations, 91, 93–94

Iacocca, Lee, 195
Immigration: baby bust and, 42; labor market and, 26, 45; projections for, 20
In the Age of Uncertainty (Galbraith), 27
Incentives: behaviorist theory and, 91; benefits as, 12, 239; individual vs. group, 113; worker response to, 112
Income. *See* Compensation; Wages
Indoctrination messages, 176
Industry Week, 4, 55, 66, 112
Inflation: baby bust and, 42; unions and, 168
Information: accessibility of, 178; analysis of, 136; computer sources, 206; disclosure laws and, 130; electronic vs. print, 132; employee need for, 6, 46, 79, 239; exchange process for, 152–153; Federal Express approach to, 218; flow of, 147–150, 177– 179, 207; grapevine transmission of, 158, 167–168; half-life of, 61, 204; oral vs. written, 137; overload, 197; productivity and, 52; quality of, 86, 155; screening of, 151–152; security classifying of, 178–179; sources for, 127, 155, 206, 208–209; surveying needs

Index

ABOUT THE AUTHOR

E. W. BRODY teaches public relations in the Department of Journalism at Memphis State University in Tennessee and maintains a public relations counseling practice in Memphis.

Communicating for Survival is his second book in as many years. *The Business of Public Relations* was published by Praeger in 1987.

Dr. Brody's articles on public relations have appeared in *Public Relations Journal, Public Relations Review, Journalism Quarterly, Legal Economics, Health Care Management Review, Journal of the Medical Group Management Association, Modern Healthcare, Hospital Public Relations, and Public Relations Quarterly,* on which he serves as contributing editor.

Dr. Brody holds degrees from Eastern Illinois University, California State University, and Memphis State University. He is accredited by the Public Relations Society of America and the International Association of Business Communicators and is a Fellow of the American Society for Hospital Marketing and Public Relations.